OUT CAME THE SUN

OUT CAME THE SUN

OVERCOMING THE LEGACY OF MENTAL ILLNESS, ADDICTION, AND SUICIDE IN MY FAMILY

MARIEL HEMINGWAY

WITH BEN GREENMAN

Regan Arts.

Regan Arts.
65 Bleecker Street
New York, NY 10012

First Regan Arts hardcover edition, April 2015.

Library of Congress Control Number: 2014955526

ISBN 978-1-941393-23-9

Interior design by Alex Camlin
Jacket design by Richard Ljoenes
Jacket art by © Sebastian Kim/Management + Artists

Printed in the United States of America

10 9 8 7 6 5 4 3 2 1

To Bobby Williams, who has given me the gift of always seeing me as whole and complete. You challenge me daily to look at myself honestly. Thank you.

And to Dree and Langley for allowing me to love you and cherish you in your confidence, beauty, and creativity.

CONTENTS

THE SOUND IN MY DREAM

I HEARD THE NOISE IN MY DREAM FIRST. I couldn't remember the dream, not exactly, but I knew there was a shelf and something teetering on it. When it toppled, it smashed to the floor with a loud crash.

My eyes fluttered open. I was safe in my bed. My sister was on the other side of the room, safe in hers. A night-light glowed warmly in the corner. All was good. It was just a dream. I closed my eyes and tried to sink back into the comfort of sleep.

But then there was another crash, and a dull thump, and words I couldn't quite make out, spoken at high volumes by two voices. The voices were coming from downstairs. One was clipped and efficient, unemotional even in anger. That was my mother. The other was louder, deeper: my father. The higher voice stabbed at the air. The lower voice responded. My eyes came open again.

The night had started promisingly. We were hosting a dinner party at our house. My parents were like many other American couples in the mid-sixties. My father, Jack, was big and broad. He wore fishing shirts and khaki pants during the day and transitioned to something slightly more formal in the evenings: a cleaner shirt, maybe plaid, and corduroys. My mother, Puck—her real name was Byra Louise, but no one called her that—was skinny and impeccably dressed; she favored blouses paired with skirts or slacks. My mother mostly did what most mothers did back then. She took care of the house. She cleaned and she tended to the children and she straightened up and made sure that the furniture wasn't getting too worn and that the plants and flowers on display were fresh.

Above all, my mother cooked, and when my parents had a dinner party, she took control. She marched into the kitchen with a determined look on her face and spent the afternoon filling the house with the smells of rosemary, garlic, and thyme. She smiled when she cooked: she was at her happiest when there was a task in front of her, especially a task she knew would bring pleasure to others. She didn't need time to do her hair because it was done weekly at the beauty shop, sculpted into an impressive stack that was almost a beehive. She wore flats, never high heels. The women in my family were tall enough without help from their shoes.

At seven, the doorbell rang. The door opened to show other couples, professionals from town: doctors, lawyers, maybe academics. They tended to be older than my parents, people who had made a little money elsewhere in the world and fancied themselves intellectuals. They came to our house for the conversation. Stories were told. Jokes were traded. Bottles of wine were opened, maybe bottles of whiskey. My older sisters made small talk with the guests.

As the youngest daughter, I was too small for small talk, so I helped with the food. I baked pies with my mother and twice-baked potatoes. I even helped with the drinks. I was trained in basic cocktails by the time I was six, and I knew how to twist a bottle of wine just right so that not a single drop spilled. When I went to bed at ten or so, a half-dozen hands waved at me. "Good night," everyone said. I was exhilarated but also exhausted, and I usually fell asleep the second my head hit the pillow.

While I slept, the world changed. My parents, with others, could be charming and happy. They were the life of the party so long as there was a party. When the party ended, though, the air went out of the room. My mother and father took up positions in separate corners. She perched on the couch. He collapsed into his armchair. That's when the trouble began. The first comment might be innocuous. Maybe my mother would observe that my father hadn't let one of the other men talk, or my father would make a joke about the way that one of the other women had looked at the food. But that first remark would trigger a second, and a third. Comments about the dinner bloomed into comments about everything else: the house, the family, the marriage. Alcohol accelerated my parents toward their destination. My mother snarled. My father shouted. Insults were hurled, and sometimes bottles along with them. One of them, thudding into the wall, woke me.

The battles and the bottles didn't happen every night, but they happened on the nights when guests came over, which were also, inevitably, the nights when guests left—and left my parents to their own devices. Those fights remade the house, changed it into a minefield. I stayed awake in bed, eyes open in the dark, and tried to imagine safe places I might step. I toured the first floor in my mind: the yellow kitchen cabinets and robin's-egg-blue walls around them, the brown-paneled family room with Western-themed paintings hung next to the bookcases, the brown leather recliner where my mother sat, my father's dark green armchair, the thick orange shag carpet in the formal living room. It was an ordinary suburban house, but when I went through it in my mind, every inch seemed perilous.

The fights went on, sometimes long into the night. I listened as long as I could, never quite hearing specific words, instead hearing bass tones and treble tones, sometimes overlapping. Arguments like that claim many victims. The participants, of course, are the primary victims. They say things they wish they hadn't said and hear things they wish they hadn't heard. But those within earshot of the fights are victims as well. From the moment I woke to the sound of shouting until the moment I fell back asleep, I wondered why my parents couldn't get along, why they couldn't control their drinking and their angry words, whether the fault lines that ran through my family ran through me also.

Saddened and scared, I stayed in my bed and stared around my room, knowing that behind the darkness were clean white walls. It was a small kingdom and I was the sovereign, and that meant that I controlled every aspect of it. I was, even then, preoccupied with that idea of control. When I woke up in the morning, I made my bed until the sheets were perfectly flat, without a single errant crease. Before I went to bed at night, I arranged my toys carefully on the shelves. I didn't know what else to do. And when I heard my parents fighting downstairs, when I heard voices raised in anger, when I heard thumps and crashes, I burrowed even further down into my sheets, cocooned myself even more in the perfect little world I had created for myself. I fought chaos with order. Later on, that obsession with self-control would touch every aspect of my life—my relationship with food, with men, with work, with my own emotional honesty—but at the time it saved me. I controlled my immediate environment so vigilantly because I didn't know what else to do. I knew that there was no way I could dissolve my parents' anger, no way I could make the bottles fly backward through the air into hands—and then, even before that, refill them with the wine and place them back onto the shelf. You can't reverse time, even when you lie there in bed and wonder why you can't. But this book is the story of how you can go back in time. I will go back to the beginning. I will travel from Monte Nido, where I live now, to Mill Valley, where I was born. It's a day trip up the California coast, only four hundred miles, but it's a million miles too.

2

THE BABY IN THE HOUSE

MANY GREAT WRITERS have written about family. It's one of literature's primary subjects because it's one of life's primary subjects. The
most famous quote, of course, is from Tolstoy: "Happy families are
all alike; every unhappy family is unhappy in its own way." It's used
so often that it's a cliché by now. Even though I come from a family
that could easily be classified as unhappy—and I, at times, have classified it that way—I won't use that quote.

The quote that I think I'll start with is one that risks being a cliché for entirely different reasons: "The world breaks every one and
afterward many are strong at the broken places." That quote comes
from my grandfather, the American author Ernest Hemingway. It's
from *A Farewell to Arms*, the novel he published in 1929 that became
his first best seller. It's a book about war and how it affects both the
people who are in it and those who are near it, and how there's not
as much difference between the two as it might initially appear. The

quote goes on, in a slightly more depressing vein: "But those that will not break it kills. It kills the very good and the very gentle and the very brave impartially. If you are none of these you can be sure it will kill you too but there will be no special hurry."

He wasn't writing explicitly about family, but the passage always makes me think of family. Specifically, it makes me think of *my* family, which was a family he helped to create when he and my grandmother had my father a few years before *A Farewell to Arms*. My family—my father, my mother, my two sisters, and myself— is the kind of family that, in today's era of euphemism and double-speak, gets called "dysfunctional." In the plainspoken language my grandfather favored, it was a family torn by sadness and disappoint-ment, one in which human frailty and flaws were on constant dis-play. There were emotional problems. There were mental problems. There were addictions. There were suicides. There were problems within people and problems between people. We felt alone when we were together.

It was a family with breakage, though it never actually broke apart. My parents stayed together for years and years. But that means that the breakage also persisted—it became a central part of how the family was built and how it operated. My sisters and I grew up inside that environment, became defined by it, tried to find ways to nego-tiate it, and ended up contributing to it despite our best efforts. And yet as I grew up in my family, I didn't think much about whether or not it was broken. That's an outsider's thought. When you're inside a situation, moving through it day to day, you just think of it as the life you're living, as this intimately and permanently linked group of people with specific challenges and triumphs.

Throughout my life, people have spoken about the Hemingway curse. They pointed to the many difficult things in my family:

alcoholism, mental illness, suicide—all of which happened to Hemingways before I was born and would continue to happen to Hemingways throughout my adult life. I was confused. I learned to scoff at the idea, to dismissively say that the people who called us cursed didn't know what they were talking about. But also, to be honest, *I* didn't know what they were talking about. I didn't like the term. It was a nasty word that suggested a lack of control—and there was another dimension too, because it's what my mother used to call getting your period. In my mind, those meanings collided and produced the sense of something dirty: of physical uncleanliness, of moral rot, of a sense of blame laid at the feet of those very people who were suffering. At the same time, though, when people talked about the Hemingway curse, I paid closer attention. I tried to see if I felt its weight upon me.

As I have gotten older, as the events of my youth have become more distant, I have started to think back through the days and months and years, not only to make sense of them now but to think about how I made sense of them back then. Most of what I did back then was a mix of instinct and analysis, of love and fear, of luck both good and bad. Very little of it was done with a sense of larger insight. Sadly, life is laid out in such a way that you do things long before you understand them. (The key quote here is from Kierkegaard, rather than Tolstoy or my grandfather: "Life can only be understood backwards; but it must be lived forwards.") When I was a child, acting the way I did, obsessed with cleanliness and control, constantly at war with the unruliness of the rest of my family, was I aware of the reasons? Hardly.

There's also the issue of other people's behavior. It's narcissistic to assume that everyone else in my life—even everyone else in my family—acted in ways whose primary purpose was to affect me.

In most cases, they were just being themselves in the only way they were capable—imperfectly, injudiciously, moving forward with a mix of blindness and sight. Remembering that, remembering them, I have to resist the temptation to make them into part of my story at the same time that I have to acknowledge that's the only thing I am capable of doing.

Here, too, I look to my grandfather for inspiration. My favorite book of his is *A Moveable Feast,* his reminiscence of Paris in the 1920s. It's a book that's meaningful to me because I went to Paris with my father when I was eleven, and he toured me around the city, bringing the pages of the book to life. But it's also a tutorial on how to convert life into literature without giving in to certain temptations. *A Moveable Feast* is not, on its face, a dramatic story, and yet it deals with deep feelings of love and sadness, of creative triumph and personal memory.

This book exists in that same spirit, though it's different in many ways—possibly in all ways. But it's a watershed in two respects: It separates the turbulent flow of the past from the calmer waters of the present. And it also represents a turning point in the way I see my own history. For years, I pushed aside the most painful and difficult aspects of my family history, or buried them deep inside so that I could move forward with everyday tasks. I am done pushing things aside. Instead, I have decided to look at my life directly, to be clear-eyed about its sorrows but also its joys. This book not only gives me voice—it *is* my voice.

Most important, my book isn't only for me. It's for the rest of my family, though most of my immediate family are gone now, taken by time and their own frailties. But beyond that, it's for anyone who has ever been part of a similar family—and by that I mean a family rich with both triumph and tragedy. I hope that this book encourages others to investigate their own families and their own difficult memories. Tell your story. Look at yourself by looking at those who were around you from your earliest days. A family is a cracked mirror that nevertheless reflects us accurately. At long last, I am willing to look in that mirror. My family made me, and through an act of memory I can now remake it. Life happened to me—happened all around me—and I learned, slowly, to make myself happen.

*   *   *

MY FIRST MEMORY is something I can't possibly remember, which is my older sister, Margot, dropping me on my head. I was premature by about two and a half months—my mother smoked and drank during the pregnancy, as many women did back then, and there was a joke in my family that I came out because I needed the air. Being ten weeks early meant that I was tiny, only about three pounds, and I had to stay in the hospital an extra month. When I finally came home, it was just before Christmas 1961.

We lived in Mill Valley, just north of San Francisco, in a ranch house surrounded by other ranch houses in a nondescript suburban neighborhood. There was a long gray hallway that ran right down the middle of the place, and my mother stood at the head of the hall while everyone else clustered down at the other end. She held me up for them. That was my announcement and that was my arrival: Mariel Hadley Hemingway, welcome to the family.

Who did I see standing down at the other end of the hall? I saw a tall, strong man and two girls. Joan, who everyone called Muffet, was eleven, a strawberry blonde who already had an elegance about her. When she spoke, it was precise, almost lyrical. When she moved, it was like dancing. Margot was seven, also pretty, with darker hair than Muffet, prominent buckteeth, and a mischievous and demanding personality—she was always testing, needling, needing. That first holiday season, my parents left me in a room alone with her, and after ten blissfully quiet minutes, there was a piercing shriek. They rushed in to find me on the floor. She had dropped me on my head. Margot got sent to bed without dinner, and she wasn't allowed to watch TV even when she asked nicely. I don't think I thought much about either punishment or crime back then. I doubt I thought much of anything other than feeling terror as I saw the ground rushing up at me. But now, a half century later, on the other side of childhood, with grown daughters of my own, it makes sense. Margot had been the baby of the family, and I came and took that all away from her, a three-pound grenade lobbed right into the center of her world.

Memory skips ahead. There are comforting stretches of blankness, and then it's my second birthday. I rode the crest of that wave through the day, proudly. I wore a dress with puffy sleeves that made me look a doll, and I loved that feeling. Dolls got attention and pride of place and special treatment.

"I'm making a cake," my mother said, and disappeared inside the kitchen. I wasn't certain exactly what that was, a cake, but I heard the word enough times that it acquired magical properties. Though I had a bad angle from down on the floor, I could see the flour on her hands and the expression of concentration on her face. I could smell the warmth in the kitchen, the sugar and the batter. Whatever a cake was, I was certain it would change my life.

Then, all of a sudden, my mother stepped away from the bowls and the pan. She washed her hands in the sink quickly. I wasn't on the floor in the kitchen, smelling that sweet hot smell anymore. I was with my parents in the living room, watching our tiny black-and-white TV, first for a minute, then for ten minutes, then for an hour, then for an eternity.

"Quiet," my mother said, though no one was talking. A man on the screen, carried along by a car, waved and then staggered back. A woman in a hat went to his side. It kept happening, over and over again. Then I started to pick out words I didn't know: president, assassination, tragedy. My parents were devastated, even though they were Republicans. The phone started to ring; my parents talked in hushed tones to friends and neighbors. My sisters, who were in their teens, came into the room and stood stock-still. They understood the gravity of the situation. When the cake finally emerged, the day didn't feel like a celebration anymore. Ever since then, I have had a strange relationship with my birthday. It feels both important— it's the anniversary of the only day on which I came to exist—and dwarfed by history. And because of that, I learned a broader lesson: that an individual is always part of something larger, in both good ways and bad. Whenever I feel like I'm the center of the world, I remember that I'm only ever in orbit, subject to larger forces I can't control. And whenever I feel like I'm alone, I remember that islands are part of archipelagos.

*   *   *

I FOUND OUT PRETTY EARLY that I was a mistake, that my parents hadn't sat down and planned out a family that went daughter, daughter, seven-year gap, daughter. But there had been a drunken fishing trip to the Umpqua River in Oregon that had caught my parents careless—and there I was.

My mother was not young when I appeared, especially by the standards of the day. She had been in her late twenties when my oldest sister was born, and she was almost forty when I came along. "We thought you would be a boy," my parents said to me, and though they said it in a joking tone, there was a hard truth at the core. After Muffet, my mother had miscarried a baby boy, and the memory of that son who never was hovered over the family. That may have affected Margot, the very next child born who wasn't that son, and it certainly affected me.

Being a surprise also meant that I was a wild card, dealt into a game that was already in progress. From fairly early on, I noticed that Muffet and Margot competed for my father's attention. Or rather, that Muffet had his attention and that Margot was always trying to get it. Muffet's natural elegance, her ease of being, was complemented by various other talents and abilities. She was amazingly smart. She spoke French wonderfully. She was naturally athletic: give her a tennis racket or a golf club, and within an hour she'd make it look like she was ready for the pro tour.

Muffet was the apple of my father's eye, as the cliché goes. But that meant that the other apples started to feel neglected hanging up there on the tree. Margot took it especially hard. In today's world, where every child is subjected to the most meticulous analysis, Margot would have been assailed by diagnoses: dyslexia, attention deficit disorder, hyperactivity. Back then, she was just considered a problem kid. She was bad at school, disobedient at home, messy, loud, and the source of much of the conflict in the family. Or maybe it's more accurate to say that Margot made herself the source of much of the conflict as a way of getting attention. It was the main way in which she could ensure that she was seen. Sandwiched between a golden girl (Muffet) and a protected baby (me), Margot worked the corners, always doing her best to make enough noise to be noticed.

Through most of my childhood I was called Marielzy, though sometimes there were variations: Mertels, Mertz, or (courtesy of my father, who loved puns, spoonerisms, and all other kinds of wordplay)

Hariel Memingway. Everyone in the family had nicknames. It was as if no one could remember anyone's real name. Joan was Muffet, of course, and Margot was Marg or Mar-gott, with a heavy Germanic emphasis on the second syllable. My mother had been born Byra Louise Whittlesey, and she had been nicknamed Puck by the Shoshone Indians who used to come into her family's drugstore, Whittlesey Pharmacy in Pocatello. (*Puckinuck* meant "little one," or so we were told, though I've never been able to find it in any books about American Indian languages. I hated her nickname from the start because it sounded stout and hard, and my distaste only intensified as I got older and learned how many unfortunate things rhymed with it.) And my father we called Daddy Jack, which was a more palatable version of his full name, John Hadley Nicanor Hemingway, an unwieldy vehicle for various tributes—Hadley for his mother, Nicanor for a bullfighter friend of my grandfather's. We also sometimes called him Dr. Hemingstein because he seemed to know everything encyclopedically, or Hemingtrout because of his lifelong love for fishing.

I had the same middle name as my father and also the same last name. It carried weight from the very start. The Hemingway name was central to American literature. I can't say that I knew very much about my grandfather's literary reputation in those very early years. It's hard to grasp the importance of a famous writer before you can read. But even in those early years, I thought of him as more than just a writer. He was an icon, the kind of person who was never referred to in an ordinary tone of voice. Sometimes his name was whispered, and sometimes it was spoken with a proud ripeness, but it always got a special spin. And Papa, as everyone called him, he was more than just a writer. He was a heavy drinker, legendarily so. He lived that life and he wrote about it and he suffered from it. He was also an adventurer, a man who traveled around the world remaking it in his own image. He went on safaris and took to the sea and sat in the bullfighting arena and watched as matadors delivered the killing thrust to bulls.

That's what he was to the world. To me, he was the trunk of my family tree. He had created the man who created me, and because of that he was a source of fascination. Before I was born, before my parents even settled in Mill Valley, they had lived in Cuba near Ernest. Margot would have only been a baby, still in diapers, but Muffet always claimed that she had clear memories of my grandfather and his circle. There's one particular story she told more than once. She liked to draw, and she was at the pool at the finca with a pencil and a piece of paper. She was working away on a little landscape, and a man came up behind her, appraised her work, and showed her how to draw a flower better. That man? Pablo Picasso. Given Muffet's penchant for outlandish storytelling, it's hard to say whether that is true, or even partly true, but I like to believe it.

There are pictures of my parents in Cuba, a young couple looking alive and excited. My mother and my grandfather got along very well. He was proud of her, he approved of the match his son had made, and she rewarded him by acknowledging his greatness, maybe even flirting with him a little bit in the way that daughters-in-law can. She was conscious of having married into the Hemingway family, and that always turned her toward my father a little bit, even when other forms of unhappiness turned her away.

What other forms of unhappiness? There were many, and maybe the best wat to present them is to list them now and explain them later, or let them try to account for themselves. There was unhappiness with self. There was unhappiness with situation. There was unhappiness with the mind and its limits. There was unhappiness with the body and its limits. There was unhappiness being placed in close quarters with others who were also unhappy. There was unhappiness that despite those close quarters, the dominant feeling was one of loneliness. There was man-woman unhappiness. There was parent-child unhappiness. There was sibling rivalry and there was solitary pain. I remember one afternoon when I was in my room, making my bed and remaking it so that it would look smooth and almost empty. Margot was sulking because she had argued with my parents. Muffet was out with her friends. My parents were sitting downstairs, about to have guests over for dinner, which meant that they weren't far away from fighting with each other.

The family's problems pressed down upon us all. There's no question about that. They pushed some people toward the bottle, and others toward irrational anger, and others toward depression, all of which were contributing to the family's problems in the first place. This was the cycle, and as a result life was extraordinarily stressful in some ways. And yet, in other ways, we were just an ordinary family. The English pediatrician D. W. Winnicott, who was born just a few years before my grandfather, popularized the idea of "good enough" parenting, by which he meant that a young mother didn't need to be perfectly aware of all of her baby's needs and moods. All she needed to do, in the end, was protect and provide for that child. I think about that idea when I think about my family. There was chaos and there was craziness, and it did some of us in, but others emerged from it largely intact. Does that mean that it was, in some ways, good enough? Should the goal of revisiting my history be to detail the ways in which we were troubled or to highlight the ways in which we were not? When parents make mistakes, should they be condemned or forgiven or understood? When children suffer from those mistakes and make mistakes of their own, should they blame their parents or take responsibility themselves? And does that answer

change as those children grow up and become parents themselves? I
sometimes felt that I went too easy on my parents, that I accommodated behavior that no one should accommodate. At other times, I
felt that I was being too hard on them, that I wasn't mindful of the
challenges they had overcome. Learning to balance those two feelings has produced a third feeling—one of stability and peace and, at
length, wisdom. The story of my life, the story of this book, is a story
of how unhappiness can bloom like a black flower, and also of how
people find ways to prune it back.

*   *   *

EVEN THOUGH I SOMETIMES WOKE to the sound of drunken
voices raised in anger or saw venomous looks pass between my parents, I didn't have a clear sense of whether their marriage was func-
tioning properly or was desperately damaged. I was a child. I had no
emotional experience, no basis for assessing adult relationships.

At first, in fact, I think it's fair to say that I didn't care about my
parents' relationship with each other. Children assess the world only
in terms of how much it provides for them and protects them, and I
was no different. What was important to me was that each of them
had a relationship with me. I was too preoccupied with noticing how
my mother held me (or didn't), the way she praised me when I did a
good job (or withheld praise when she observed something that dis-
pleased her). I remember stroking my mother's bony hand and thinking that I loved her more than I would ever love anyone in the world,
even if I was the only one who saw how perfect she could be. As for
my father, he was affectionate and playful and wonderful except for
those moments when he wasn't, when drink would take hold of him
and drag him into what I only faintly understood as a world of adult

anxieties and preoccupations. I remember the smell of dinner wafting through the house and interpreting it as a kind of code. If the food had an American smell, like fried chicken or lamb chops, it meant that my father probably wouldn't be home for dinner. If it had a more exotic bouquet, French or Italian or Japanese, then it meant he'd be there at the table—he thought of himself as a man of worldly refinement, and international cuisines were one way of expressing that sophistication.

I was also fully engaged in the process of watching my older sisters. There was enough of an age difference between us that I was still at tadpole stage while they were hopping around the pond. Each of my sisters provided a highly specific example of how to move through life. Muffet was a shining beacon to me, someone I idolized beyond reason. Everything she did was perfect. She had bright eyes and what I thought of, at that age, as good breeding: she said the right things and held herself properly and never seemed crass or unkind. Negotiating my way around Margot required a bit more care and strategy—she could be unpredictable, even mean. Each of them had a specific way of dealing with me, but I was most interested watching them interact with each other. When they fought, which was fairly often, Margot would yell angry things at Muffet, things I was sure that she didn't mean, and Muffet would pretend she was a princess who was above the fray, who couldn't hear a thing that was being shouted at her, and she would dance away.

In Mill Valley, I shared a room with Margot, where each of us had a twin bed. I tried to keep mine looking like I had never been in it. The sheets were pulled tight, and the blankets pulled even tighter over the sheets, and at night when I went to sleep, I tried to get in the bed without disrupting any of it. I wanted to be visible only to the fairies I was sure whizzed around in the high corners of the room.

Why did I do that? Some of the reason had to come from Margot, in the sense that she was the opposite, a whirlwind that needed to toss and tumble everything. She was a world-class slob who never put away clothes or toys or anything. She just dropped them when she was done with them and left them where they fell. She moved around restlessly all night and sometimes even got up out of her messy bed and thundered around in the room. This disorder, this need to disarrange, struck me as something unacceptable, something dangerous. It was like sharing a room with a monster. In my terror, I sometimes ran down the hall to my parents' room, where I slipped into bed without waking them. One night my dad, still sleeping, shifted and accidentally knocked me out of bed onto the floor. I didn't cry. I just lay there still, breathing hard, trying not to breathe at all.

It wasn't like my father to push anyone. He didn't like conflict or confrontation. He had grown up in a family in which his father, Ernest, always held him at arm's length, sometimes showing love but more often demanding a certain reserve. My grandfather had rigid ideas about how a boy should become a man. You sent that boy out into the world to find his inner bravery. If there was hunting, you sent him to hunt. If there was fishing, you sent him fish. A little while later, you sent him to a bordello to learn about women, and then suddenly you had a son who was no longer a boy. My father never had much training on how to communicate, ironic for a writer's son, and he carried that mix of frozen emotion and active engagement with the world into his adult life, into marriage and fatherhood. When he was bothered by tension in our house, which was often, he escaped to hike or fish or hunt. He was more comfortable in the larger world than in the small world of his home, where faces and voices at close range overmastered him quickly. This put him at odds with my mother, who was immensely judgmental and critical and always spoiling for a fight. She wanted to talk about why things were bad and how she feared they would never get better, while he didn't want to talk at all.

Alcohol, which was as much a part of the family as any of us, inflamed all aspects of the problem. It made my father more distant and my mother more combative. There were many complicating factors having to do with nearly everything else that adults feel as a form of pressure—money, sex, health, broader issues of parenting and mortality and philosophy regarding the place of human beings in the world. But the fights, rooted in choices that happened long before I was born, accelerated by drinking, often came down to an unbridgeable gap. On the one hand, there was a woman who desired a certain kind of emotional intimacy but who couldn't restrain herself from looking judgmentally at the people in her life. On the other, there was a man whose discomfort with that glare blinded him to any intellectual sense he had that it might save his marriage.

When you fight as husband and wife, you also fight as parents. I remember my mother as a hard woman, partly because of the way she looked—bony, severe—and partly because of her tone, which was clipped and critical and rarely without some moral point. "Ladies don't act that way," she would say. "We're not that kind of family," she would say. She had unpleasant things to say about people who were different than we were, whether they were different as a result of religion or race or culture, and she wasn't especially supportive of people under her own roof. My mother loved me. I knew she did, but it wasn't easy for her to show it. There were only a handful of times when she held me close, and I remember them all. She was better at making her affection known through her actions than through her words. She was in the kitchen often, not just on my second birthday—she had studied cooking with Julia Child in Paris when my parents were first married—and I remember her baking bread. I can recall the smell of the bread, which was also her smell.

But then in the evenings, that smell shifted. The scent of bread disappeared, and in its place was whiskey or wine. Voices were raised, along with objections. My parents retreated to different sides of the living room. Accusations crossed and recrossed the space between them, picking up momentum. They traveled slowly at first but, in the end, went quickly enough to pierce whatever was in their path.

* * *

I WAS WATCHING AN OLD MOVIE recently about a miserable marriage. The wife paced around the living room. Finally, she wheeled around, hands on hips, her eyes wild. "I feel like I can't get out of here!" said the (over)actress. For me, as a kid, escaping the pressure cooker of the house was easy enough. I just walked out the front door.

From the time I was little, I was always out in the yard or the neighborhood, exploring groves of trees, skirting the edges of neighbors' lawns, looking closely at bugs or lizards. I ran away when I was four years old, hoping that someone would come and get me. I waited for a while and eventually turned to make the long journey back home—I was probably only halfway down the block—only to reenter a house filled with cocktails and tension. I'm not even sure they knew I was gone.

I wouldn't say that my parents didn't worry about me, but a melodramatic decampment by a four-year-old couldn't really compare to the demands of a middle child who was putting up a fight at eleven, or for that matter an older one who was venturing out into the world at fifteen. They had their hands full with Margot—and then, suddenly, unexpectedly, with Muffet.

When I was young, Muffet had been my beacon. When I was a little older, she only shone more brightly. I loved her for her fashion sense: She had one long black velvet jacket that could look purple in the right light. She wore tall black kneesocks that were just the right mix of demure and provocative. Even when days were drab, she lit up the family. If I was too quiet at times and Margot was too loud at times, Muffet was perfectly modulated. She knew when to have fun and when to buckle down and do work. She knew when to affect maturity, joining my parents for a glass of wine, and when to act more like a kid. Part of the reason I idealized her came from the distance in our ages. When I started going to elementary school, she served as a kind of surrogate parent. She made sandwiches for my lunches, tuna with the crusts cut off.

But that side of Muffet wasn't the full story. When I was five or so, Muffet started going into San Francisco to hang out in the Haight with musicians and artists. It was an exciting time for her, and an exciting place, far different from the conventional and constricting environment at home. The Bay Area was the epicenter of youth culture then. My sister got into all the music that helped make that scene legendary: Jefferson Airplane, Big Brother and the Holding Company, not to mention dozens of bands whose names have been lost to time. She was part of the Grateful Dead's inner circle during their early days.

At first, those visits to the city didn't change much except her choice of food. She started to add in strange things to go along with the tuna: alfalfa sprouts, bean curd. Then she started to bring philosophy along with it. She started talking about how food could change the way that you saw the world, how certain vegetables or grains were more in harmony with the universe.

One night, she came home from the city talking a mile a minute, not just about food but about life in general. She had a theory about how she was a butterfly, because butterflies could fly free if they wanted. "And what is freedom, anyway?" she said. "It's not just an idea, but the only idea. It's an element in the air just like oxygen. It flows across the earth like water. We're in a river of freedom, whether or not we know it."

She went on. My parents narrowed their eyes and told her to stop talking nonsense. She didn't. She ended up in Margot's and my bedroom, pacing excitedly and insisting that dreams could be real, that they *were* real. Margot wasn't there, I don't think; at least I don't remember her being there. She probably wouldn't have stood still for Muffet's monologue. She would have challenged it or mocked it. But I stayed perfectly still and didn't say a single critical word. I loved it. I fell asleep listening to the sound of her voice.

In the morning, she wasn't on my bed anymore. She wasn't in the house at all. The next time I saw her was a few nights later, when she burst into the house with her speech already in progress. The difference was all internal at first, but it quickly started to colonize her appearance: her hair became wilder, her clothes less elegant.

One night, the stars were especially beautiful. "You can see them all," my mother said.

Muffet got up from the table. "I'm going outside to look at them," she said. "And then I'm going to fly into the city." No one took her seriously until she neared the edge of the deck. And then my father bolted toward her, moving fast enough to reach her before she got her feet up on the railing.

Muffet's personality change was scary and sad for my parents.

It was accelerated by drugs, but I didn't understand that as a small child, and I'm not even sure that my parents grasped it fully. They were part of a generation where the dominant drug—in some ways, the only one—was alcohol. They tried to keep up with youth culture in the sense that they listened to the music or evolved their attitude about hairstyles (maybe it was okay for them to be that long) or hemlines (maybe it was okay for them to be that short). But drugs were a bridge too far. Whatever they thought was causing Muffet's increasingly erratic behavior, it was a weight that settled over us. I remember once, late at night, hearing my parents discussing Muffet downstairs. It wasn't an argument with her. It wasn't even an argument about her—it was a mostly hushed, sometimes intense conversation. "I don't know what to do," my father said. "We need to get her back."

"Whatever has to happen, that's what will happen," my mother said. "We'll do it."

The voices trailed off, and I heard someone coming up the stairs. I was supposed to be asleep, so I closed my eyes. The door to my bedroom opened. It was my father, and he sat on the edge of my bed and cried. I didn't like it when I was pulled into the adult world by hearing my parents fighting downstairs, and I didn't like it when the adult world came to me. Was I supposed to console him? Was there anything I could say? The burden flattened me, and in response I flattened myself further: I pressed down into the sheets again, seeking invisibility. I don't know if he knew that I was awake and could feel the bed shake with his weeping.

3

THE TRIP IN THE CAR

"I THINK THAT MIGHT BE A COW OVER THERE," my father said. He said something else after that, but I had closed my eyes and drifted off.

I was five years old, in the front seat of the family station wagon. My head rested in my mother's lap, and my feet were stretched across my father's legs as he drove. Kids could ride that way in the late sixties and early seventies: no air bags, seat belts optional. It was so comfortable, like a sixty-mile-an-hour bed. I loved going out for Sunday drives, watching the trees flash by outside the car.

But this wasn't a Sunday drive. We were moving. Though my father worked as a stockbroker in San Francisco while we lived in Mill Valley, he never liked the job, and at some point he disliked it so much that he couldn't continue. When I was four, he started to get a small yearly inheritance from my grandfather's estate, and as that money accumulated, he decided that we would leave Mill Valley and move back to Idaho. Idaho had a good case. Not only was it where the Hemingway family homestead was located, but my mother had been born there too, in Pocatello. My parents bought a place in Ketchum, right near where my grandfather had lived, and packed up the car and left Mill Valley. I was old enough to know we were moving but young enough that I didn't really understand what it meant. I walked a meaningful circle around my room and then waved good-bye to the house.

For the beginning of the drive, my father told us facts about Idaho. He seemed to have a limitless supply of facts. It had become a state in 1890, only a few years before his father was born. It was nick-named the Gem State. It was shaped like a rifle stood up on its stock. I dozed off in the car and woke to the sound of my parents shouting at each other. "Things will be better for her there," my father said.

"Unless they're worse," my mother said. They were fighting about Muffet and whether the move would bring her back into line or send her spinning further out into orbit. My mother was needling and criticizing, and my dad was tightening up with anger. In the backseat, both Muffet and Margot were ominously silent. I pulled my blanket around me. It was the same one that had been with me in my crib, tattered down to almost nothing but still soft, with a ribbon of satin trim. It was blue, which was probably because my parents were hoping for a boy, but it was mine. Even that's an understatement. It was me, as much a part of me as a limb or organ. I loved it. I couldn't exist without it.

And then, suddenly, the fight accelerated and my dad snapped. His face went beet red. He grabbed my blanket and threw it out the window of the moving car. I went rigid with shock. What had I done to deserve this punishment? My mother screamed for him to stop the car, to turn around and go get it, and he narrowed his eyes and raised his hand and said that he couldn't be responsible for what would happen if she said even one more word.

There was no screaming now. The car was dead silent. I pulled my legs up close to my body and felt all the air go out of me. For miles I prayed that my dad would come to his senses, that he would turn around and go back for it, but he didn't. I cried as quietly as I could all the way to Idaho. I don't even remember arriving there, because I still felt like I was back in the spot where I had been tossed out the window.

Those first weeks in Idaho, my mother spent hours calling back to San Francisco, trying to find a store that sold that same blanket. I slept uneasily at best.

Then one night a package came in the mail. "Look," my mother said. She reached her hand into the envelope and took out a blue blanket. I couldn't run fast enough to hold it.

"It's the same one," my mother said, but when I smelled it, I shook my head. It was new, harsh, almost chemical.

"No," I said. I buried my face in my hands. I was even more inconsolable now. But I held out a shred of hope while my mother washed the blanket and dried it on the clothesline. Finally, she brought it to me again. This time, it passed the test. I kept that blanket for almost a decade, wore it down to the smallest rag, wrapped it around my pillow when I was a teenager.

That was only the first trauma in Idaho. Getting adjusted to a new place wasn't easy. I felt like I couldn't make new friends, in part because of shyness, in part because of how I looked. My mother had cut my hair like a boy. The haircut made me self-conscious. And then there was the matter of my teeth. Back in Mill Valley one morning, Margot and I had been waiting for the school bus when I saw some girls coming down the street. There was one girl who was everyone's ideal of beauty: blonde, long hair, already charming in all the right ways. I was moony-eyed with admiration. Margot was off to the side, making herself dizzy by swinging a baseball bat around and around. As the girls approached, I stepped toward them to say hello and Margot stepped forward with her bat, and it was like the Big Bang, but inside my head. My front teeth were knocked right out. They were gone until I turned eight.

My looks were shot. My confidence wasn't there yet. And then there was the fact that the Ketchum school wanted me to repeat the kindergarten year I had just completed in Mill Valley. "No way," I said. I put my foot down. Or at least that's how I remember it. More likely is that my parents spent hours in consultation with each other and decided that I could afford the year off. Whatever the case, they let me skip kindergarten that first year. Instead of sitting in a classroom, I learned to ski. My father bought me a season pass—my picture was all gums and cheeks—and signed me up for lessons with a woman named Mrs. Sherntanner. She was pregnant and also holding a new little baby in her arms—as I would learn over the years, this seemed to be her permanent state. Mrs. Sherntanner was nice to me in ways I couldn't have imagined: warm and open, funny, and supportive. She nursed her infants constantly, which was entirely foreign to me, almost forbidden. And she was Catholic, which made her exotic and, to my mother, problematic. Our own religious beliefs were self-styled, somewhere between Episcopalian and Jack-Catholic, some of the faith, none of the confession. One thing we weren't, though, was the kind of Catholic that Mrs. Sherntanner was. My mother didn't come right out and say she didn't approve, but it was easy to tell. She had a certain kind of derision that you came to know intimately if you lived with her. She would go off on someone once, and from that moment on, that person was fixed in that unfavorable position. She never changed her opinion back, no matter how much evidence there was to the contrary.

But I loved Mrs. Sherntanner and everything around her. She was a steady beacon, a reliable source of everything that was hard to come by at home. She had babies she loved unconditionally. She could be stern, but she was never harsh. And I saw her when I was doing the thing I loved most in the world: skiing. I liked nothing more than to bundle up in my ski clothes and head out for the morning; it was the closest thing to swaddling for a five-year-old. I loved the snap of the cold air. I loved my charge account at the Sun Valley cafeteria, which came with a J number to tell the cashier: mine was J3547. I loved the hot chocolate that I had every morning with the tiny gems of marshmallows that never dissolved. Beginning skiers learned on Dollar Mountain, and my father drove me there every morning.

When I started skiing, it was pizza pie—they called it that because it's the shape your skis make, the wedge of the snowplow. I smashed into lots of people when I was skiing pizza pie. But after only a week or two with Mrs. Sherntanner, I closed the pie up and wasn't smashing into people so often, and before long, I was going up and down Dollar all by myself. By December of that first year, I was friends with everyone on the mountain: the people who operated the chairlift, the other teachers, the cafeteria staff.

I was one of the youngest students on the mountain, which meant that it was hard to find friends my own age, so I invented one. I had a Skipper doll—Skipper, of course, was Barbie's younger sister. Barbie was fine, but she had weird bumpy breasts that I couldn't understand as anything real. I named my Skipper doll Skippy and created a whole biography for her. She liked Skippy peanut butter rather than Jif. She was braver than Barbie, at least when it came to skiing.

I bundled Skippy up in wool pants and a tiny little sweater that my godmother made for her and stashed her inside my jacket sleeve. On the chairlift, Skippy and I talked nonstop about the fastest route down the mountain, how my missing teeth made me look strange, how my hat didn't match my outfit. As I got more confident on my skis, I decided that Skippy needed more action, and as we went up the lift, I would take her out and toss her down into the snow. The second she left my hand, I would start screaming to her: "I'll be there in a second! I'll save your life!" I came off the chair like a rocket and sped back down the hill to get her. She was so happy to see me, an expression of joy and relief on that beautiful unchanging face of hers. Once I threw her off to the side into a drift, and I was so worried I'd lose her that I jumped off the lift. It wasn't as scary as it sounds; there was so much snow that year that it was more like stepping off the chair.

*   *   *

AFTER ONLY A YEAR OF SKI-SCHOOL EDEN, I was given the fruit of knowledge. It was back to school, which meant back to social life and back to new opportunities for triumph (or, more likely, embarrassment).

That year, first grade, was also the first time that I started to understand the magnitude of my family legacy. From the minute we arrived in Idaho, people had talked about my grandfather in a way that made me understand that he was someone important. When we went to people's houses, they sometimes had a bookshelf devoted to his work or a picture of themselves with him. "I was just rereading this," they would say to my father, holding up one of my grandfather's books, and my father would nod politely.

But then I reported to my first day of first grade at the Ernest Hemingway Elementary School, and that was a different matter entirely. The school was my school, with my name on it. I went around with my chest puffed out. But soon enough, kids started to talk behind my back. "Do you see how she acts?" "She's stuck up." "She's acting like some kind of rich bitch." I was mortified. I couldn't talk to my parents about it, and I was almost sisterless: Muffet was in her final year of high school, and Margot, already partying too much as an early teen, had been sent away to boarding school at Catlin Gabel in Portland.

So there I was, with my Hemingway bloodline, stranded in the middle of first grade at a school named for our family. I particularly remember the pain of writing papers. When I turned in my assignments, teachers took them from me gingerly, as if they didn't quite know what to expect. Did I think I was brilliant? And what if I was?

Those heightened expectations collided with my heightened shyness. In my mind, I was sure that I was doing things right. I thought that I deserved to have my thoughts heard. I spent lots of time at a typewriter writing things down, certain that every sentence was a golden insight. The same thing happened at the piano, where I spent hours composing, or at least thinking that I was composing.

Reality descended. I turned the paper in, and it came back scarred with red ink. I got piano lessons, and it turned out that I was terrible. I was horribly frustrated. Why was there such a drastic separation between who I imagined I was and the way that I showed up in the world? And why wasn't the world doing its best to help me understand my own talents?

The limits of the body were just as perplexing as the limits of the mind. One afternoon, we did the President's Physical Fitness Test. It was a big deal back then. If you did well, you got a note from the President. There were a variety of events: push-ups and sit-ups, running for speed, running for agility. "Time for the rope climb," the teacher said. One kid went, and then another, and they got to the top of the rope quickly. When it was my turn, I got three feet off the ground, and then my brain locked up. I started thinking about how my feet were supposed to hold the rope with my toes. Were my knees involved? That's when I let go. It was a three-foot fall, tops, but it felt like I was tumbling from a mountaintop.

I hit the ground, feeling the sting of failure, and looked around to see if people were laughing at me. They weren't. They weren't paying attention at all. Most of them were already heading out of the gym, the boys telling each other jokes, the girls twirling their fingers in their hair.

I sat there for a minute and tried to imagine attacking the rope again. I willed myself to see myself at the top. I sat quietly, immobile, until the gym was empty, and then I tried it again. I was a quarter of the way up the rope, then halfway up the rope, then at the top. My victory was even more confusing than my failure. Why could I do things alone that I couldn't do in front of other people? Was it shyness? Was it that same old desire for invisibility? I didn't talk to my parents about it. They weren't the kind of people you could go to about that kind of thing.

*   *   *

AT FIRST, AT LEAST, Idaho was markedly better than Mill Valley. My father was especially happy with the move. When he was a boy, my grandfather wouldn't let my father fish very much, so as he got older my father fished whenever he could. In fact, during World War II, when my father enlisted in the army and was sent as an intelligence officer to help with the French Resistance, he brought his rod and reel. He was almost captured by a German patrol after his first mission because he went fishing. Mill Valley limited him, but in Idaho he returned to fishing. He made it his life's work—he was a fish and game commissioner some of the time—and became one of the best fly fishermen in the world. He wrote books about fishing and, to the degree that it was possible when you were the son of one of the most famous writers of the century, came into his own.

Idaho didn't solve some of my father's problems, however. It didn't teach him how to deal with my mother's criticism or to be honest about what he was feeling—or, for that matter, to manage his drinking. But it gave him one great gift, which was that it reconnected him to the outdoors. From early on, he was a powerful and almost spiritual advocate of nature, and it brought out his eloquence. "Nature never makes you feel bad about yourself," he said. "It's a living presence that only wants you to experience it and love it. It's the closest thing to recapturing the pure heart you had before life made you feel bad."

In retrospect, I see that he was talking about his own life and his own bad feelings: his drinking, his marriage, his fears that he hadn't lived up to the example his father had set. But I heard his words in terms of my own doubts—the petty cruelties of kids at school, fears about my own shortcomings—and they gave me relief. I accepted what he was saying about nature, that it forgave you and renewed you and restored the possibility that the choices you made would be happy ones. Nature was all of what I understood about God. I would go outside with my father all day, fishing and hunting and hiking, learning to identify birds by their calls and fish by the insects amassing near the water's surface. My fishing technique was good, especially when it came to casting, but I didn't always catch enough fish for my tastes, and much of the time I just dangled my feet into the river or looked at colorful rocks. Bugs landed on my knees. Hawks circled around in the air looking for a mouse or groundhog, and after they made their kill the crows followed to pick at the bones. Those were some of my fondest memories with my father. He was always loving, deep down, but he wasn't always able to find a setting where he could display his love comfortably. Nature gave him a place where he could be himself without compromise or complication.

Even then, I had questions about how people fit into the circle of life. Were we really part of the food chain, and if so, why did we have such an unnatural advantage with our guns? My father never hunted for deer or elk, because all us women at home told him we'd never speak to him again if he did. But we used the guns on birds; we hunted for chukars and doves and ducks and stored them in a huge freezer. Sometimes a dove would be paralyzed from terror, not dead but not moving either, and our dog, a Labrador named Elsa, would bring it back to us. I built a huge outdoor cage and nursed those doves back to health. I even wore a homemade nurse's cap. The results were mixed. Sometimes they got better and were released. Sometimes our cat got into the cage.

I don't think the other girls took to nature quite the way I did. Muffet absorbed it with ease and elegance, like she did with everything. Margot, because she knew it was something that my father valued, tried to like it too, but I don't know if her heart was really in it, except for skiing. She would go up on the mountain and smoke pot, drink out of a bota bag, and ski back down drunk. She would go to parties and get bombed, and she was proud that my father had taught us how to drink wine at the table, which was something that I saw as a source of embarrassment.

*   *   *

MARGOT'S DRINKING AND RISK-TAKING were part of what she thought of as the Hemingway legacy. They were her way of echoing my grandfather's dedication to adventure. But of course, even that appetite for adventure was extremely complicated. Life had its limits, and one of those limits was death.

In Ketchum, in 1961, about five months before I was born, my grandfather had gone into his basement, retrieved a twelve-gauge shotgun, carried it up to the foyer, and shot himself in the head, ending his life at the age of sixty-one. Local clergy called the death accidental, even though everyone knew better.

The suicide had followed a period of intense depression and frequent electroshock treatments at the Mayo Clinic. He had been in a bad way most days since he and his fourth wife, Mary Welsh Hemingway, had left Cuba in the summer of 1960. Some said that he had been failing even longer than that. His eyesight was poor. He had trouble working. A. E. Hotchner, one of his closest friends and collaborators, visited Papa in Cuba in early 1960 and described him as confused and hesitant. He was heavily medicated and also self-medicating, and he had gone for the shotgun at least once before he used it. People like to use his own words to explain his suicide, especially quotes like "Every man's life ends the same way. It is only the details of how he lived and how he died that distinguish one man from another." But the truth is that no one knew what was in his mind except him, and he took the secret with him when he went.

Ernest's suicide was shocking to my father, in part because it was so common in his family. Back in the late nineteenth century, Ernest Hall—Ernest's maternal grandfather—had put a Civil War–era pistol to his head and pulled the trigger. But the bullets had been removed by his son-in-law Clarence, my grandfather's father. Though Clarence acted to prevent his father-in-law's suicide, he had no one to stop him when he took his own life in 1928. My grandmother Elizabeth Hadley Richardson—the woman whose name my father and I both carried—had lost her father, James Richardson Jr., in the same way back in 1903. In both cases, financial pressures were involved, though it's strange to call that the cause of something as fundamentally inexplicable as suicide. Others would follow. Ursula Hemingway, my grandfather's younger sister, would die of a drug overdose in 1966 after battling cancer. And Leicester Hemingway, his younger brother, would use a pistol to end his life in 1982.

None of those things were mentioned at Ernest Hemingway Elementary School. Any inkling I had of the suicide came from the party that his widow Mary still held for him every summer. It was a strange event, to say the least—a birthday celebration for a man who was no longer alive. People shared remembrances and offered tributes; most of them were memories of drinking with Papa. At one of those parties, I overheard my father in conversation with another man, talking more openly about his father's suicide. But even once I was able to piece together what had happened to Ernest, I don't think I had anything close to an appreciation of his adult pain and the sense of hopelessness he must have felt as his ability to engage in life ebbed, and the writing that he thought depended upon that engagement ebbed along with it. How could I possibly understand? People in Ketchum weren't sad that he had killed himself, not really. He had left behind a great deal of celebrity for this little town of a few thousand people. Most of them weren't related to him and couldn't be expected to feel any connection beyond fame or literature. Even within the family, he had a strange status. Grandfathers weren't quite real beings. My mother's father had died when I was very young, and I had a persistent vision of him burning up in a fire while we were visiting him, though that wasn't what had happened at all. However I processed death and departure, it wasn't straightforward; grandfathers were mystical beings who existed beyond what could be known and explained.

But Ernest was a presence, always, especially in Ketchum and Sun Valley. When I was on the ski lift, heading up the mountain, I would sometimes be paired with adults who weren't locals. When they asked me my name, I would answer politely. They would blink and repeat it: "Hemingway?" After that came a furrowed brow, then a pause, then a smooth brow, then a nod of significance and admiration. At seven or eight, I wasn't sure what I had done to deserve it.

Other than that, my relationship with my grandfather was like that of any other kid: his books came to me in the classroom and the library. I read *The Old Man and the Sea* in grade school and thought that in my naïve childhood way I really understood him, that I had a special access to him that no one else did. But that thought, even at the time, passed quickly: I wrote it off as a kind of self-absorption, as the feeling that I wanted everyone to see me at the center of the universe at the same time that I wanted to remain invisible.

4

THE FATHER IN THE HOSPITAL

"MARIEL," MY FATHER SAID. "WAKE UP."

I turned in bed, opened my eyes, and closed them again immediately. It was either too late or too early. Either way, I wasn't moving.

"Come on," my mother said. "Let's go." I blinked and looked around my room: white bedspread, white dresser. It was pitch black outside the window. Was I sick? Had someone died? Were we moving again?

"Mariel," my father said again. It was his quiet voice, not deep and loud like when he was mad, but scratchy, a little constricted. He was being gentle when he spoke and also when he put his arm on mine. He guided me downstairs and then up the driveway to the car. I slid into the backseat still in my pajamas. In the front seat, my mother and my father talked in rapid, hushed voices. I was still mostly asleep, so I picked out only the words I already knew: Muffet, problem, worried.

Muffet had made the move to Ketchum normally. She found herself a group of friends, did well in school, seemed to be going along like any other teenager. But here and there, we saw flashes of the behavior that had alarmed my parents in Mill Valley. And then I was rousted from my bed and packed into the car.

The voices in the front seat started to become frenetic and upset. My mother may have turned and pressed her face against the window. Before I knew it, we were in town. I saw my older sister running naked down the main street of Ketchum, a strange flowing scarf up over her head and the expression of someone who believed she could fly.

I wasn't awake enough to be scared. The whole thing was dreamlike, but I definitely knew that something was wrong. My father got her into the car, which involved more than a little wrangling, since Muffet was possessed by an idea of herself that couldn't be contained or controlled.

At home, she kept insisting that she had only taken one hit of acid. The next day, the doctor came and gave her a shot, and she slept for two days. After that, she was sent away to school. The house was lonely, and Muffet's strangely calming presence evaporated without her. My father became more withdrawn. My mother became more brittle and critical. Margot wasn't the kind of person to calm things down—she liked to spark conflict—and she was already away at boarding school, so the day when Muffet was sent away may have been the beginning of my official role as the family's peacemaker and facilitator. None of these things are precise. It's not like an election, in which candidates throw their hats into the ring, the votes are counted, and a winner is declared. Family roles evolve. But I know that when Muffet went to school, I quickly became more aware of my parents' frailties and conflicts, along with the fact that someone in the house had to provide order and stability. I was only eight years old and not ready for any real responsibilities like this, but they were falling to me nevertheless.

After a little while, we went to visit Muffet, and that's when I found out that the school was in fact a different kind of place—a hospital up north where people went who had "mental difficulties." What were mental difficulties? I wasn't sure, but it seemed like Muffet had them.

The place was called Blackfoot, and when we arrived, we had to wait outside a building that had big black iron bars on the windows. Muffet came out in full American Indian regalia: high moccasins, a short leather skirt, hair in braids, everything beaded and fringed. Her skin had turned yellow from the drugs she was taking. We took her out of Blackfoot and brought her home, at which point she immediately stopped taking her medication, which she said saddened and dulled her. That launched her on a cycle that would characterize the rest of her life, right up to the present: she would act in ways that people deemed normal for a little while, act in ways that alarmed people for a little while, provoke response, receive treatment, reject treatment, act normal for a little while. No matter how she acted, Muffet never scared me. She was my sister and she loved me, and she was generous and smart and entertaining. But even as a young child, I knew there was something wrong, even before people started using words like "schizophrenia." She spoke in different voices. She claimed to hear voices. She was violent only very rarely, though I remember she once held scissors near my mother's neck. For the most part, she was the Muffet I had always known, but with less control and regulation and a greater sense of vulnerability.

Muffet's departure not only promoted me into the center of the family but also indirectly recharged her competition with Margot.

My family was all about whose problems were able to draw the most notice, and when Muffet got sick, Margot got even angrier—worried for her sister, of course, but furious that there was now another obstacle preventing her from being the center of attention.

When Margot was back from boarding school, she was even bossier with me. She wouldn't let me use the bathroom or open the refrigerator on my own. "I hate you," she said. "You're a little tattletale." She was right in one respect: she ate strange foods like Mars bars and Cheetos, sometimes even hiding them under her bed. That infuriated my mother, and it bothered me too. I couldn't stand the idea of food kept so close to the floor. "Why do you have to go and tell Mom?" she asked. "No one should ever trust you."

Margot would grab her coat and rush out the front door. "I may or may not be back," she'd say. When she wasn't at home, she was at the house of a friend, maybe on a basement couch with a boy who had his hand up her shirt. She had a reputation in town for being loose, which wasn't a word I even really understood, except that it made me feel dirty and wrong. Sex wasn't on my mind yet, but Margot's example pushed it even further away. Her behavior worked on me as a negative example. It made me want to be a better girl, a different girl, clean in mind and body.

*   *   *

THE DOG PAWED EXCITEDLY at a spot by the front door. It was Elsa, our yellow Lab, and she could tell that my dad was getting ready for an all-day hike in the mountains. He was dressed in what we thought of as his uniform: khaki corduroys, fishing shirt with buttons and pockets, medium-weight jacket with more pockets, brown boots. They were meeting a friend of his and going to high altitude. "See you later," he said, and he and Elsa went out the door.

Elsa came back in the late afternoon. My father followed her by a few steps. But he didn't say hello or tell us stories about the mountain. "I don't feel well," he said, and sat down in the chair. "I have a tightness here." He drew a line across his chest with his right index finger.

"You shouldn't smoke," my mother said, though he wasn't smoking at the moment. "It's probably that or stress."

My father didn't answer. He didn't look at my mother directly. That wasn't uncommon—it usually took him a while to take the bait—but the expression on his face was grim. He was rubbed his left arm from the shoulder to the elbow. "It's numb," he said. His face was gray like cardboard. "I think I'm dying," he said.

My mother opened her mouth to give more unsolicited advice, but something in his tone scared her. She moved quickly to his side and got an arm around him and helped him up out of his chair. We hustled him to the car and drove to Moritz Hospital in Sun Valley. The doctor, who was a fishing buddy of my father's, determined that my father was having a heart attack. "No question," he said. "It's a good thing you got him here quickly."

To a kid, a heart attack is the scariest illness imaginable. It's simple and vivid. Your heart, which is what keeps you alive, decides that it hates you for some reason and attacks you. We all had a mental picture of someone who was having one, probably from movies: a man would widen his eyes, clutch his chest, and drop dead. It wasn't until my father's heart attack that I even understood that it was something you could survive.

My father was in the hospital for six weeks or so, resting and recuperating. The kids weren't allowed to see him, for the most part, although the nurses snuck me in a few times. "Daddy," I said, my voice fluttering. He would always smile at me, though the smile seemed weak. And he would always console me. "It'll be fine," he said. "Don't worry about it. I'll be back home soon." The strangest thing about my father being away was the smell in the house. My mother was terrified, and that made her cook more, and the foods she cooked were all the American foods she loved that my father resisted: fried chicken, chops, macaroni and cheese. One of my clearest memories about my father's heart attack is the smell of lamb chops filling the house.

One night, at dinner, my mother said she had news about Daddy. I tensed up. Was it bad news? It wasn't. It was great news: he was coming home the very next day. We cleaned up the house, and I went to sleep excited and grateful.

But my father returned a different man, with different rules. He had to quit smoking, which meant that he wanted my mother to quit too. She complied as long as she was in sight, but she would sneak cigarettes in the tiny laundry room, which was the size of a closet; she didn't open the windows when she was in there, so when she came out, billows of smoke would follow her.

My father also had to eat healthier, so butter disappeared and came back in the form of margarine, which tasted like plastic (and it turns out, was one ingredient away from being plastic). I liked the Imperial Margarine man, though: he wore a big red crown and was king of his castle. My father followed the Imperial Margarine man's lead. When he came back from the hospital, he placed himself in charge of everything. There was to be no more stress, no more arguing, no questioning his authority. "That's enough," he'd say, and it had to be enough. He wasn't allowed to get upset.

My father's heart attack also meant an end to his drinking—in theory. What it meant, really, was that the drinking shifted from hard liquor to wine, which was considered a milder and even healthier form of alcohol. We evolved a drinking ritual called Wine Time. It happened at five o'clock in the evening, though they had one of those gag clocks that said five o'clock all the way around. At Wine Time, a huge bottle of red wine suddenly appeared, and everyone was given a glass. Muffet—when she was back—drank right along with my parents, as did Margot. To make sure the wine was at its healthiest, they would put ice in it, which I guess took the edge off. And that's how it went: glasses of watered-down red wine, one after the other.

Watching wine take effect is like documenting evolution in reverse. After one glass, they were funny and nice. After two, some of them were a little short-tempered. The third glass touched off a fight about food or politics or household finances. If a child spoke at that time, my father might snap at them: children were meant to be seen and not heard, he'd say. It happened to Muffet and it happened to Margot and it happened to me. It didn't matter what I said, whether I was joking or just making an observation. He'd shut me right down. He and I were the two most athletic members in the family, and we liked to compare notes on exercise. I would tell him where I had hiked that day, how long it took, who else was on the trail. When he was sober, he would listen enthusiastically and ask encouraging questions. But when he was drunk, he would push back competitively. If I said I did the trail in two hours, he'd say he did it in an hour and a half. If I said I was out with the dogs at eight, he'd say he was out at two in the morning. His three-drink self was almost the opposite of his normal self.

Often, that third glass was just the end of the first act of the Wine Time drama. Then there was an intermission. Adults would regroup. Kids would go to bed. The fourth glass would start the cycle all over again. A fifth and sixth would often follow.

After the heart attack, there were new things to fight about too. "What about her?" I would hear my mother say. Or: "Maybe she would care." I didn't know who she was talking about, but I had older sisters to help me out. Margot, in particular, loved to torture me with information. She's the one who told me that while my father was in the hospital, he had some kind of affair with a nurse. I don't know how far it went. It may have been more romantic than sexual. I imagined kissing, at least. For my father, of course, an affair with a nurse while recuperating was hardly a neutral event—his own father had fallen in love with Agnes von Kurowsky while he was in the hospital in Milan during World War I, and she had been the inspiration for Catherine Barkley in *A Farewell to Arms*. The affair with the nurse, Hemingwayesque though it might have been, further bruised my parents' already fragile relationship.

One evening the three sisters were in Muffet's room, getting ready for bed. Margot asked me if I had heard. "Heard what?" I said. Margot turned and looked at Muffet meaningfully. "What?" I said again.

Margot sat down and clasped her hands. She had big news to deliver, and she was going to be as dramatic with it as possible. "Mom and Dad might get a divorce," she said.

I was horrified. The idea knocked me back onto the bed. Then I thought about it for a minute. "Wait," I said. "What's divorce again?"

*　*　*

SLOWLY, MY DAD SETTLED BACK in to the swing of things, and life in Idaho moved along smoothly.

Summer was the yang to the yin of winter. I took my puppy, Mr. Bubba, out to the lake and climbed rocks without using ropes. I swam in the river and rode my bike back while I was still wet, letting the sun dry me and feeling the satisfaction of athletic challenge. I hiked back to the resort and charged food to the J account at the Sun Valley snack bar. I had also started buying myself stomach medicine. I was preoccupied with the idea that germs might appear in the house if we weren't vigilant, and I kept a small stash of medicines in my room to protect us. I also developed a mortal fear of throwing up. I had seen my parents throw up from alcohol, probably, and I didn't like those implications at all. A little later, I would see Margot throw up from bulimia, though it's possible I saw it earlier than I think. Whatever the cause, it wasn't a normal fear, the aversion that nearly everyone has to the feeling of queasiness; it was something extreme.

Slowly, my dad settled back in to the swing of things, and life in Idaho moved along roughly. There was no divorce—my parents seemed committed to the marriage, no matter how fraught it became—but the tension intensified. It was especially bad whenever company came over, because that meant a promise of happy times and the inevitable disappointment of departure and unhappiness, and more drinking, which meant more fighting. Around this time, I started sneaking into my parents' bed while they were still downstairs. I would stay there and listen to the conversation, trying to separate the laughter from the angrier tones.

I often fell asleep, though usually not for long. Sometimes the noise that woke me was yelling. Sometimes it was my mother coming into the room. She wouldn't intentionally wake me up, but she would make a ruckus: she would drop the toilet seat loudly, run the water too long, turn the lights off and on. Then she would get in bed and sit with me and cry and tell me about her sad life with my father. One night, she might lament that my father no longer showed her affection. "I used to have beautiful clothes," she'd say. "Your father used to give me all the money I needed for them. Not anymore." Another night it might be about the road not taken. "I wanted to be a flight attendant," she'd say. "But I was too tall." In those moments, she inhabited a world that was even worse than the real world, one where none of her dreams or destinies were available to her, where she was ill-used and neglected. It was almost like a grand old dame of the theater or the silver screen complaining that the world had passed her by. Her stories were never especially detailed or imaginative; she got quickly to the central point, which was that she was deprived, and after a little while she seemed to lose her head of steam. That's when the TV went on, mostly with detective or cop shows.

When she dozed off, I would tiptoe downstairs, careful not to wake anyone. By that time my father was asleep on the couch or, more often, downstairs in the basement, and I would make sure that the living room was clean. It was easy to do in the middle of the night. It was just me and the water in the sink and the wine poured down the drain. I would clear away not only the dishes on the table but also the broken bottles that were sometimes thrown, and occasionally I'd have to wipe off spots of blood from the walls where someone had cut themselves. The house smelled nice during the day, of food or baking, but it was different after a fight: staling wine and the strong smell of cheese left out for hours. Our cat, Kitsy, would watch me from the little box where she ate, which was on top of the food warmer. I would wash the good crystal glasses by hand. My goal was to make the evening invisible, to create a situation in which people could wake up the next morning, come back to the living room, and not remember even a shred of the night before. Sometimes it worked like a charm, and the next day was normal again; I'd help pull weeds in the garden, and then my parents would let me ride my bike to town.

I found new ways to occupy myself. I fancied myself a fabulous modern dancer, which basically meant that I would dance on my own to whatever was on the stereo: the Moody Blues, Antonio Carlos

Jobim, a Doug Sahm song called "Sunday Sunny Mill Valley Groove Day" that reminded us all of where we used to live. I was in love with Carole King like nearly every other girl in the country. Certain bands, though, struck me funny, in the sense that they gave me a bad feeling: "Spinning Wheel," by Blood, Sweat & Tears was something I associated with a fight between my parents over Muffet, and whenever I heard it I tried to hear another song in my head immediately. The same was true of the Grateful Dead. They reminded me of Muffet before she began acting strange, and thinking of her as she used to be was too sad to bear.

My mother wasn't as interested in music. She listened to talk radio and watched morning television; she had been a *Today* show regular since it debuted in the early fifties. My mother was also the one who sat with me and watched television shows. She liked cop shows and crime shows, and I watched them all with her: *Mannix, Hawaii Five-O*. I thought I was a genius because I could always figure out *Mission: Impossible*. And then on my own, I watched *The Waltons*. I loved it for all the reasons I was supposed to: the big family, the intimacy, the low levels of conflict. It was proof that there were families that said good night to each other and houses where no bottles were thrown.

*   *   *

EVERY SUMMER, FOR A WEEK, my parents would send me to Oregon to stay with Mary Kay and Dan, my godparents, who lived on a farm with no kids and lots of animals. When I was with them, I sewed, fed chickens, and picked baskets full of vegetables out of Mary Kay's garden. They had an attic filled with dolls and dollhouses, toys and baby clothes, all handmade, and I could stay up in the attic or in a room right next to theirs. My choice. I also was drafted into helping Mary Kay with her booth at the state fair. She dressed me to match it. She won ribbons, and I felt like I was winning them too. Mary Kay and Dan loved me with all the love they had stored up for babies that they couldn't have. It was so easy to be with them. They didn't drink, so no one ever changed. I was just me, Mariel, in the orchard or the attic or on the porch swing doing nothing at all. I was the center of the world there. Or, more accurately, I was away from being the center of the world I knew. Without Margot, without Muffet, without my parents, I didn't have to worry about cleaning up after a fight, or being picked on, or feeling sad as I watched people I loved injure each other. I also noticed something strange, that I seemed to fit well in this other world. So much of my identity up to that point had come from being the calm in the storm, the stable daughter in a family that was always spinning out of control. When I was stable within stability, it felt strange: not unpleasant, but unfamiliar.

* * *

MUFFET AND MARGOT kept our bathroom filled with products: hair sprays, skin creams, oils, lotions. As we all got older, I inherited a larger share of the bathroom, which meant that I inherited a larger share of the clutter, and clutter wasn't something that I could tolerate. "Clean this up," I would say to no one, and then I would do it myself.

One Saturday morning, a few days before fifth grade was set to start, I went to clean the bathroom. It was tricky, because while Muffet probably would have been okay with it, Margot didn't like anyone to interfere with her world. She didn't really see the mess she was making, but she was certain to see the absence of it.

I started to clean, but right away I was distracted by a bottle of Sun-In. It was a hair lightener, and it made you look like you were "kissed by the sun." I loved the sound of that so much that I repeated it out loud. "Kissed by the sun," I said. My hair was blond, but my mother called it "dishwater blond," which meant that it didn't glow the way that other girls' hair did. Maybe Sun-In was the answer.

I read the directions on the bottle and sprayed a little bit on my head, but after five minutes of watching the mirror, nothing was happening. I sprayed again, and then one more time, and then I started watching myself in the mirror again. Still nothing.

I put the bottle away and left the bathroom. It was August, and there were other things to do: swim in the river, go to the pool, lay out on the deck. My mother loved to go out on the deck and tan. She had a huge reflector that she tilted up so that her face caught the most sun possible. I sat with her as long as I could, but out of the corner of my eye I saw a range of things beckoning to me: pets like Kitsy and Mr. Bubba, the trampoline in the yard, the cage with our new parakeets. The next day, I swam in the pool and then sat outside in the sun; the day after that, I went swimming in the river and biked home.

The third day, I noticed my hair getting blonder. I was thrilled, and then I was nervous: it didn't stop at yellow blond but went right on through to orange and then a kind of reddish blond, and then suddenly it was the first day of school. "I don't want to go," I said. "My hair looks weird."

"You're going," my mother said. I held my breath right up until the front door of the school, and then I exhaled with relief. Sun-In was everywhere that year, and plenty of kids, boys and girls both, showed up with hair the color of brass. By the time school pictures

were taken, my own real hair had grown back in, darker than anything from the Sun-In. I looked like a bumblebee.

*　*　*

MY FATHER'S LIFE after his heart attack, and his determination
to keep the family in line, only meant more separation from my
mother. And that separation made him isolated in nearly every way.
He accommodated his isolation most of the time, but then there
were the moments when he would rebel against it. At some point,
I noticed a marked change in how my father dealt with my sisters.
There was a turn in the way that he showed them affection and in
the way that they allowed him to do so. Over the years, I have sometimes wondered if there was anything going on behind closed doors
that I didn't know about, anything improperly intimate or even sexual. To be clear, I didn't see anything untoward. No one ever said
anything to that effect. It's hard for me to even imagine. But I force
myself to wonder because there was such a persistent sense of unease
in the house. In the contemporary world, where children are vigilantly protected, people do some of the wondering for me. They use
words like "violation" and even, sometimes, "molestation." I reject
those words because they seem like impossible words to use without proof. I know only that my house was defined in large part by
a father who was sad and lonely and who could only really admit it
to himself when he drank. My mother, whatever her strengths and
dreams, was cruel to him at a basic level. She dismissed him and
made him feel smaller. My father was then left with some aspect of
his basic humanity untended. He turned elsewhere in the family for
affection. He may have made my sisters feel uncomfortable when
they were adolescents and young women. It may have been more

than simple discomfort. But I can't say exactly what it was. It isn't that I won't say. I can't say. I don't know. I never saw anything to suggest specifics. We lived in a complicated house. All the relationships were unhealthy and unbalanced. They were messy, not necessarily sexually, but emotionally and psychologically. Who got attention? Who deserved it? How was basic affection parceled out? What was the cost of feeling good about yourself?

Years later, I raised these issues in a documentary about my family, and when I went to promote the film, I would talk to crowds after screenings. More than once, someone in the crowd would stand up and thank me for my frankness regarding sexual abuse. The first time it happened, I was stunned. I didn't know what to say because I didn't think that's what I was talking about. In my mind, I was talking about the fact that human beings are fragile, even into adulthood, and that the things they do to shore themselves up are sometimes done without concern for the fragility of others. As an adult, I have seen other adults be inappropriate in their affections with children because they were mad at spouses or disappointed in themselves. The vast majority of the behavior isn't sexual, and it's not abuse in any clear way, but it's unquestionably an aggressive and unkind continuation of an unhealthy family dynamic.

Much of my thinking on this topic has come together in the years since I was a child, of course, but some of my instincts are the same as they were back then. One of the central questions that occurs to me is this: Why, when people hear about discomfort in a family, do they immediately imagine the most taboo acts? As a culture, we've singled out one kind of interaction and decided that it's the worst thing that can happen to a person. But that's misleading, not because it's not horrible, but because it obscures and trivializes the hundreds of other ways that a family can betray a child, most of which are far more nuanced and complex, more interwoven into everyday life. When we draw a bright line, when we put certain things on one side of that line and call them abuse in such an obvious way, it prevents us from dealing with the other things. You could make a real argument that my mother's behavior was just as sick if not more so, that her relentless criticism put conditions on ordinary affection. When she was nice to me, nice without any complication, I remember feeling like her kindness was a valuable secret that belonged to me and me alone. But that also meant that I couldn't share it with anyone else or it would be a betrayal of her trust, and she might withdraw even that small amount of affection from me.

None of this is to excuse or absolve my parents but to try to explain their behavior—and, most of all, to explain the way my sisters and I behaved in the face of their behavior. I remember that my father was sad much of the time and that he grasped at ways of feeling better, whether through drinking or through escape. He reached out and all too often found nothing there to comfort him.

5

THE MOTHER IN THE HOSPITAL

"STOP IT," I SAID. Margot was telling me what I should and shouldn't do, bossing me around.

"Shut up," she said. "You don't know what you're talking about."

"I do," I said. I was eleven. I didn't have to put up with her anymore. I thought about standing up and leaving the room. But we weren't in a room. We were in an airplane, winging our way east toward London. After a few days there, we were going to continue on to Paris, where we would meet up with Muffet, who was working with a French author, translating his work into English. She was heavily medicated, and as long as she stayed on her regimen, she was more than functional.

The flight was an hour long, and then another hour. It seemed like it might never end, especially with Margot next to me. I closed my eyes, leaned back in the seat, and thought about my peacoat. My mother had taken me to the store and bought it for me before

we left, and much of what I thought about myself in London came
from imagining myself in that coat, warm and safe in the cold wet
weather.

The plane finally landed. The tires screeched on the runway, but
I had never been so relieved to hear an unpleasant noise before.

We were tourists in London like any other tourists, doing all the
things that Americans do: walking the streets endlessly and pointing
at landmarks like Big Ben and City Hall. I especially liked the Tower
of London, where the royal jewels were kept under guard. I marveled
at the way that the Beefeaters at the Tower stayed emotionless and
rigid, eyes looking straight ahead. They were charged with focus and
duty, and they were honor-bound not to react to anything in their
field of vision, no matter how distracting or ridiculous. To me they
were the strongest people in the world, and they also were familiar:
that's how I felt at my house, like I had to see things and not do anything, to observe and not react.

I loved being in our hotel, the Cadogan on Sloane Street; our
room was beautiful, and we went downstairs for high tea and scones.
In a sign of early-actress syndrome, I spoke with an accent while
we lifted our teacups and sipped from them. "Lovely," I said. "Just
lovely." Margot tried an accent too, but she couldn't keep a straight
face, and it was hard for her to hold the hot tea while she was laughing. I thought that I would never see anything as impressive as the
hotel until we went out walking one day and ended up at Harrods. It
seemed like the biggest store in the world, and it was: there were entire floors dedicated to dolls or to chocolate. I bought a dress for my
baby doll, Sylvie, and also fancy red shoes for myself that made me
feel like Dorothy in *The Wizard of Oz*.

As magical as London was, it paled in comparison to Paris. My
father had been born in Toronto, but he had gone to France while he

was still a baby, and he had spent the first years of his life there. My grandfather's book *A Moveable Feast*, which wasn't published until after his death, was a memoir of his life as an expatriate in 1920s Paris, when he and Hadley were young and new in the city. My father is in the book, called by his nickname, Bumby. He often asks questions that move the narrative along, or he is at home, comfortable in his tall cage bed. There's even a piece devoted exclusively to him: "The Education of Mr. Bumby," which recounts a conversation between my father and my grandfather in which they discuss everything from the difficulty of the writing life to parental discipline to the tenuous health of F. Scott Fitzgerald.

We stayed at the Ritz, which was even fancier than the Cadogan, and because my grandfather had been there frequently—frequently drinking—they had named a bar and a number of cocktails after him. We were treated like royalty, and the place felt like a palace: everything was gold, from the bathroom faucets to the picture frames. My parents had a huge suite, and Margot and I shared a room that was attached to it. Muffet would visit some mornings. High tea in London had been one thing, but this was something else entirely: the hotel staff woke us up in the morning and opened the curtains, as if they were ushering the sun into the room, and they brought warm croissants and coffee with milk, which I drank, feeling more adult by the minute.

My father was energized by Paris in ways I hadn't seen before. He took me to visit places from the book, which were places from his life: crooked streets with their strange small hotels, lavish gardens that had been central to the city since the seventeenth century, the good café on the Place Saint Michel. We went to the zoo. "I came here when my dad needed the place quiet so he could write," my father said. We went to the Gare de Lyon, the train station in the southern part of the city. "This is where my mother lost my grandfather's manuscript," my father said. It's one of the most unforgettable scenes in *A Moveable Feast*. Ernest was in Switzerland, writing about the peace conference in Geneva. Hadley was coming to meet him, and she put her bags aboard the train and went to get a drink of water. When she returned, one small bag was missing—it was the bag that contained a manuscript of short stories, pieces about Nick Adams in Michigan. She and the conductor searched the whole train, but it was gone.

Ernest wrote about greeting my grandmother in Switzerland and how she broke the news to him:

> *I had never seen anyone hurt by a thing other than death or unbearable suffering except Hadley when she told me about the things being gone. She had cried and cried and could not tell me. I told her that no matter what the dreadful thing was that had happened nothing could be that bad, and whatever it was, it was all right and not to worry. We could work it out.*

My favorite stop was the Louvre. My father paused in front of a Cézanne canvas, a painting of pears. "My father," he said, "wanted to write the way these pears are painted, to be simple but somehow give the full picture of something. You don't need a million details. You just need to show what something truly, purely, is."

Most of the memories were like that, nostalgic in the best sense. They kept my father warm. The truth was that he hadn't really ever had a normal life with his father, not in Paris and not afterward. By the time he had real, thoughtful memories that he could put color to, Ernest was gone, already separated from Hadley and on to his second wife, starting another family, fathering two more sons, raising them somewhere else. There's another famous quote from my grand-father that speaks to this: "To be a successful father, there is one ab-solute rule: when you have a kid, don't look at it for the first two years." When my father was a little older, he had gone to Cuba to spend time with his dad, but mostly he spent time with the women in Ernest's life, who orchestrated things so that the great writer could work. Periodically Ernest was kind. Paris was the one place my father remembered being completely connected to his father, and that's what the city gave me in turn. It also calmed down the rest of our family. Margot and Muffet got along wonderfully, which was rare: Muffet showed Margot the city, took her to all the cafés that she had been to with her boss, wore scarves and flowy skirts that Margot imi-tated, though it made her look like a cowgirl.

After Paris, we stayed in a village called Pérouges, near Lyon. It was so small that no cars could drive into it at all. The whole time we were in Perouges, it was stormy and cold, and our rooms felt like something from a dollhouse, with small fireplaces and high-canopied beds. When you returned from a chilly walk, the hotel staff would greet you with hot chocolate made with real milk and melted choc-olate. Perouges was like a fairyland from a book, and while my par-ents fought, they were far less contentious than they were back in Idaho—when either of them reached a breaking point, they would just read the newspaper or take a nap. Muffet was with us in Per-ouges, and we three girls enjoyed the glorious room service. Margot and I stuffed as many croissants as we could into our mouths. I think I fit four in there. I ran to my parents' room to show them, and when I got back, I saw Margot sticking her finger down her throat and throwing up the breakfast we had just eaten. I hid out, not making a sound, because the scene felt awful and wrong. Why would anyone want to throw up their food?

*   *   *

THOUGH SKIING was part of our life in Idaho—it was part of most people's lives in Idaho—getting my mother onto the slopes was always a challenge. "I'm not good at this," she said, and she was mostly right—she wasn't a natural athlete, and she never really had confidence on the snow. When the rest of us went on to intermediate and expert trails, she stayed on beginner runs.

One bright afternoon when I was eleven, we left my mother on the easy part of the mountain and went to take the ski lift up the mountain. The next time we saw her was in the hospital. She had crossed too closely in front of an equally uncertain skier, and they collided hard. The accident shattered her leg. For months she was in a full cast from toe to hip.

At first, under the influence of painkillers, she was uncharacteristically pleasant. We all drew on her cast. Margot painted a Picasso-like self-portrait. Daddy drew some fishing flies. She smiled and traced the lines with her fingers. But when the pain pills wore off, so did her pleasant mood. She needed help with nearly everything, and she wasn't shy about saying so: "I want a glass of water," "I need to go to the kitchen," "Can someone bring me the mail?" Since my father was spending more and more of his time in the basement—it was almost like a separate apartment down there—the job of helping my mother fell to me. I was only eleven, but I essentially took on a full-time job. I cleaned. I organized. I cooked. I fetched whatever needed fetching. And slowly but surely, I started to inhabit the caretaker role. It had an immediate effect on the house. I saw that my mother was less likely to snap at me than she was at my father. I saw that my father was happier keeping his distance. Caretaking was an extreme version of what I had been doing for years: creating artificial order so that the house didn't descend into chaos. Mostly, I remember being exhausted. At night, my mother needed help limping to the bathroom. While she was in there, I would fall asleep in her closet, sprawled on top of her shoes, and she would nudge me with a slipper to let me know she was ready to go back to bed.

After four months, the big cast came off, and she got a little one that only extended just above her ankle. She could cook again and get up and down the stairs more confidently. My father bought her a recliner, and she took her meals in the chair, legs stretched out. That's when we stopped eating dinner at the dining table and switched over to meals in front of the TV. They weren't TV dinners—they were as gourmet as before—but they were served on trays after Wine Time.

* * *

"DON'T HAVE TOO BIG A SNACK, GIRLS," Kelly's mom said. "We're going to stop for dinner soon."

"Can we have a little one?" Kelly said.

"Sure," her mom said, beaming.

It was the perfect American family in the perfect American vehicle taking the perfect American trip. I was with Kelly and her parents, and the four of us were driving down to San Onofre, California, in their camper. Kelly and her parents talked excitedly the whole way, pointing out the windows at interesting buildings, cool cars, herds of cows.

The only issue I had was food. We were near the coast often, and they liked stopping for seafood. Seafood wasn't something I was ready for: I was still obsessed with controlling my food, which meant knowing exactly where it came from, and imagining my way into the murky depths of the ocean was beyond me. I was positive that if I ate anything from the sea, I would end up bent over a toilet for hours. "No thanks," I said to shrimp and lobster and fish that was probably delicious beyond my dreams.

When we got to the beach, the trip was perfect. We drove the camper out to the ocean and swam, and Kelly, who was a year older, flirted a little bit with a local surfer boy: blond hair, blue eyes, dark skin. I flirted a little with a friend of his, though with less success. "Hi," he said, and I turned away, blushing and giggling.

About a week after we got there, Kelly and I were on our stomachs tanning when something blotted out the sun. It was her parents, standing over us. They were stiff as statues, and I knew that something was wrong. Finally, her father's face cracked. "You have to leave," he said. I must have looked horrified. Had I done something wrong? An apology rose in my throat. He rushed to clarify. "It's your mom," he said. "She's not feeling well. You have to go visit her."

"Back to Ketchum?" I said.

He shook his head. "Your parents are in Portland, where your mom is in the hospital." He explained: She had been feeling weak ever since her broken leg, and the doctors in Ketchum were concerned enough to send her to Portland for more tests. "They discovered something," he said.

"What?" I said.

"They're not sure," he said. "But you need to get on the plane immediately." We packed up the camper and drove to the nearest airport.

It was the smallest plane I had ever seen, more like a chair lift on a ski slope, and two men who weren't dressed like the pilots I was used to flew me up the coast. The plane shook and shuddered the whole way. I counted the minutes and sipped the air so that I wouldn't throw up.

When I got to Portland, my father met me. "Hi," he said, but there wasn't any bounce in his voice. We drove to the hospital, where the two of us sat in his car in the parking lot and he tried to tell me what was happening. "Your mother…" he said. "Your mother…" Then he started to cry, which stopped him talking, and then he started to talk again and said we needed to go inside to meet his friend Dan. I was cold and also numb, and he put his jacket around me to warm me up.

We went upstairs to a sparse room that held only a couch and dresser and coffeemaker. Dan came in and sat with us, and after a little while my father was able to talk. "The doctors had to knock her out," he said. "They needed to cut into the space above her chest and remove a tumor."

"So they removed it?"

"They couldn't. It had already spread into other parts of her body." That meant that she was sicker than they had expected. "She might not have been feeling well for a while. It might have had something to do with why she broke her leg, or why she stayed in the hotel room most days in London."

As he talked, I noticed that he was wearing a khaki fishing shirt, and that Dan was too. Had they gone fishing while the tumor spread through my mother? I was suddenly furious with them. Couldn't they see that she needed us? The shirt filled my field of vision. It was a symptom but more than a symptom. It was a symbol. It stood in for all the loneliness in our family, all the attempts at escape, all the anger that couldn't be expressed. I couldn't express mine either. "Can I see her?" I asked. "Now?" My voice was small, not hard-edged like I wanted it to be.

They led me down the hallway, which smelled like the senior home where my grandmother lived. I couldn't bear any of it: not the tumor, not the smell, not the cold rain in the parking lot or the way my flip-flops were squeaking on the floor. Just before we got to my mother's door, my father reached over and laced our fingers together. I knew what this meant. I had seen it before. It meant that he was sad and scared himself, and that he didn't know what to do. I forgave him the fishing shirt.

My mother was on the bed, sleeping. She looked beautiful even with the oxygen mask that was lying on her chest. Mary Kay, Don's wife, was with her. "Puck," my father said. "Marielzy is here."

My mother opened her eyes. "Hi, baby girl," she said. She held out her hand—with its prominent knuckles and pink nail polish and a hospital band that was too big for her wrist—and I took it between mine.

"You look pretty, Mommy." I said. "Not sick at all. You did your hair."

"Mary Kay helped me fix it up this morning," she said.

She pulled me close to her. I had to hop up onto the metal bar of the hospital bed. The back of her hand was cool on my cheek. "Daddy says you're sick," I said, and the rest came in a rush: "You can't die. I love you. I'll pray, and you have to promise that you'll pray too. You have to." I had already started negotiating with God, or whatever my understanding of God was—I figured there had to be some power that could turn things around.

"You're blonder," she said, "and nice and tan too." Then she laughed, louder than she should have, which scared me. It was the kind of laugh she laughed when she was watching a TV show and something surprising happened. She wiped tears from under my lashes. "Okay," she said. "I promise. I will be okay for you." I put my head on her stomach. I was scared to get too close to her chest or her throat. If I pressed down on the tumor, would it leak more poison into her? The cold rain was still coming down outside, and I watched it through the wires in the window, feeling her breathing underneath me.

We stayed an extra week in Salem at Dan and Mary Kay's house. I slept by myself in the attic room, but it wasn't the same. I couldn't give the dolls my full attention. I thought only about my mother, which was a way of not thinking about the possibility of a world without her. Every day, we trekked back to Portland, to the hospital, as Mommy got stronger and Daddy met with the doctors to decide what to do when we got home. They decided that she would start chemotherapy and radiation in Boise. The treatments would be weekly. Daddy would drive her. When he couldn't, I would. He had already taught me to drive, because I had to make trips to the market when Mommy had her broken leg the year before.

*　*　*

MY FATHER TOLD ME LATER that my mother was only given a few months to live. She made it though those months and hundreds more, but her cancer shifted the entire dynamic of the house yet again.

We all had problems, some more than others. Muffet had her mental issues. Margot struggled with her disorganization and insecurity. My father had suffered a heart attack. I was obsessive and worried too much about my stomach. But whatever we were dealing with, it paled in comparison to the cancer. That was something we all understood. My mother, by falling ill, became the undisputed center of attention. One thing the cancer did, immediately, was eliminate any remaining chance of divorce. If my parents had discussed it at times after my father's heart attack, it was taken off the table after my mother's diagnosis. Splitting up was no longer an option.

The main result of my mother's cancer was that I became her full-time caretaker. The jobs that had fallen to me when she broke her leg remained, and they were extended and expanded. I needed to bring her meals, help around the house, pick out clothes, make sure she made it to her appointments on time. Like my dad's affair with the nurse, this repeated a family pattern: my grandmother, Hadley, had spent her twenties caring for her mother, who came down with, and eventually succumbed to, Bright's disease. But for me, at the time, in Ketchum in the early seventies, becoming my mother's caretaker was a singular event, the end of my carefree childhood. It isolated me in ways that I couldn't have anticipated—from classmates, neighborhood friends, kids I would see on television. What was that girl in the movie doing playing in the yard? Wasn't there an ailing relative in her family who needed everything? Caring for an sick parent is rewarding, but it's also hard, and it's especially difficult at that age, when I probably needed all the things I wasn't getting: a sense of self, a sense of separation.

People sometimes ask why I didn't get angry. The first few times I heard the question, it sounded like nonsense. Get angry? That wasn't even on the menu of possible outcomes. My reaction was to make myself invisible, almost like a servant of the house. I didn't rebel. I didn't subvert. I didn't make a scene. What I did was to slowly and subtly learn to manipulate a tense and treacherous set of emotional circumstances. I learned to pick my way through the minefield of ailments and alienation.

Soon enough, it became second nature. I would learn when it worked to my advantage to cozy up to my mom a little bit, spend more time with her than she was asking, and when it made more sense to go down to the basement and spend time with my father. I operated the home like a machine whose purpose was to produce the least amount of tension possible. That was the beginning of a habit that would last for years and even decades: do whatever possible to engineer an easier life in the short term, even if it relied on evasion and caused blockage. My family made it easy for me, in the sense that no one openly confronted any problems or issues. We moved along, locked together, locked in place.

It wasn't a drab existence, just an extremely focused one. When I watched TV with my mother, she liked me to entertain her with burlesques of the commercials, so that's what I did. I learned to apply my mother's makeup, and to feel a vanity that she didn't. She was content to leave the edges of her base makeup sharp and exposed, but that looked strange to me, her head and her neck were different colors, and so I smoothed the lines.

Summer lost its sense of freedom. I stuck close to home. I jumped on the trampoline in our backyard and perfected front and backflips. My friends Kelly and Sara came over sometimes, but I found myself trying too hard to convince them that everything was okay, and that was exhausting.

A few times a week, I took my bicycle and rode north to Galena Lodge, a spot about twenty miles north. On the way home, I sometimes stopped at Easley Creek, where there was a church camp filled with big-city kids who came in jaded and then, after a few weeks, found themselves totally bewitched by mountain living. I watched them jump into the river for the first time. One of the kids, a boy about my age, detached from the group. "Do you live around here?"

"Pretty near," I said. "I'm from Ketchum."

"Why are you allowed to ride so far by yourself?" the boy said.

I shrugged. I didn't really know the answer. Was I privileged because I had more freedom, or just neglected? Part of me wanted to tell him the whole story: the cancer, the alcohol, Muffet, everything. But I wasn't the kind of person to vent to a stranger. I didn't even really talk about those things to my friends. I just wanted them to feel that everything at my house was okay. So whenever I spoke about my mother's illness, I emphasized normalcy and routine.

That strategy had long-term consequences; it short-circuited my ability to recognize and respond to emotional problems. That would last decades, resurfacing now and again to upend my life—or, more to the point, to make sure that inertia won and productive change was impossible.

At the time, though, I didn't do much of anything about it. I broke down only once, when I was with my aunt and my uncle, my mother's sister and her husband. We were in Boise, where my mother was getting chemotherapy. "I wish..." I said, and trailed off.

"What?" my aunt said. I think she thought I was going to say something about where I wanted to eat dinner or get ice cream.

I was suddenly crying. "I wish I could change everything," I said. "I wish that Mommy wasn't sick, and that she and Daddy were happier, and that Muffet was better too."

My aunt and uncle put their arms around me. They consoled me with genuine compassion. "Things will get better," my aunt said. "You'll see." I looked into her kind face and saw only platitudes. I knew that I couldn't change things by wishing.

And because I couldn't change anything near me, I started to change things inside me. I went from being terrified of throwing up to being completely obsessed with food. I wasn't anorexic or bulimic. I never went through a period where I didn't eat at all, and I never really threw up. But I became fixated on certain types of foods and certain eating habits. I told myself that the foods I was eating were for my mother, that I was minimizing any possible shock to her system—Muffet always liked to talk about food that was in harmony with the universe—but the truth was that they were for me too. I remember passing through a period where I would only eat peanut butter and honey sandwiches, nothing more, for close to a year. I rationalized it: they were soft, so they wouldn't upset anyone's stomach, they had enough protein and nutrients, and they wouldn't spoil easily.

My list of permissible foods grew slowly. "Here," I'd say, giving my mother brown toast and jam made from only berries, along with wild rice. "This has nothing unhealthy in it," I said. "It won't cause any stress." Nothing came out of a box. If my father caught fish, I prepared it on the barbeque with butter, salt, and pepper. I learned to forgo any and all guilty pleasures, from cheese in a can to sugary cereal to Ritz crackers and Wheat Thins, even though the woman in the Wheat Thins ads was a gymnast and seemed healthy enough.

When my mother felt stronger, she cooked with me. We might make whole wheat bread and eat it while it was still hot, with honey and French butter. When she was weak, I cooked on my own. We made lots of the recipes that irritated my father—good, solid American food—though I adjusted for my new ideas about healthy eating. I tried a fried chicken recipe in a skillet, and it was delicious, but the frying was unhealthy, so I tried again with a flour made from nuts. That was too dry—not enough butter—and I tried yet again, succeeded, and fed the failed first experiment to the neighbor's dogs.

My food habits were healthy enough, but they were connected to other forms of compulsion. On the school bus, I only breathed out of my nose—furthermore, I stuck my face as close to the glass as possible so that I imagined I was only getting the air from outside the bus. Maybe every kid has these private rituals, these ways of mastering their immediate surroundings. Later, when I was a mother, I saw that kind of behavior in my own children and their friends. But at the time, I had no perspective on those beliefs. They were both my private magic and private science, the only things holding the world together.

6

THE DAUGHTER IN THE MAGAZINE

IN THE EARLY SEVENTIES, Evel Knievel hatched a plan to jump over the Snake River Canyon, a huge scar cut into the earth in southern Idaho. The stunt required extensive planning: he had an aeronautics engineer design a rocket-powered motorcycle that he hoped would take him across the canyon, which was a quarter-mile wide in places and five hundred feet deep. Much of the operation was local—staking out the canyon, checking things like winds and sight lines—and they needed neighborhood kids to help out, deliver notes, get coffee, that kind of thing. Margot had a friend who was working on-site, and then Margot, too, went to work there.

That first week, a man who was also working the event was staring at Margot. "What?" she said. She wasn't the type to let something like that go.

"You're very beautiful," he said. Margot thanked him, I'm sure, and then probably went and partied with him and his friends. At any rate, she didn't come home for a few days. It had happened before.

Her early-teen habit of getting drunk at a party and calling my dad to come and pick her up had evolved to the point where she would frequently crash at friends' houses. A week went by. Maybe we got a phone call, but she didn't resurface. No one was worried. And then she reappeared. To our shock, it wasn't in person. Rather, it was on a national magazine cover.

In retrospect, it may not have been quite as sudden as it seemed. She had traveled to New York with my father the year before and made contacts in the fashion world. But it seemed like it was an overnight transformation. There was a marked physical difference too. She had left town with light brown hair, and suddenly there she was, on a magazine cover, with blond hair. She had left town struggling with her weight, always a little heavier than she wanted, always wearing these huge wide belts, which she must have thought covered her up but actually created the impression of thickness, and there she was wearing the finest clothes and looking sexier than anyone ever had. She also had a new name: Margot was gone and she was now "Margaux," which sounded more cosmopolitan and worldly and came with a funny story about how she was conceived, something having to do with my parents and a bottle of Chateau Margaux.

In some ways, Margot's rapid rise, and the appearance of Margaux, made perfect sense. She was always a very social person, always good at getting along in the outside world. She had a talent for surviving, certainly, and she was more experienced—which isn't to say sophisticated—when it came to the riskier aspects of teenage life, especially sex and drugs. But nobody ever expected that she would be famous. When I thought about it hard, it made me a little dizzy. It was as if somebody had twisted my head on backward.

That first Christmas, she came home. Hemingways always came home for Christmas. She had a serious boyfriend with her, a guy named Errol Wetanson, whose family ran the burger chain Wetson's.

His older brother was the actual businessman, the true heir of the hamburger empire. Errol was a social butterfly and a playboy. He had an image, to say the least—he had black curly hair and a mustache, and he wore white pants and shoes. "Where does a person find clothes like that?" my father wondered.

Errol filled in some of the gaps of how Margot had become Margaux. He had met her when she was visiting New York with my father, and then they had been together when she had returned to the city. He claimed that he had introduced her to the big names in the fashion world—to people like Marian McEvoy, who was the fashion editor at *Women's Wear Daily*; to Frances Stein, who was the fashion editor at *Vogue*; to the photographer Francesco Scavullo; to Halston. Errol also talked about how smitten he was, how he would meet her plane with flowers whenever she returned to the city from a trip. It was, for me, a glimpse of an adult life that was very romantic and not entirely convincing. The people around Margaux seemed to want something from her, even if it was something she seemed more than happy to give them.

Within about a year, she got the Babe campaign, which made her the spokesperson for a Fabergé perfume. That meant more than magazine covers; it meant advertisements everywhere, on billboards and in magazines and even in television commercials. In June 1975, she was on the cover of *Time* magazine, with a headline that read "The New Beauties," and that September *Vogue* called her "New York's New Supermodel," which was a word that hadn't been used very often at that point. It's what they had called Twiggy and Jean Shrimpton and not very many other women.

Over the years, I had to think about Margaux's fame, either as an independent idea or in relation to my own, so many times that it's hard to recapture that first phase of it. How did it make me feel? I felt confused, for starters. It's an exaggeration and maybe an inaccuracy to say that I was jealous. I was too young to be jealous. But there was something patently unreal about the way she became so famous so fast. Margaux had become one of the most recognized women in America: one of the faces everyone wanted to see, one of the standard-setters for beauty. During one of her vacations home, a magazine came out to Ketchum to do a piece on our family, and there was a photograph of the three of us—me, Margaux, and Muffet—walking down the highway with the mountains in the background. We were immortalized in the caption as "Margaux Hemingway's sisters." I hadn't thought of us that way before, not exactly, and it felt like a nice way to redraw the picture.

*   *   *

GROWING UP IN KETCHUM, we didn't have lots of movie theaters. We had exactly one, in fact: the Sun Valley Opera House. The Opera House was built in 1937, the year my grandfather published *To Have and Have Not*, a story of love and smuggling set in Cuba and the Florida Keys. *To Have and Have Not* was also a movie, of course, with Humphrey Bogart and Lauren Bacall. In it, Bacall speaks her most famous line: "You know how to whistle, don't you, Steve? You just put your lips together and...blow."

The movie, I'm sure, screened at the Opera House, though I don't remember seeing it there. But I saw tons of other movies there over the years. Every Friday and Saturday night, they had fifty-cent showings, and all the kids went. Most of the time we didn't even watch that closely. We crawled under the seats and popped up next to friends. Now and then, a boy would reach for your hand in the dark. For me, in third grade, that boy was Sean Paterson. He was a real-life dream, a paragon of male beauty and virtue. I would catch him looking at me when I was looking at him. He talked about how he would defend me against other kids who might have thrown a cup and accidentally hit me in the head. I developed a theory of love after that: people were there to increase your safety, to stop cups from hitting you in the head, and you rewarded them by letting them hold your hand. I was good at that.

After those few perfect months, Sean and his family moved away, and the movies became ordinary again, just a loud place with lots of kids and seats that you could crawl under. My social life wasn't ideal. Maybe that's the case for any teenage girl, but I felt like I was especially insecure. I was too tall—taller than all the boys—awkward and leggy and flat-chested and self-conscious to a painful degree. Everyone in my family was tall. I dealt with almost everything by giggling: comedy, tragedy, even ordinary information. I noticed early on that girls weren't straightforward with their loyalties. They would be nice to me in one-on-one conversations, but in groups they would pretend that they didn't like me. It was like a form of gaslighting, really: they would have normal conversations with me when we were on our own, reject me as soon as someone else showed up, and then reassure me as soon as that other person left. Once I was sitting under a portico by myself, wondering why none of my female friends would sit with me. They were off in a separate group, probably trying to attract the attention of guys. As luck would have it, the guys noticed me, and two of them came over to talk. Except that they weren't interested in talking. They walked right up to me, swung back their ski-booted legs, and kicked me in the shins. I fell over, trying not to cry. It hurt so much I couldn't even giggle. None of the girls came over to see how I was, but then later that day one of them called me to apologize. None of that behavior was that uncommon, or that extreme, but I had a hard time finding kids who could rise above it.

I found some. There was Kelly, who was my partner in crime

in everything. We created our own radio show, the Kelly & Mariel Hour, which went straight to cassette. We did fake interviews, sang songs, tried out accents—I was best at French and Kelly did a perfect Frito Bandito voice like the ads on television. Her house was the opposite of mine: messy (Christmas tree still up in April), warmly noisy, openhearted, and relaxed. Her mother smiled as much as my mother frowned. Her father disciplined her, but with humor and patience rather than anger. Kelly's parents had two much older boys, and by the time Kelly came along, their parenting had relaxed significantly. Kelly would tell me about trips that she would take to the beach in Mexico, her family in the camper for a solid month, and I couldn't even imagine. My family had trouble being in the same car for twenty minutes on the ride to a dinner party. Then, if we went somewhere, it was in segments: I might go fishing with my dad in Oregon, or driving with my mom to see friends in California.

My other best friend was Sara. We bonded over horses. She had her own horse, called Chocolate Revel after the ice cream, and I borrowed a horse from the Sun Valley Center. We adventured around the valley on trails or took the horses into the shallow parts of the river. I wanted to show my parents that I was responsible enough to get my own horse, so I put in my time in the stables, mucking the barn and feeding the animals. The horses were rewarding to be around. They always responded to affection and watched carefully as you moved around in their space. They also talked to you all day long if you knew how to listen, pinning their ears back in frustration or flicking a glance to let you know that they were ready to go out. Starting around sixth grade, I also worked as a guide, leading trail rides for tourists, which were an entirely different kind of animal. They would say they were experienced riders, but the second they were up on the horse, they'd freeze up, and the horses would sense their terror. Sometimes they'd overcompensate for the lack of control they felt and start kicking at the horses, or screaming at them, and the horses didn't take very kindly to that. But since they were tourists bringing in money to our little town, I was instructed to tell them that their horses were skittish, and to take them back to the barn and get them a Pokey Joe horse. Every once in a while, I would get revenge on one of the more arrogant tourists by leaving them on a real horse, which would grow more and more fed up with the incompetence and the clumsiness and the cruelty and eventually take off running back to the barn, tourist clinging on for dear life.

I worked hard that summer, cleaning and guiding, making my case for a horse. But I was operating from a deficit. Two years earlier, my parents had made the same deal with Margot and gotten more than they bargained for. She wasn't careful with her horse, didn't take the time to train him and run him, and he jumped the fence daily and had a habit of parking himself out on the highway. That was Exhibit A for the prosecution. My mother kept asking me who would take care of a horse if they ever decided to get me one, which they were pretty sure they wouldn't. So I dreamed of it instead, as hard as I could. I imagined that I had magical powers to make one appear.

* * *

WITHOUT A HORSE, I threw my energies elsewhere. Around that time, I redecorated my bedroom. It had been mostly white, with a white bedspread and a white dresser. I kept the white walls but redid everything else in red: red curtains, red furniture, a red bedspread that I made myself. I moved furniture around every few months, just to give myself the feel of a new room. I liked nothing more than pulling the desk against a wall where it hadn't been before, or rear-ranging the figurines on my dresser.

When I wasn't interior decorating, I was outside, mostly with Mr. Bubba, my yellow Lab puppy. He came along with me and Sara whenever we went riding or playing by the river. "Bubba," I would say, and he would run to me, big feet fast over the ground, and jump into my arms.

One morning, I let him out to play in the garden and run over to the neighbors' house to beg for a little snack of bacon. Before I rode my bike into town, I went to say good-bye to him until the afternoon, when my dad would bring him to the river. I didn't see him in our yard, not even making a mess of the lettuce patch, so I rode over to the neighbors'. He wasn't there, either.

I went out onto the highway—even though he wasn't allowed to go there, he didn't always obey the rules. I reached the road, looked around, called his name, and headed north. A few hundred yards from our driveway, there was a drainpipe where he sometimes liked to play. As I approached, I heard a scuffling noise. I couldn't see into the pipe from the road, so I ditched my bike, slid down the shallow hill, and climbed into the large end of the pipe. Down at the other end, I saw a heap of yellow fur: it was Mr. Bubba, breathing heavily, trying to stand. I got close enough to see that something was wrong, and then close enough to see what was wrong. He had been hit by a car.

I picked him up and ran back down toward the driveway. He was almost as big as I was, and I couldn't quite get clearance off the ground, so as we ran his rear legs dragged. He was bleeding on my shirt. I started talking to him, faster than I had ever talked to any-one, even my Skipper doll: "Please," I said, "please, Bubba, listen, we'll get Daddy, he'll take you to the vet, hold on boy, you'll be fine, you need to be fine."

Halfway down the driveway, I screamed for someone to come

outside, and my father appeared in his tennis shorts, shirtless. His
eyes swept across the scene, and he didn't even pause. In a second he
was next to us, lifting the dog from my arms, and in another second
we were all in the car, my father driving, me in the backseat holding
Mr. Bubba's head. I couldn't see well through the tears in my eyes,
but I could tell the bleeding wasn't getting better. It was coming
from his side and from his mouth.

"I think he's choking on the blood," I said.

"Your mother called ahead to the vet," he said. "They'll be ready
for us when we get there." The vet's office was past Ketchum, and my
father ran all the lights in town.

At the office, a nurse in a pink dress was standing outside to take
Mr. Bubba. I wanted to go in with him, but I wasn't allowed. "He's
the best vet around," my father said. "He'll do everything he can."
What could I do?

I waited with my father and listened to the cars pass by on the
road and watched the sky, where hawks circled over the field across
the street. My father had found a fishing vest in the car, and he was
wearing that with his shorts, and he waited with me but couldn't be
still. He did some squats and fake tennis swings. When the vet came
out, he was bloody too, and his head was down. He told us that Mr.
Bubba had fought hard but that the cuts inside his body were too
severe. The nurse directed us to the back door, to a sheet covering
something that was still warm. It was Mr. Bubba, but it wasn't Mr.
Bubba anymore. Just a few hours earlier, I had been looking right
into his eyes, telling him how much I loved him, watching him listen
to me say it.

"Come here," my father said. He was standing near the car. I
walked over there and felt myself crumpling. I couldn't breathe. My
father held me. I wished that I could simply feel consoled, but there
was too much else going on along with it: a slight sense that I was

being melodramatic, even though I was sadder than I had ever been; a twinge of regret that my parents didn't show that kind of affection more often.

The shirt I wore was yellow with flowers on it. I had wanted it so badly. I threw it away.

*   *   *

"INTO THE POOL, GIRLS." The man pointed down at the water. Margaux and I got in. She splashed me and I splashed her back. We were in New York City, on a rooftop, the city stretched out in the distance.

I had been in swimming pools before, but never in New York City, and certainly never on a rooftop. At one point, as my hand went down to scoop up more water, time hiccupped for a split second, and I forgot how I had gotten there. Then I remembered. About a month before, still riding the crest of fame as America's premier supermodel, Margaux had been offered a role in a film. The movie, *Lipstick*, was about a model who was being stalked by a musician. The script also called for a second female role, the model's little sister, and Margaux asked Johnson if he could see me in the part. She thought that it would make her entry into acting easier, more comfortable and more natural. And so, the winter I turned twelve, I flew out to New York City with my father to meet with the director, Lamont Johnson, and the producer, Dino De Laurentiis. We stayed in the Plaza Hotel, which awakened all kinds of glamorous thoughts: it was where Eloise lived, of course, in the children's books, and there was even a big portrait of her in the lobby, leaning on a wall with her dog at her feet and a fancy dinner unfolding behind her. I woke up the next morning feeling like I had hardly slept a minute and not missing it at all. Energy was going through me like I was a live wire.

We walked over to a tall building and took the elevator up. I imagined we'd meet in an office with some chairs and a big oak table and a picture window. I didn't expect to come off the elevator and see a swimming pool. Margaux was there already, along with two men I had never met, one tall and the other short. The tall one introduced himself as Lamont and shook hands with my father and then with me. The short one, who I guessed was Dino, just smiled and watched. "Into the pool," Lamont said. "Just act like sisters," he said. Margaux and I splashed around, which was an acting job in and of itself, since we rarely played like that. Mostly, I just giggled.

After I auditioned, such as it was, the men went off and consulted while my father took me to FAO Schwarz. Back at the hotel, my father made a call. "There's another meeting tomorrow," he said.

Another morning, another day shot through with energy. We woke up early and walked across Central Park, which was crowded with people throwing baseballs and Frisbees, roller-skating and piloting little sailboats in ponds. "Look," my father said, pointing to a statue. It was Alice in Wonderland, with the Mad Hatter on one side and the March Hare on the other. We exited the park through an opening in a big stone wall and went into another tall building with another elevator going up. There was no pool in this building, only a room with the biggest desk I had ever seen, and behind it was the short man from the pool. He looked like a little kid in a car, trying to drive when he could barely see over the steering wheel. "Dino," my father said. In his heavy Italian accent, Dino told me that I had the part. He told me that I was going to be a big star. "It will be perfect," he said.

We went home, waited for a little while, and then flew off to California for the shoot, this time with my mother as chaperone. We stayed in the guesthouse of Stephanie and Efrem Zimbalist, who were friends with my father—well, she was, through fishing. The

Zimbalists had a kind of mirror image of my parents' marriage: Efrem was also the son of a famous man (his father was a concert violinist), and he and Stephanie seemed isolated from one another, though she was the one who spent time on her own taking trips into nature. Their daughter, also named Stephanie, was beautiful in pictures on shelves. She was at Julliard studying to be a musician, though later she would end up being an actress too. And what was an actress, exactly? I'm not sure that I understood what I was getting into. Acting in movies wasn't anything I had thought about, even when I was watching movies. I wanted to be an architect, because I loved controlling spaces, or a marine biologist, because my family had visited Sea World when I was young, and it seemed like an impressive mix of science and entertainment. Acting was very abstract at that point.

I'm also fairly certain that I understood almost nothing about the movie's subject. *Lipstick* is a dark story of rape and revenge; Chris Sarandon plays the musician, Gordon, who turns out to be a monstrous villain. I didn't know that the movie was about sex and rape. I had read the script. Maybe I had even seen the word. But the concept didn't sink in. I was so defiantly naïve about those matters, and so put off by the darkness of the adult world, that in my mind I blocked that out. Sex in general was an unknown world for me, a source of real anxiety. Part of it was related to Margaux. Kids around Ketchum commented upon it often, and I didn't want to be a bad girl, so I went the other way. But intimacy was also a problem. I never saw healthy affection between my parents, except maybe a peck on the cheek on Christmas Eve. Sex felt disconnected from what good people did. It wasn't part of a marriage (as far as I knew), and it wasn't part of a productive adolescence (again, as far as I knew), and when you did it, in any way, people whispered about you behind your back. I didn't see how you could participate in it at any level and still be a good person. That was only one of the ways that the movie asked the impossible of me. There was also the matter of the film's villain: Chris Sarandon was so nice, and it made no sense to me that he was also this horrible stalker and attacker.

Despite this, I had to act. There were plenty of scenes in which my character, Kathy, had to show confusion or terror. Everyone on the set wanted to make sure that I wasn't too scared, that I understood it was only make-believe. But that was a kind of paradox: If I knew that it was all fake, how could I deliver a realistic performance? Somehow, when the camera came on, I felt like I knew what I had to do. I understood the broad outlines of my job—that I was supposed to react a certain way—and I suppose I instinctively knew that the way to create emotional nuance was to imagine myself in a similar situation that I had already experienced. So I could draw on scenes of humiliation and fear in my own life, memories of peeing myself on the ski slopes or being kicked in the shins by the boys under the portico. The people watching the movie would have no idea what I was thinking; all they would see was the reaction, which would match up perfectly with what was happening with my character.

I loved being on set, not just for the acting but for all the other aspects of the movie world. Watching the crew was a revelation: there was an entire world of support staff, all working to make this project happen. They would bring snacks, or drag cables, or pour grape juice in place of wine, or make sure that your watch didn't jump ahead visibly in time during a scene. The actors were warm and welcoming. Chris Sarandon, as I said, was a perfect gentleman, the diametric opposite of his character, which made the scenes with him both comforting and disorienting—in one of them, I had to run while he chased me through the Pacific Design Center, an unfinished building that was a labyrinth of dark corridors and tight turns. Anne Bancroft played my lawyer, and she was nice and supportive. And even the actors playing smaller roles fell into place as sometimes more than colleagues: I hung out with some young women playing dancers, and one of them was drinking carrot juice, which looked healthy enough that I requested some for myself—actually, I request-ed it for my mother, but I ended up drinking it, and my mother chided me for my obsession with health food. For the first time in years, I felt like I had a home that wasn't filled with various insolu-ble problems: alcohol, illness. I created a family for myself. When I turned fourteen, on set, I got a surprise birthday cake, the first one I really remembered since Kennedy was shot.

The sense that the set was a safe zone was reinforced when we got back to Idaho after the shoot. We drove to Boise to check on my mother's health, and the doctors found new cancer in her spine. I felt like at some level it was my fault, that I had created an unhealthy sit-uation in which she wasn't able to get enough rest—or, worse, that she sensed the ways in which I was growing accustomed to my new movie family and growing apart from her. I confessed that to my fa-ther one afternoon, during a walk, and he stopped in place. "That's ridiculous," he said. "Mommy is alive because you love her so much, not sick because you had a good time making a movie. She had a good time too. The movie made her happy." My father pitched in then, as much as I ever remember. He cared for my mother during the days and I managed her during the nights, and scarves arrived from Margaux in Italy to cover my mother's head, bald again from the treatments.

*   *   *

"LET'S HAVE A SLEEPOVER," Kelly said.

"What?" I said. I was stalling. Sean Paterson had moved back to town, and Kelly had started dating his brother Mark. They were officially a couple, and I knew that Sean still liked me, but a sleepover? With boys? What happened at those?

"You know," Kelly said. "A sleepover. It's simple. We'll just take sleeping bags out in the backyard."

"Your parents won't mind?"

She shrugged. "Come on," she said. "I don't see the problem."

I saw nothing but problems, or at least potential ones. It could end in embarrassment, shame—or even worse, some kind of sex. It was all a minefield to me. But I found myself agreeing with Kelly. "Okay," I said.

That night, we met Sean and Mark after dinner. The four of us pulled our sleeping bags out into the yard and then lay there looking up at the stars. After a little while, Mark and Kelly got into the same sleeping bag, and they started groping and kissing. I watched them from the corner of my eye while I tried to carry on a conversation with Sean.

"So," I said. "Are you going to ski this year?"

"I guess," he said.

"I wonder what movie is coming to the Opera House next," I said.

"Not sure," he said.

Finally, I stopped talking long enough to let us both feel the space between us. He started to inch closer to me.

"No way," I said. "You're not going to do that to me." Then I burst into idiotic laughter: full, out-of-control giggling, to the point of breathlessness. Needless to say, nothing happened, and then later that week Sean sent me a note through someone else explaining in kind but firm language that we were pretty much finished as a couple. My heart was broken, but I couldn't have done anything differently.

*   *   *

WHEN *LIPSTICK* WAS RELEASED in April 1976, I didn't go to an official premiere. Instead, my father took me to New York and we sat and watched the movie in a theater on 42nd Street where people yelled at the screen and cheered on Margaux in every revenge scene. That's when I realized that my parents had let me be in a movie where I got raped. It was a shock. I wouldn't say that I felt violated all over again—that's melodramatic, and not true at any rate—but I had a number of different emotions all at the same time: fear and surprise and a little uneasiness at the inappropriateness of it all and, deep down, in ways I couldn't even admit to myself, maybe even a little excitement, not because of the sexual violence, but because I was being allowed into an adult world.

It was also shocking to see how Margaux's performance was received. On set, she was the recipient of a tremendous amount of attention. She was New York's New Supermodel, a huge earner, the star of tomorrow. All that attention got to her, in good and bad ways; she had always been the girl who needed to fight to be noticed, the neglected middle child, and there she was being noticed at a previously unimaginable level. Throughout the shoot, she used to say that the movie was sure to be her breakthrough, that she was giving an Academy Award–caliber performance. Sometimes she stated it even more simply. "I'm an actress," she'd say. Or "I made it." But when it was released, the movie was roundly criticized, and Margaux more than anyone. She got nothing but horrible, mean-spirited reviews. People called her talentless. They said that it was annoying to watch her. They made fun of her voice. One of the gentler assessments came from Roger Ebert. "How does Margaux do in her acting debut?" he wrote. "Well, not terribly well. She has an interesting voice and is pleasant to look at, but she doesn't really seem in command of her more difficult scenes."

Ebert wasn't particularly mean, but the whole thing just seemed unfair. Margaux wasn't a natural actress, it's true. She hadn't grown up watching other people carefully and positioning herself to react. It wasn't her personality. She was more about her own needs and ideas. And even I could tell on set that there were certain scenes in which it was really difficult to get her to be natural. But she had nothing to hold onto, no training: she had been thrust into a movie simply because she was a famous model—and worse, it was a movie *about* a famous model, so critics and audiences somehow resented her more, as if she couldn't even give a convincing performance as a character who was so similar to herself. Critics and other writers were willing to begin writing her off, even though she was still in her early twenties.

What made matters worse was that I got generally good reviews. Ebert again: "She has some difficult scenes and handles them like a veteran, she's unaffected and convincing on camera and, whether she knows it or not, she can act." And Vincent Canby, at the *New York Times*, said that my performance was "immensely moving" and "utterly unaffected." That was fine, though I cringed when he went on to say that I made everything else in the movie look like "a calculated swindle." The reviews, and particularly my good reviews, hit Margaux hard. She didn't want to look at newspapers or hear things people were saying, even if they were being related in a supportive tone that mocked the critics. She was deflated and frustrated and also just plainly sad. It's as if her movie career was already yesterday's news, as if critics had decided to discard her and move on to next year's (non) model.

Lipstick put me in a nearly impossible position. I was proud of the work I had done. I did feel that I connected to something in the role, and that I understood how to do this strange business of realistic pretending. At the same time, I didn't want to be used as a weapon to disappoint and dishearten my sister. She had set her sights on an acting career, and it seemed like maybe it was over before it had even really begun. I felt a tangle of emotions that ranged from gratification to shame to a kind of survivor's guilt, and everything in between. Inside of all of it was an important lesson about movies and the way they worked—or didn't. Films are a collaborative medium, for better or for worse. When you're an actress, you show up on set and do whatever you can with to bring your character to life. That requires you to plumb certain emotional depths and use certain techniques to communicate those emotions to the audience. But when you're done with your part, you have to just stand down and hope for the best. There's nothing else you can do. The process is always a gamble.

Whatever mixed feelings I had about the critics, the movie changed my life at least a little bit. I felt pretty good about myself for a while, and even when other kids were mean to me, I had a silent response at the ready: "Oh, well I don't see that *you've* made a movie." I probably got more attention from boys my age, but it never even registered. One thing that I did notice was that it suddenly felt like old men were interested in me—and by "old men" I mean anyone older than twenty. I could hold conversations with them, and I had begun to collect some more interesting life experiences, and that was ultimately more comfortable for me than trying to have normal conversations with boys my own age, which would inevitably end with my clamming up or, more likely, giggling uncontrollably.

* * *

WHEN I WAS FIFTEEN, I got another acting job, a TV movie called *I Want to Keep My Baby*. I was Sue Ann Cunningham, a high school girl who has to reassess her life when she gets pregnant. We filmed in Boulder, Colorado, and I was fifteen playing sixteen, outfitted at first with a fake belly and then with a padded bra so that I would look more full-figured. The movie was easier than *Lipstick*, and just as fun. I started to expand my emotional range as an actress. All that meant, really, was that I learned more ways to map memories onto actions. Want me to show sadness? Just let me imagine Mr. Bubba, and I'll be in tears. The character couldn't have been less like me, which made it a challenge and also a vacation from self-absorption. I could pretend to be something I wasn't and would never be: the popular girl with the cute jock boyfriend.

I was also reminded of how much I liked being on set. The people there were tremendously supportive, from the director down to the makeup and hair people. Everyone had a job that they took pride in, and that made me proud of my job. Just as before, the crew came to be a temporary family, which was superior to my real family in that it was all of the proximity with none of the problems. Even better, it had a defined end: after the shoot, I waved good-bye and hopped on a plane, well in advance of that inevitable moment when everyone's bad traits would surface. Even then, I was learning to live through a series of temporary, intense experiences, setting up a rhythm of change.

While the set was similar to *Lipstick*, the release of the movie was completely different. I didn't have to wait a year: it was out within a matter of months. And people in Ketchum didn't have to go to the theater to see it—it just showed up on their television set one night. I was proud of the movie, proud that I was in another one, but it was also embarrassing. I worried that everyone in town—my classmates, my teachers, store owners, neighbors—would see through the superficial physical transformation and know that I was just faking.

They didn't know. They praised me—not lavishly, but enough that my confidence and sense of my own competence bloomed again. Maybe I wasn't great in school. Maybe I was too shy and self-conscious to absorb enough information, or to arrange it in the way that the teachers wanted. But here was something else that I appeared to be good at, and it was enough to know that something like that existed. For the first time, too, I started to notice that there were other actresses around my age doing the same kind of thing that I was doing: Tatum O'Neal had done *Paper Moon* in 1973, and Jodie Foster had done the TV version of *Paper Moon*, then *Alice Doesn't Live Here Anymore*, and she was just about to break big with *Taxi Driver*, *Bugsy Malone*, and *Freaky Friday*. I started to set career goals, which were really personal goals. When I saw Tatum O'Neal, I thought she was terrible: not the actual girl, but the image that people had of her. She seemed spoiled and misbehaving, attention-seeking in all the wrong ways. In my mind, I leaned more toward the Jodie Foster side of things. She seemed quiet and really smart, as if she had everything under control. I was in awe of her and a little bit jealous.

One of the best things about acting was that it kept me out of normal school. On set, I had a tutor, which was great. You never did anything worse than anyone else, and there was no class to stand up in front of, blushing uncontrollably. When I went back to Ketchum after the TV movie, the sense of being special lasted about a week, and then I was the same old Mariel. That made me miserable. At the time, my father had helped found a new school in town called the Community School. It started in the basement of the Episcopal church and was run like a prep school: lots of work, high expectations, better-qualified teachers. My father even taught French and Spanish. I begged my parents to let me go there, and finally they consented. From the beginning, it was a problem. The school was just too demanding, though I wasn't willing to admit it. I had done well in elementary school, but suddenly I was falling behind. We had so much reading assigned, and I had a physical reaction to it. I read so slowly that it felt like I was in quicksand, and before I knew it I would start to doze off. That was a strange turn for me, because it marked out some negative space, a zone of failure, which was something that I hadn't exactly experienced before. More and more, being an actress seemed like the best choice.

And I was one at home: still acting like things between my parents could be okay. In some ways, things had changed greatly between when I was twelve and when I was fifteen. My parents had officially retired to their own corners of the house. They hosted fewer parties, and my father went on more fishing trips, and for longer each time. That's not to say that when he was home it was easy. My mother would cook for him, even going to the trouble of avoiding the foods he disliked. He would eat in silence. Then, a few hours later, he would go back down to the kitchen, pour himself a glass of port, and make a snack. My mother, upstairs, would smell the burnt toast, and it would just infuriate her. "That son of a bitch," she'd say. "He's making a fool out of me."

*　*　*

"I WAS WAITING." It was a few days before Christmas, and I had gone to the airport to pick up Margaux. In my mind, her name was starting to be spelled the way the world saw it: the famous supermodel rather than the infamous sister. Her flight was early, though to hear her tell it, I was late. "I was waiting," she said again.

Margaux's star was rising. Through the late seventies, you were just as liable to see a picture of her at Studio 54 with Bianca Jagger as you were to see her on a magazine cover, and when she wasn't there she was jet-setting. She had a place in New York and a place in LA. She went to the Alps and to the Amazon. By this point, she had already left the burger heir and was married to Bernard Fauchier, a Venezuelan photographer. "I'm painting," she said. "There are things I need to say that I can only say through art." But she wouldn't show us her paintings and wasn't even confident enough to discuss them. She just announced it: I'm an artist now. That was how Margaux was then. She kept a running monologue about what she was accomplishing and the surprising new directions her life was taking; she was a little hard to pin down.

Margaux was mostly about Margaux. Now, with the wisdom of the years, I can see that it was her insecurity that made her seem so selfish, but back then it was mostly irritating. We could be most of the way to the house before she asked a single question about anyone else.

Oddly, you could see her selfishness most clearly in her most generous act: giving holiday gifts. When she came into town, she came loaded down with packages, though it turned out that mostly she was just regifting all the free stuff she got as a model. "This is for you, Mom," she'd say, and it would be a basket of lotions that clearly came from a cosmetics company. "This is for you, Dad," and it would be some strange scarf in a color he'd never really wear. The irony was that she wanted everyone to give her very special presents, and she was upset if you didn't hit the target perfectly. When I was little, I loved surprises, and at the holidays she used to torture me by waiting until my parents were out and then forcing me to watch as she opened all the presents. Even then, she always compared her gifts with mine and decided that mine were better, that they somehow marked me as the favorite, and later on she would try to engineer complicated trades: she might get a glimpse of Muffet's new skirt and then follow her around the house asking her to trade.

Margaux's visit also gave me a chance to look at Muffet again the way a new arrival might. At that point, Muffet was heavily medicated, which was the main way that mental illness was treated then. By modern standards, she was certainly bipolar, with periods of mania, though the word "schizophrenia" was also used. My father explained it to me as a matter of brain chemistry: If your brain could be stabilized by lithium, it made sense to take it, the same way that an anemic needed to take iron pills. But the side effects included severe bloating, and then sometimes she would go away during the year for electroshock treatments. She went in manic, if highly attuned to her surroundings, and came out different, with less clarity in her thoughts and some memory gaps. She dealt with those gaps by inventing elaborate stories, and she was usually the heroine of them.

Every year was the same. I would go to the airport to pick up Margaux, and the ride home would be filled with all kinds of love and generosity, a new hopefulness that old wounds might heal and old habits might change. When we came through the front door, my mother would be cooking, and she'd look up with a smile. "Hi, girls," she'd say.

But the evening settled in. Wine was poured. People had the chance to sleep in their own beds. And in the morning, the newness had evaporated and we all went back to being the same people we were before. My mother went back to carping about my father and how he didn't make her feel loved. My father withdrew into his version of the same complaint. Margaux fought. Muffet rambled.

I developed my own Christmas rituals. I would leave the house early, just to get away from the claustrophobia of it all, and take a long walk into town. I would spend time with whatever animals were around. And I would go through family albums obsessively. As the third child, I was the least documented, by far: there were hundreds of pictures of Muffet, dozens of Margaux, and just a few of me. That sent me into corners of the house looking for more evidence of my life, trying to fill in the gaps. I found an old school picture on a bookshelf. I found a ski picture in a drawer.

Looking for photographs over the holidays, I found a box in a closet, and an envelope in the box, and a picture in the envelope folded inside a piece of paper. The paper was yellowed at the edges, but the photo was clear: it showed a young woman alongside a smiling, handsome young man. The woman was smiling too, which is what slowed me up in recognizing my own mother.

I brought the photo to her. "What's this?" I said, holding it out. I tried to speak as gently as possible, but her mouth tightened anyway as if she was being challenged. When she saw the photo, though, she softened. "That's me and my first husband," she said.

I had a hundred questions but couldn't ask a single one.

My mother paused for an eternity and then sat down next to me. She started to speak but could not. After another equally long pause, she explained. She had been married when she was very young. "He was a fighter pilot in the war," she said. "He was shot down after we were together only a few months. A little while after that, your father came on the scene." As if on cue, my father appeared. He nodded at everything my mother was saying, but he had a distant look his eyes.

That night, at dinner, there was another argument. Maybe that's an overstatement. There was a disagreement. Margaux was telling a story about a friend in town, and my mother interrupted to say that she had never trusted the girl. "You say that about everyone," Margaux said. "You're never satisfied." She glared at my mother and stormed away from the table.

"Well," my mother said. "Maybe now we can have a pleasant meal." In bed, later, I couldn't shake that idea: never satisfied. My mother had been a girl as full of hope as any other girl. She had found her Prince Charming, only to have him taken from her. My father arrived on the scene determined to do his best, but who could live up to the standard set by a dead hero? Everyone in my family was in an impossible shadow. Margaux was in the shadow of her perfect older sister, Muffet, who in turn was in the shadow of her own mental disarrangement. My father was in the shadow of my mother's first love. My mother was in the shadow of her own past. All anyone wanted was to be out of those shadows, to be recognized and appreciated for what they were rather than dismissed for what they were not. As the youngest, I was trying to learn to come into my own, to come into the light, but the examples all around me were examples of failure and compromise and frustration. I got up and switched off the lamp.

7

THE DAUGHTER IN THE MOVIES

THE MOVIE WAS WEIRD. That was my first thought, and for a long time my only thought. I was at the Opera House, watching a comedy—or what people said was a comedy, at least. It starred this strange-looking guy, a skinny redhead with oversize glasses, and he kept making sex jokes, including one where he stroked this giant egg. I didn't pay much attention to it. I was still heartbroken from Sean, but people around me were laughing, and afterward I heard some older boys repeating the lines from the movie.

A few weeks later I was at home before dinner, doing my homework, when I heard my mother calling up the stairs: "Mariel, you have a phone call." Her tone was excited, almost girlish. She never sounded like that. I hurried down to the kitchen. My mother held out the phone. Her eyes were shining. "Mariel," she said. "Woody Allen is on the phone for you."

"What? Who?"

"Woody Allen," she said. "You know."

"I don't know," I said. The phone was still in her hand, with this person I didn't know waiting on the other end of it.

"The guy who made that movie you saw a few weeks ago. The little guy with the glasses. Apparently he wants to talk to you."

"Ew," I thought, "the egg."

I took the phone. The voice on the other end was immediately recognizable as the man from the movie, but he was calmer and in command. Even better, he was saying nice things about me. He told me that he had been watching my work, including *Lipstick*, and that he wanted to meet me in person and see if I might be good for his new movie. "All right," I said, and that was that. When I hung up I was confused. What had I agreed to? More to the point, where had I agreed to go? I didn't know that he was in New York, but that's where we went.

I had never really auditioned for *Lipstick*. It had been me and my sister in a swimming pool. So my meeting with Woody was my first official audition. An assistant brought me into an empty theater and gave me a script. It was dark, and I couldn't really concentrate on the pages. "You'd be Tracy," the assistant said.

When Woody came in, he was funny: funny for me to look at, because he was short and had that hair and those glasses, and also funny to talk to, with a quirky way of looking at me while I talked. "Do you mind reading with me?" he said.

He read some lines, and then I put the script in front of my face because I was so shy and unsure of myself.

"Well," he said, "I would like to see your face while you read."

I pulled down the script a bit.

"Better," he said.

I read the words on the page, but mostly I just giggled. I was so shy and embarrassed. I don't think I understood much of what I was reading, but I tried to make it sound like I did. It was over quickly, and we went home, or rather went back to my grandfather's apartment on Madison and 67th, in an ugly blue building. That afternoon, the call came in: Woody wanted me to be in his movie. We went back to Idaho for a few months, finished up the summer, and got back to New York for the fall. Woody loved to shoot in the fall.

The movie was *Manhattan*. I would be playing Tracy, the girl-friend of Woody's character, Isaac. I don't remember how much preparation I did. I watched *Annie Hall*, which I think was just out, and some of Woody's earlier movies too. Since I was sixteen, I still needed a guardian, so my mother came to New York with me for the duration of the shoot. Her cancer had retreated—I don't know if anyone talked formally about "remission" or "cure," but she was better, even if she was still weak. When we arrived back in the city, shooting started quickly. Woody kept his set loose and fun—he would go out to lunch with some of the cast and the crew members who were close to him, and we would sit and order food or whatever while everyone told jokes. Everyone was nice to my mother, and she was as optimistic and lighthearted as I had ever seen her. And making a film in the city was the most enjoyable thing I could imagine; seeing New York through Woody's eyes is something that has entranced generations of film audiences, and it was amazing for me too.

Playing Tracy was another matter. I prepared for the role the same way I prepared for any role, by trying to find something in it that was similar to things I had experienced, and in that sense it was easy. I had been moony-eyed over boys, and I had reacted with suspicion to others, and I had felt the pain of rejection from friends and classmates, and even gone through a little heartbreak of my own after that disastrous evening of the sleepover with Sean Peterson. Of course, there was a great distance to cover from that to actually imagining myself in the position of a seventeen-year-old dating—and, as the script made quite clear, sleeping with—a man in his forties. The real Mariel would never have gone out with Woody, not in a million years, but I could see someone like Tracy, a sophisticated New York girl, being attracted to him as part of her emotional education. Plus, much of my part called for me to laugh at his jokes, and that was easy, since I was laughing all the time anyway.

The one thing that threw me was the sexual innuendos—and sometimes they weren't even innuendos but outright sex talk. There's a moment in the movie when Tracy and Isaac are in bed, eating food. "Let's do it some strange way you've always wanted to do but nobody would do with you," Tracy says. Isaac is shocked by her forwardness, and then he says, "I'll get my scuba-diving equipment and really show you." When I ran across that line, I asked my mother what it meant, and she got a mortified look on her face. I asked again. Her expression darkened. "Don't ask stupid questions," she said. My mother wasn't against the movie. It broke up the boredom of her life, and she liked being close to celebrities. I remember wondering if other women I knew, like Mary Kay or Mrs. Sherntanner, would have let their daughters act in a Hollywood movie with considerable sexual innuendo—but then I pushed it out of my mind, because I didn't want to imagine a world where I would have been denied the experience of *Manhattan*.

That scuba-diving line came during the scene in the movie that gave me the most difficulty. It wasn't because I had to show emotion or hold my own against more experienced performers. It was difficult because we were supposed to be eating Chinese food, and that was one of the foods on my forbidden list—the same list that had kept me away from seafood when I drove down to California with

Kelly's family. I didn't know what was in there, what the meat was between the noodles or what the noodles were for that matter, so I put granola into my Chinese food container. That started a lifelong tradition of making trouble for myself during scenes where I was required to eat on camera.

When I started the shoot, there were other people on set that Woody dealt with more regularly—other actors and crew members. At some point, I started to notice that he was listening to me. If we had bad weather, he would take me to a museum or art gallery. I remember one show made up entirely of tiny objects. "This scale is weird," I said. "Does something like this make us imagine we're small, so that we can use these things, or that we're even bigger than we are?"

Woody had been walking to the next room. He stopped and backed up a step. "I like that," he said. "Maybe both are true, but that's a great question." His reaction was very different from what I was accustomed to in school—teachers who thought that I wasn't smart because the essay I had written didn't fit their idea of what a good paper should be. I'm sure that in part he was just trying to make a young actress feel comfortable, but I also felt that he was really listening. He was also a Francophile, and we talked about my trip with my father, and my grandfather's book. "We should go to Paris, just me and you," Woody would say, and I would laugh.

Manhattan did wonders for my confidence—not only did it teach me that I was capable of being interesting to people I admired, but it helped strengthen my still-fragile self-image. I was still fairly certain that I was too tall and boyish, but for the first time I started to notice that it was a stylish look. It may have made me feel worthless in Ketchum, but I started to see that people in New York liked it. Maybe being too long was a good thing. I started to slouch less and make more of my height. Not incidentally, it also helped with the comedy of the movie: if I stood up straight, I had a solid half foot on Woody.

When the movie ended, I was heartbroken. The film crew had served as a kind of surrogate family, and I had developed close friendships with people who were unlike me in every way except for the fact that we were united in a common purpose. I knew that that crew wasn't invested in the movie in quite the same way I was. They were normal people with normal families who lived nearby. Their kindness wasn't inauthentic by any means, but it was circumstantial—they wanted things to work as smoothly as possible so that they could go home. I sensed that, but I also found that I liked it. There was no blood-is-thicker-than-water angst, no fear that you weren't doing what you needed to or getting the care that you deserved. You showed up, acted professionally, and developed a kind of intimacy. It was unlike my family, in the sense that it didn't require exhausting amounts of work to maintain at a basic emotional level, and that was immensely rewarding.

* * *

WOODY ALLEN—Hollywood director, New York celebrity, urban neurotic extraordinaire—arrived at the small airport in Hailey, Idaho, on a private jet. It was early November, not a very pretty time in the Gem State, and when he got off the plane all he saw was a dingy, overcast landscape. There was no snow yet, and everything was gray. "Oh, my God," he said, with perfect Woody Allen cadence. "I felt like I was landing on the moon."

I had been back home in Ketchum for a month, maybe more, but my head was still filled with Manhattan. I tried to get back into the rhythms of normal school life, but I couldn't. I hated it. The time away from home had been a source of liberation but also one of guilt. When I came back, I was reminded immediately how tenuous my mom's health was, and I worried so much about it that I couldn't concentrate on schoolbooks. Every time I started to read, I fell asleep. I would wake up at four in the morning and try to do my homework then, when it was quiet, and that worked for a little while, until I started to get tired in the mornings also. The irony was that when there was no pressure involved, when I had time to read on my own, free of any assignments, I liked it. I took to it. But the idea of school suffocated me, and I didn't see any way out.

Well, there was one way out, but it wasn't going to work. Woody's initial joke about taking me to Paris kept resurfacing. He brought it up more and more often, to the point where I started to think that maybe he wasn't joking. Our relationship was platonic, but I started to see that he had a kind of crush on me, though I dismissed it as the kind of thing that seemed to happen any time middle-aged men got around young women. And I encouraged the conversations and the walks because they validated me.

Back in Ketchum, I told my parents about the Paris offer, hoping they would squash it immediately. Instead, they were impressed and even a little enthusiastic. I repeated myself, thinking that maybe they had misunderstood: he wants me to go to Paris with him. And they repeated themselves: Paris with Woody Allen, no problem, sounds interesting. I tried to raise the threat level further. I told them that that I didn't know what the arrangement was going to be, that I wasn't sure if I was even going to have my own room. Woody hadn't said that. He hadn't even hinted it. But I wanted them to put their foot down. They didn't. They kept lightly encouraging me. I pretended to be happy that they were giving me my independence, but the truth is that I felt abandoned and angry. Weren't parents supposed to look out for you? Weren't they supposed to set limits? My parents didn't, and I didn't understand why they wouldn't. Was it that they didn't care enough? That night I pressed myself down in the bed again, trying to feel invisible.

One day, Woody called. "I'm going to come see you in Idaho," he said.

I was so excited I clapped my hands together after I hung up the phone. I wanted him to visit. I had seen where he came from, and I wanted him to see where I came from. We had talked often about how beautiful the place was, the mountains and the lakes. The season worked against us a little bit, the November grays, but it was still majestic: mountains towering over lakes and forests. I drove him back to the house, which was maybe forty minutes away, and he asked questions about everything and listened to my answers.

At the house, he met my parents and stashed his stuff downstairs in the guest room off my dad's quarters. About ten minutes after that, we were sitting in the living room talking to my mother when my dad appeared in the doorway. "Get your boots on," he said. My dad had a dog whistle, which he used to call Elsa, our Labrador, and off we went.

Across the street from our house, there was a hiking trail, and we were headed in that direction when my father stopped. "We don't need to go on a trail," he said, and started bushwhacking right up the mountain. Woody looked back at me to see if we were serious, and then he followed my dad. My dad was going at a clip, whistling symphonies, using the dog whistle to keep Elsa near, and I was keeping up with him and then peeling off to go back and check on Woody, who fell behind. He was at altitude, 6,500 feet, just off the plane from New York, and he was winded and then some. He looked horrible.

"Dad," I said, "Maybe this isn't a good idea."

"Come on," he said. "We're almost there. This is great. He's got to see the view." We finally got to the top: my dad and Elsa and I, and then, after a slight delay, Woody. We were standing there for maybe a minute when all of a sudden we were socked in by fog and then, right on its heels, a massive snowfall. It was like a quick cut from gray and cold to the biggest flakes you've ever seen, wet and white and heavy. I apologized to Woody, and we turned and went right back down, my dad whistling again.

We got to the house just before dark. My mother had been cooking while we were hiking, and she met us with the news that dinner would be ready in ten minutes. Woody, wet and miserable, went to shower and change into dry clothes, and he joined us at the dinner table for pheasant and wine. We hadn't eaten in the dining room for years, but this was a special occasion. We sat down and started to eat, and it was fantastic. My parents were laughing and getting along and being more charming than I had ever seen them. They were a great audience for Woody, but they also held their own, telling fascinating stories and making witty observations. Woody was making a great show about how much he liked the food, as he was cutting into the pheasant, he let out a satisfied murmur. "What do you think?" my father said.

"What do you mean?" Woody said.

"Of the bird," my father said. "I shot it this morning."

Woody's whole face fell. In his mind, chicken came from Gristede's. But he got over it quickly, and it was back to the conversation and the laughter. After dinner, we were sitting in the living room, and Woody clapped his hands. "So," he said. "Now what do you do?"

"Now?" my father replied.

"At night, I mean," he said. "Are there clubs?"

I laughed. For starters, I was kind of young to go out to the clubs. And then there was the fact that there weren't any. There were bars in town, but they were for hard-core barflies only. Most people just stayed at home and watched TV. Woody ended up in a long conversation about fly-fishing with my father, who could make it the most interesting topic in the world, and I stayed and listened for a while and then went to bed. I should have been tired from the hike, but I couldn't sleep. I was suddenly panicking about the whole Paris trip; I had somehow pushed the invitation out of my mind, but now it flooded back in, and I started thinking through all the angles, none of which worked to my advantage. It was a great offer, and we were great friends, but were we really friends at all? Would we get our own rooms? We would, wouldn't we? I dozed off, flailing, and woke right back up with the certain knowledge that I was an idiot. No one was going to get their own room. His plan, such as it was, involved being with me. In the middle of the night, I went downstairs to the guest room and roused him from what was probably the deepest sleep of his life. "What?" he said. "What?"

"I'm not going to get my own room, am I?" I asked him.

"What?" He was squinting at me like I was speaking a foreign language.

"If we go to Paris," I said. "I don't get my own room, do I?" He was terribly flustered, not quite awake, not quite in focus, feeling around for his glasses. "Listen," I said. "I just want you to know. I can't go to Paris with you."

He was still pretty disoriented when I left the guest room, and the next morning he was clearly disconcerted. He called the plane to come and pick him up, and I drove him back to the airport in Hailey as cordially and casually as I could. Deep down, I was really sad. I loved him as a friend. He had made me feel important in ways that

I hadn't, up to that point, felt. But I also knew that it was an impossible situation. I had agreed to take a part in his movie where I was playing more sophisticated and more adult, and if that was confusing for me, it was also probably confusing for him. It was intimate, but it wasn't. I couldn't give myself over to it completely, even as an idea.

Woody didn't abandon me. He was more careful, but we continued to talk through the years. Right after *Manhattan*, he made *Interiors*, which was a movie about strange WASPs who lived their bizarre lives and never talked about it. He showed me an early cut and asked my opinion. I thought that it was very interesting, a legitimate investigation of these people's damaged lives like the Ingmar Bergman films that he loved. I told him it was admirable and dark. What caught me up short, a little bit, was that at some level I thought he was romanticizing the lifestyle. He fashioned a world of gloriously wealthy WASPy people who kept things at the surface while all these passions roiled underneath. What he didn't get to was the possibility of a kind of base ugliness. When people are trapped in an unpleasant family dynamic, when parents are at each others' throats, they're not wearing beautiful sweaters. Or, at least, that wasn't the case in my house. I often wonder if he found my family disappointing, if we were too ordinary an example of dysfunctional seventies America.

*   *   *

DURING *MANHATTAN*, Muffet was at a point in her life when she was thin and gorgeous and happy with herself. She met a man, and the two of them decided to get married. Shortly after that, probably out of optimism, she went off her medication and went through a minor manic episode, and when the two of them visited Idaho, her fiancé was having second thoughts. He told my family that he didn't know if he could go through with it, that Muffet might be too much to handle.

"It'll be fine," I said. "She'll be happy, and you'll be happy." I don't know where I thought my authority was coming from—a teenage girl making a case for her sister's fitness as a wife—but I wanted someone's marriage to work. I must have made a decent argument. Muffet went back on her meds, her fiancé calmed down, and the two of them got married.

They lived in New York, and when I visited her, I saw that she was protected, by which I mean that she was protected from herself. "I have a whole schedule," she told me. "Everything is taken care of." In the morning, her husband helped her pick out her clothes. Then yoga, then a short walk, then lunch at La Goulue. She was beaming. Having a life that was under control was important to her, even if it was under her husband's control.

A few months later, they went to Paris and stayed in the small hotel his parents owned. That time, Muffet must have gone off her medicine completely, because she had a full break. She wandered off one night and didn't come home for a day or so, and when she finally returned, she was completely split off from reality. My father had to fly to Paris to get her and talk her husband down from the brink. The marriage was done, though. It wasn't what her husband had bargained for, but it's what he had feared. Muffet returned to Ketchum, to my parents' house. At first, I'm not even sure she admitted that her marriage was over; she rationalized the move home as somehow related to my mother's care. And she did help tremendously. She would make coffee in the morning, clean the house, sit with my mother in the kitchen, and plan the week's worth of meals. Being forced to help run the house made Muffet entirely functional. It muted her own illness and gave her a blueprint for survival: when there were tasks in front of her, she could see them without seeing her fears or self-doubts. She could move forward without backsliding. For me, her return was a mixed blessing. I was glad to have her back. The house was less lonely with her around. But it also made me fixate more on my own moodiness, because I worried that it might turn into something more permanent and serious, something that would harden around me. Becoming like the others in my family was a powerful and constant fear. They were the people I loved the most and the people whom I was the most like, but they were also terrifying examples of how balance could be thrown off and an otherwise regulated existence could be overwhelmed by emotional blockage or mental disarrangement.

*   *   *

MY FATHER WAS BACK IN FRANCE soon enough, but it was Cannes this time rather than Paris. He took me for the premiere of *Manhattan* at the Cannes Film Festival. I had never been to an event like that, and it was overwhelming in every way. Photographers were lined up on both sides of the stairs, and as each actor or performer went up, they erupted with yelling and flashbulbs. I looked from side to side trying to smile but feeling like I wanted to run.

Once the lights went down, I was calmer. The audience loved the movie. Woody was a favorite of theirs, and the film compared favorably to *Annie Hall*, its immediate predecessor. I didn't mind watching myself on screen so much. There were ways in which it was an interesting process. But the enormity of the whole experience started to work on me. "Dad, I feel funny," I said. "I don't think I can stay." He took one look at me and diagnosed a panic attack. We went out through of a side door, past security, back to the hotel.

I was just as uncomfortable back in Ketchum. After *Lipstick*, I had some trouble readjusting to daily life, and it was worse after the TV movie. But *Manhattan* was the breaking point. I loved Idaho, but I also started to hate it: the claustrophobia of school, the sameness of home. Being my mother's caretaker made things seem even worse.

I got it in my head that I wanted to quit school, and once that idea was there, it took root and grew. I became obsessed with quitting. My friend Sara, who was older than me, was leaving Idaho to go to school in New York, and I decided that I was going to move with her. I planned obsessively. On a magazine shoot to promote a movie, I had befriended a woman who worked as a hair and makeup person in the city. She lived on Park Avenue South, and when I contacted her, she told me that there was a vacant apartment in her building. "Send me pictures," I said. The rent was $1,200 a month, maybe a little more than that, but I figured I could afford it with the money from *Manhattan*, which was coming to me in a few months, when I turned eighteen.

I didn't say anything to my parents until it was all in place, and then I convened a meeting before Wine Time. I sat down in a chair and asked them to sit down too. "I'm moving," I said. "I'm going to New York City." I was clutching the sides of the chair so hard I thought my fingernails would go right through the upholstery. I expected an earthquake: you're too young; there's no way we're going to let you leave; you better think again, young lady.

They looked at each other for a split second and then nodded. "I'll be sad to see you go," my mother said, "but I understand."

"I'll drive you," my father said. "We'll go across the country together."

I couldn't believe it. I had prepared for a protracted negotiation. I had my reasons all outlined in my head. I was willing to go to the mat to fight for the right to move to New York. But no one even objected. It was a replay of when I had been asked to go to Paris with Woody Allen. I looked around to see if I was in the middle of a *Candid Camera* skit, but there was no one hiding behind the couch. It was simpler than that. Yet again, I had overestimated my parents' capacity for being engaged in my life.

And so, a month later, my father and I packed my life into a U-Haul—my bed, my clothes, some pots and pans—and headed for New York.

*   *   *

SARA STILL HAD TO FINISH UP high school, so for months I was in the apartment by myself. I had some friends in Manhattan, mostly from *Manhattan*. The hair and makeup director, who lived downstairs, had cats, and I got one too. At first, we got along great, the cat and I. I could snuggle with the cat or talk to the cat or take care of the cat. But it was a studio apartment with wood floors and only a little bit of furniture, so every time the cat found a penny or a pebble it was like an echo chamber in there. I was so frustrated that I started leaving the windows open. "Go on," I told the cat. "Don't you want freedom?" But all he did was play with the blinds or, occasionally, slap something out onto the street. I finally got some throw rugs to muffle the sound.

I didn't do much acting work at that time, though I dabbled in theater and occasionally read scripts. While I waited for my *Manhattan* money to come through, I did odd jobs, including walking a dog that belonged to Bryan Bantry, a friend of mine who was a rep for makeup artists and photographers. It was a year of cats and dogs.

My romance with the city that had started during the filming of Woody's movie continued. I loved to go to diners by myself, order some food, watch people. I loved standing in the middle of Central Park and looking at the tops of buildings in the distance. Mostly I just walked and walked. The city had a specific effect: you could feel so lonely and so taken care of at the same time. I got recognized fairly often—mostly by cabdrivers and construction workers, it seemed. But they were polite enough. "Hey look," they said. "It's that girl from that movie."

Part of the reason that I didn't mind the cabdrivers and construction workers was that they made me feel less lonely. When I left Ketchum to come back to New York, I assumed that the camaraderie from the *Manhattan* set would continue. At first, it did, a bit. I ran into Michael Murphy, who had played Yale in the movie. I hung out with the Salad Sisters, Fern and Romaine, who did hair and makeup. But then I wasn't running into Michael as often, and the Salad Sisters and I drifted apart. Sara came to rescue me from solitude, but within about a month, she had a serious boyfriend and slept over at his place all the time.

I had family in the city, of course, but that didn't fix things. In some ways it made it worse. Margaux didn't look out for me or protect me or even spend much time with me. After *Lipstick* and the way she had been treated in reviews, you could tell she was off the rails. She wasn't doing as much work—the professional life span of a model was so short—and she was casting around for the next thing. Now and again, she would call me. "Let's have dinner," she would say, or "I'll meet you in the park and we can walk around and look in store windows." She was quiet with me and seemed unsure of herself. But then I would see her on a TV talk show acting like things were grand, and it would upset me. I understood that she wanted to create a positive impression for the audience, but I could see right through her. And I assumed, at some level, that everyone else watching on TV could see through her and thought the same thing. Once, she was on *The Mike Douglas Show*, and she didn't seem coherent. Had she been drinking? Then she got up off the couch to go sing with the band, and I was mortified. Why was she doing that?

I reacted to Party Margaux the same way I reacted to Chaotic Home or Heavy Muffet. I went the other way. I became extremely careful, mostly kept to myself, limited all risk and exposure. The idea of staying home and doing my own thing was nice in theory, but then the night came and it was just me and an empty apartment, with only the cat's claws on the floor to remind me that I wasn't alone in the world.

When I managed to get dressed up and go to parties, I couldn't work up the ego that was necessary to flirt, or pick up a boy, or hold court. At those parties, I thought mostly about the high school experiences I was missing. Sometimes I even talked to people about that other version of myself and what she would be doing if I hadn't come to New York. "If I was home, I'd be skiing," I'd say. Or "If I was at home, I'd be at a school dance." I pictured all the kids back home crowded into a basement, smoking cigarettes and talking about what a fool I had been to leave. It takes years of experience to realize that nobody else thinks about you quite as much as you fear they do. I had none of that experience. "Did I make a mistake?" I asked the cat. The cat jumped off the couch without answering.

8

THE NAME IN THE CREDITS

"THAT LOOKS RIDICULOUS," I SAID. I pointed at the TV. A friend of mine was over at my apartment, and we were watching a movie. In it, a handsome actor was pretending to be a skier. He looked dashing in his goggles and his hat, but whenever the movie showed him on the slopes, it cut to a wide shot where it was beyond obvious that someone else was doing the skiing. The stuntman was a completely different build, and though the actor was blond, you could see the stuntman's dark hair peeking out from under the hat. "Can you believe it?" I asked.

My friend shrugged. "Whatever," he said. "It's just a movie. No one thinks that the skiing is real."

"But it should be," I said. "It could be."

"What do you mean?"

"Imagine a movie where the actor actually knows how to do physical things," I said. I had done something more than just imagine it. I had sent my agent in search of it. "I want a part where there's some athletic work," I said. "I think it could be great."

Scripts came and went, and soon one came and stayed. It was a project called *Personal Best* that had been written by Robert Towne, who had also written some of the best movies of the past decade—*The Last Detail*, *Shampoo*, and, of course, *Chinatown*. *Personal Best* was going to be his directorial debut. The film was about a female hurdler and her intimate relationships both with her track coach and with a fellow female athlete. I loved it when I read it. "Tell everyone I'm interested," I told my agent. "I want that part." When a week went by and I heard nothing, I called back and was even clearer. "I don't want anyone else to get that part," I said. A meeting was arranged.

When I met with Towne, though, he was skeptical. He was committed to hiring only world-class athletes. They had already cast Patrice Donnelly, who had competed in the 1976 Olympics. That only made me want the part more. "Give me a chance," I said. "I'll train harder than anyone to get in shape." I persisted, and I insisted, and eventually I got the part. Scott Glenn, who had just broken out in *Urban Cowboy*, would play the track coach. I was so excited. It was an adult role, finally, and proof that I could extend my career beyond *Manhattan*.

More to the point, it was another dramatic role—specifically, a dramatic role about a character struggling with issues of identity and self-confidence. Movies back then were like that. They focused on human relationships, first and foremost. That had a benefit for the audience, I think, though I was more aware of the benefit for me as an actress. In the course of understanding a character, in the course of preparing for a role, you were forced to sort out your own issues. Movies became a complex and satisfying endeavor: both a replacement for my family and a kind of staging ground where I could work my way through my own sense of things and ask questions that were otherwise too difficult.

The clarifying power of drama was one thing, but even before I got to that, I had promised that I would train, and that's what I did. They worked us out at the UCLA track and also at Santa Monica College. The regimen was very hard. I didn't like hurdling at all. It scared me. It was one thing to clear the hurdles and another thing to do it while looking good. The girls who figured it out were amazing, but many of us looked like we were leaping into the sky, and it came off as silly and awkward, not graceful and powerful like it needed to be. One of the actresses couldn't run at all—her mechanics were bizarre—and I worried that I would end up like that and either lose the part or, worse, end up on film looking like some kind of gawky freak. Even worse, after a few months, the training started bulking me up. I was terrified of that, because in my mind I associated it with getting fat. To me, that was like punching me in the face. Most days I would end up back at home, frustrated almost to tears by my inability to figure out hurdling. But I also took my own tears as proof that I had picked the right project.

* * *

THE PHONE WOKE ME UP. "Hello?" I said. I checked the clock. It was early, which meant that the call was important. Was it good news or bad news? Maybe something bad had happened to Muffet. I tensed up.

"Mariel?" The voice was vaguely familiar.

"Yes," I said. "Hello?"

"I have good news." I relaxed. It was my agent, calling to tell me that I had been nominated for an Academy Award for my performance in *Manhattan*. "That's great," I said, and hung up.

When I woke up for good an hour later, the news had grown inside my head. An Academy Award? I didn't know exactly what that meant. We didn't watch the ceremony regularly when I was growing up, and I didn't have a clear sense of the categories or how nominations worked. Seeing my name in the credits for *Manhattan* had been thrilling enough. Was this an even bigger deal? I called my agent back, and it was quickly explained to me that it was. I was nominated in the Best Supporting Actress category, and my competition included Jane Alexander and Meryl Streep, both from *Kramer vs. Kramer*; Barbara Barrie from *Breaking Away*; and Candice Bergen from *Starting Over*. *Manhattan* was also nominated for one other award: Best Original Screenplay. And so, a few months later, I was at the Dorothy Chandler Pavilion, the longtime home of the awards ceremony, waiting to see if I would take home a statuette.

My Oscars date was Scott Glenn, my costar in *Personal Best*. Scott was a guy's guy, very easy to get along with and old enough to be safe, though I also had a little crush on him. Years later, I found out that his wife was angry that I took him to the awards. I can see her point, I suppose: I dressed up fancy, in an antique dress that was white and made me look like a bride.

But it wasn't a wedding. It was a competition. Not that there was really any competition. During Oscars week, I was at a dinner party with some other actors, and a man pointed down the table. "She's amazing," he said. "She has the award wrapped up already." He was pointing at Meryl Streep, who had been nominated the year before as well, for *The Deer Hunter*.

I shrugged. "She would totally deserve it," I said to the man. "She's great. I'm happy either way." I wasn't just saying that to protect my feelings. I was completely serious. I was nineteen years old, with two films and a TV movie under my belt. *Manhattan* had been one of the greatest experiences of my life, whether or not I won.

At the ceremony, the Academy seated people according to some complicated master plan. The nominees for Best Actor and Best Actress were really close to the stage, to minimize the travel time required for the winner. The Supporting Actor and Actress nominees were right behind them. I was sitting really close to Jack Nicholson; *The Shining* was about a month away from coming out, and posters had already started to appear, the creepy yellow one with the face inside the capital *T.* I had met Jack once or twice before through Robert Towne, who was part of that whole Hollywood playboy scene, and during that Oscars week I also met Warren Beatty, who was nice but completely lived up to his reputation as a compulsively flirtatious person. Hollywood had its craziness then as always, and when you went to parties you saw plenty of sex and drugs, but it was also a kind of club. People weren't as handled then as they are now. There weren't layers and layers of managers and agents. You were able to see the big stars as real people, warts and all. The show was hosted by Johnny Carson, who always hosted in those days. Kermit the Frog sang "Rainbow Connection." Dustin Hoffman presented a lifetime achievement award to Alec Guinness. Farrah Fawcett handed out the Best Visual Effects trophy. And there was no upset: Meryl won Best Supporting Actress, gracefully accepting the award from Jack Lemmon and Cloris Leachman.

* * *

"COME OVER," MARGAUX SAID. It was about two weeks before we were set to start shooting *Personal Best*. I hadn't seen her for months, though we had spoken on the telephone a few times. She was out in

Los Angeles, doing some modeling work, and she wanted me to visit her at the Westwood Marquis. "You can stay the night," she said. She met me at the door. "How are you?" she said.

"Good," I said. I told her about training, about how I had to both run and jump and think about how I looked while I ran and jumped. I told her about how I was screaming in front of the mirror so that I'd have a rougher voice, different from the chipmunk sound that came out every time I spoke.

"Uh huh," she said. "Uh huh." As a test, I didn't say anything for a little while. "Uh huh," she said.

Clearly, she had something else on her mind. "What's up?"

"Well," she said, "I need you to help me."

"With what?"

She clucked her tongue impatiently. "With my acting." She had an audition for a role, and she wanted me to go through her lines with her. She handed me the script, went to the other side of the room, and started. From the first word, I knew that we were in trouble. The problem was that her line readings weren't working. For starters, she had a hard time with the simple act of reading. She had a learning disability, probably severe dyslexia. But it wasn't only that. She couldn't read the lines in anything approaching a naturalistic manner. Her voice would shift into an unnatural register. Her posture would stiffen. She was acting with a capital *A*. I didn't know what to say. If I praised her effusively, she would have accused me of being insincere, and she would have been right. If I said anything negative, she would have felt terrible. If I said nothing, it would have seemed dismissive. I tried to find a gentle way to go at the issue. I explained to her that acting was no different than the two of us sitting there talking. "Just imagine," I said, "that you are a different person saying these words, but for all the same reasons, and with all the same ideas and emotions." I was trying to make things as clear as possible, but she couldn't make the jump. Whenever she went back to the script, it would all happen again: that voice, that posture, that capital *A*.

My attempt at treading lightly didn't work. Margaux could read my expression, or at the very least read my attempt to suppress my expression. She was demoralized. We stopped running lines. "Stay here with me tonight," she said. "I have to go down and meet someone, but I'll be back." Not too long after she left, I fell asleep. During training, it was hard to stay awake past ten or so. When I woke up, the room was pitch black. Margaux was back, and she had her hands around my throat. "You think you're better," she said. "You think you're better at this. But you're just the little sister." She was drunk, and she wasn't tightening her grip, but it was still terrifying. I got her off me and pushed her onto her bed. She wasn't completely there. Maybe it was a blackout situation. In a minute, she was asleep. I sat up and felt my throat where she had put her hands and knew that I would never get back to sleep. And then a heaviness settled on me. I felt every ounce of the weight of Margaux's disappointment with the way that her acting career had gone, and every ounce of the fear of where it might go. I didn't know what to do for her, or if there was anything I could do.

*   *   *

PERSONAL BEST WAS A PROTRACTED SHOOT, the longest moviemaking experience of my career. There was the training, for starters, and then the set was shut down because of a Writers Guild strike. No sooner had we started production than we were shut down again because David Geffen, who had put his own money into the project to finish it, got mad at Robert Towne. Robert was doing a ton of cocaine and rewriting scenes as we went, and that meant that a six-week shoot turned into twelve weeks, and then six months. The cast and crew would spend days on the set playing Frisbee, waiting for an assistant director to come tell us what to do.

If it was strange when we weren't working, it was equally strange when we were working. Robert was married, but he and his wife were having time apart, probably because he had gotten involved with Patrice Donnelly, who played Tory, the other main female character. Robert and Patrice left together at night and arrived together in the morning, and while no one really minded that—on-set romances weren't uncommon—we were all struck by the way Patrice looked. When she came to set with Robert, she looked haunted and emotionally drained. It was different from her normal personality, which was that of a focused athlete, but it helped her when it came to playing Tory.

It wasn't until later in the shoot that it started to occur to me that Robert was upsetting Patrice on purpose, for the movie's benefit—that he was directing her, in a sense, while they were at home. As an actress, Patrice was sort of like Margaux; when the camera started rolling, she became unbearably formal and actress-like. She somehow believed that acting a role was a process of becoming someone else. Robert must have felt at some level that he needed to engage in some emotional manipulation to get her back to acting natural and extract the best performance from her.

Watching Patrice, thinking about Margaux, I started to develop some of my own ideas about acting. I have always felt like it was grandiose when actors talked about their philosophy. For me, the only way to play a role was to find the part of myself that was the most like that character. To do that, I had to recognize that I had parts of dozens of different personality traits, many contradictory. I had a little cowardice and a little bravery, a little fear and a little lust and a little heroism and a little evil. Whenever I encountered a scene that called for any of those emotions, I just had to access them. The rest was just a matter of fidelity to the story being told. *Personal Best* brought up issues of competition and inadequacy that were central to my personality, and the issues of confusion were familiar enough—it didn't matter that my character experienced them as sexual confusion.

Or maybe it did matter. Up until then, I had never had a serious boyfriend. More to the point: I had never had sex. It was time. I had a good friend on *Personal Best*, a young guy who worked on the movie. "You know what?" I said.

"What?" he said.

"I think we should go out."

"When?" he said.

"This weekend," I said. We went for food, and I made enough eye contact to let him know that the coast was clear. "Maybe we should go back to your place," I said, and that was that.

Sex wasn't earthshaking. Or rather: sex with him wasn't. He didn't do anything wrong. Clothes were removed. Backs were arched. But I knew immediately that we didn't have any romantic chemistry. Unfortunately, opinions differed. "I think I'm in love with you," he said. "We should move in together."

As amazingly premature as his reaction was, mine was even more amazing. "Okay," I said. "I think you're right." Weeks later, we were living together. In my mind, that's what happened after sex. My parents were together, and if they had stayed together, then any couple that got together had no real options. Sex meant partnership, meant commitment. I didn't know what else to do. And so, not even twenty, I was all of a sudden in a serious relationship, living with my boyfriend.

* * *

"YOU'RE A BRAT. You're horrible to be around." I had seen Robert
Towne frustrated. I had seen him struggle to communicate his ideas
about the script. But I had never seen him this mad at an actor, not
even screaming but lowering his voice until he was almost hissing.
It was shocking—all the more so because I was the actor he was
hissing at.

We were in my trailer. Robert had called a private meeting. "Do
you have any idea why I brought you in here?" he said. I shook my
head. "It's because of how you've been acting." I shook my head
again. But in the back of my mind, I knew. I'm not sure what had
triggered my bad behavior. Maybe it was the way the shoot was drag-
ging on. Maybe it was insecurity about my performance in the film.
Maybe it was my discomfort with my relationship. Whatever the
case, I decided that everyone was wasting my time, and I got very
pissy. I gossiped with the crew, talked behind the backs of the other
actors. "Did you see how Scott looked this morning?" I said. "Do you
think he slept at all?"

One day, as we were starting to do the high jump scenes, I
started to unload on Patrice. "The problem with you," I said, "is that
you're not really an actress. I don't know why you can't get this right.
You've had enough extra help from Robert." I couldn't believe the
words that were coming out of my mouth. It was the first time I can
remember completely losing my ability to be polite or kind or even
respectful. The crew members stared at me, eyes wide. They hadn't
seen this side of me, and they weren't sure what to think.

Word filtered up to Robert, and the next afternoon, he ordered me into my trailer. "You're not being nice to people," he said.
"They're professionals too. This has been going on for a week, from
what I hear, and it has to stop."

A week? I only remembered the one day. I kept a brave face until

Robert left and then broke down and cried for four hours straight. I decided I was never going out there again. I would die in the trailer. This wasn't what I wanted to be, some spoiled-brat star of a movie, especially with a director I respected. And to think that other people, too, were looking at me in that light—it was as if all the air had left my body. I was so shaken up and ashamed. When I finally left the trailer, I vowed never to act that way again. It was one of the best things that ever happened to me on a movie set, but also one of the most complicated. It reiterated the importance of acting well, of acting professionally, and while that was vital on the job, I think it made me even less aware of how to deal with the more problematic aspects of my own personality. Act well, always: good advice if you want others to like you, but not necessarily good advice if you want to understand yourself.

*   *   *

AFTER I FINISHED FILMING *Personal Best*, I built myself a house in Salmon, Idaho, a small town about a hundred miles north of Ketchum. Let me clarify: I didn't build it. I designed it. I drew up plans for how I wanted it to look. I talked to an architect to make sure it all made sense. And then I hired a crew to make it real.

Building began in April; Salmon was at a lower elevation than Sun Valley, so there was no snow. The crew I hired were these cute Idaho guys who did construction on the side. I asked one of them to help build my house, and he brought the rest along. My brief affair with my friend on the *Personal Best* set had petered out, and I went into that summer hoping that one of them would want to go out with me. Actually, I was hoping that they all would. But they were told by the head guy, Charlie, that they couldn't fraternize with me.

It was a hard and fast rule, enforced under threat of death—or, at the very least, being punched in the face by Charlie. That was chivalrous enough of him, except that no one bothered to tell me about the rule, and all summer I felt like a leper. I'd fixate on one guy, flirt as best as I knew how, get no response, and move on to the next.

Even without romance, it was an amazing summer. We built platforms and put up teepees so that we could sleep there while the construction proceeded. Early on, my dad had someone come out to build a pond, and every morning we all went down and jumped in the cold water. We cooked together. We told jokes. We went for hikes.

At the end of the summer, we finished building and the guys all left, so I was there by myself. It was beautiful, but it was empty. My dog Stitch was there with me, and I used to look at him and think about the half-life of wonder. You get something new, a house or a friend or an idea, and it feels electric to you. You're charged by it in ways you've never been charged before. Soon enough, though, that charge dissipates, and things are normal and regular again—not bad but not magical anymore. Newness is an amazing property, an antidote to feeling tired and empty.

When I sat in the house for a little while, when I sat in the house by myself, there was a sadness that crept up on me, especially at night. It's almost as though I hadn't thought the whole thing through. I created this great world, but I hadn't populated it. There was a sense of incompleteness about the place, both psychologically and physically. When I decorated and put up curtains, I wasn't good enough at sewing, so everything was fastened with duct tape that I had taken from a movie set. That wasn't the only thing I used it for; if cushions ripped, I reupholstered them with the same tape. There were times at night when I'd see lights coming down the road and panic. Who was that coming toward the house? What did they want? I had a loft bedroom, so I would run down the super-steep stairs to get knives from the kitchen and sit just inside the front door, waiting.

* * *

WHEN I FIRST BOUGHT the Salmon lot, my dad came with me and we hiked around the land. "I'm glad you're spending your money this way," he said.

The lower altitude meant that it was a little warmer, but it also meant that there were snakes around. "What do I do if I see a rattle-snake?" I asked my father.

"Just kill it," he said. I didn't understand, and I said so. "You know," he said. "Shoot it."

"I could never hold the gun steady."

"Then get a big rock and smash it to death," he said.

Thirty seconds later, so quickly on the heels of our conversation that I thought I was imagining it, I saw the biggest rattlesnake I had ever seen. It was moving slowly across the property, right to left. I thought I was going to faint. "Daddy," I squeaked. "What do I do?"

"Are you kidding?" he said. "I told you. Get that rock. Kill it. You have to kill it. Otherwise, you'll see more and more. They'll make a nest under the house." I ran to the nearest big rock, lifted it with two hands, and threw it at the snake. I'm not sure if I killed it, but I killed some of my fear. After that, there were many times that I was on horseback when I spotted a rattler, and I just took the horse right around it.

If my father made me feel better about living in Salmon, my mother—in her own vexed way—did the same. During the entire time I had my house in Salmon, my mother never came to see it, not even once. On the one hand, it made me sad. Why wasn't she more interested in my life? On the other hand, I was relieved. Being around her wasn't easy, especially when it came to the way she responded to any move that took me farther away from her. I imagined her visit and how it might go. For starters, I'd have to make her comfortable, which would mean listening to endless commentary about her weakness and discomfort, getting her drinks, making sure that everything was the right temperature. Remaking the house to accommodate her would mean that, at least for a little while, it wouldn't even feel like my house anymore. And even that wouldn't work. She would be nice for an hour or so, and then the questions would come. "What's your plan here, Mariel?" "Why did you waste your money building a house in the middle of nowhere?" "Are you happy here by yourself?" I was constantly asking myself those questions, so I wasn't sure I could bear them coming from her.

*   *   *

AS WE FINISHED UP SHOOTING *Personal Best*, I wrote Robert Towne a letter thanking him for giving me a steady stream of challenges, for creating an environment where we were all pushed to do our best work. I told him I knew that we had done something important.

When Robert got my letter, he invited me to discuss it in person. I figured it would be a meeting of the mutual admiration society, or at the worst a meeting of the mutual flirtation society. But the second he arrived, he sat down and fixed me with an intense look. "I know what the letter is about," he said.

"What do you mean?" I replied.

"You're in love with me," he said.

I screwed up my face. That wasn't what I had meant. Or was it? That was Towne's reputation in Hollywood—that he was really good on rewrites—and he spoke my letter back to me like a master spin doctor. As his words started to pile up, I got so confused that I started to agree with him. "Right," I said. "True." Maybe I really was in love.

To make a not-very-long story short, Robert and I got involved. He wasn't with Patrice anymore, and he wasn't going back to his wife, so he went forward into a relationship with me. Robert had a condo on Venice Beach, and I spent most of my nights there, which meant that I neglected my own place, a garage in Coldwater Canyon that had been converted into a small apartment. I spent time with him and his daughter, acting as some unholy cross between a babysitter and an older sister and a stepmother. She was four years old or so and not always an easy kid to deal with, which probably wasn't her fault—he was the kind of dad who opted for indulgence and a lack of discipline because he didn't get to spend very much time with her. I tried to be nice to her, or at the very least friendly, so that she wouldn't openly resent me. But it was an unnatural situation.

It wasn't a good idea to get involved with Robert. That seems obvious from a distance. But it was good, maybe, to let myself make that choice—you're supposed to learn to make your own mistakes, as they say. Partly I allowed myself to enter the relationship because I was feeling more secure professionally. I had done a series of critically and commercially viable films, and that meant that my career was on its way. "Things are going well," I used to tell Robert. What I meant, I think, was that I had made things go well.

This increased confidence had its benefits, but there were pitfalls too. Toward the end of making *Personal Best*, I had been offered

The Executioner's Song, a TV movie based on Norman Mailer's book about the convicted killer Gary Gilmore. The producers wanted me to play Nicole Baker, the nineteen-year-old single mother who became Gilmore's girlfriend. The darkness didn't bother me. If anything, it appealed to me: I was looking for something adult and even a little depressing. I flew to Salt Lake City, where the film was in pre-production, for a meeting, but ultimately I turned it down. The reason was simple: I refused to do television. At the time, it wasn't cool, especially if you had already established yourself as a film actress. It felt like a step backward. In retrospect, that was probably a prejudice that I would have been smarter to rethink. Rosanna Arquette took the role, did a great job with it, and was nominated for an Emmy.

9

THE NUDE IN THE FRAME

IT WAS EASY TO TURN DOWN projects like *The Executioner's Song*, because my next movie had already appeared: a biopic of Dorothy Stratten. If Nicole Baker's life had been dark, Dorothy Stratten's was pitch black. Dorothy had been born in Canada, in Vancouver, and was working at a Dairy Queen there when she met a man named Paul Snider, a local nightclub promoter. The two of them became an item, and Paul began to manage Dorothy, which basically involved arranging for nude photos of her to be taken and sent to various girlie magazines. Paul thought that Dorothy would have more success if they moved closer to the action, so the two of them, then a married couple, left Vancouver and arrived in Los Angeles in 1979. Dorothy quickly became part of the *Playboy* empire. She was the magazine's centerfold that August, and afterward she worked at the Playboy Club in Century City. Paul may have been content to keep her in the nude-modeling world, but Hugh Hefner and other people at *Playboy* wanted her to cross over to legitimate acting, which resulted in small parts in television shows like *Buck Rogers in the 25th Century* and *Fantasy Island*.

As Dorothy got more and more involved in acting, she began to drift away from Paul, especially after she was cast in the Peter Bogdanovich comedy *They All Laughed* and began an affair with Bogdanovich. That was the beginning of the end for Dorothy. Paul felt more and more threatened. He sensed that Dorothy was slipping away from him forever. And so, in the summer of 1980, Paul and Dorothy met at Paul's house in West LA. Whatever tension there was between them boiled over, and Paul raped and killed Dorothy and then killed himself. The crime, brutal and spectacular, became an instant obsession for nearly everyone in Hollywood. A TV movie was rushed out, starring Jamie Lee Curtis as Dorothy. But there was a feature script circulating too, one written by Bob Fosse, whose previous movie, *All That Jazz*, had been one of the big dogs in the room the year I had been nominated for an Oscar for *Manhattan*.

The second I heard about the project, I wanted it. Dorothy was my age, more or less. She had come to Hollywood as a young woman under very different circumstances than me, but they weren't so different that I couldn't imagine my way into her life. I started reading about her life immediately, researching. I was hell-bent on knowing her. My agent at the time was Bob Fosse's agent, and he encouraged me to go after the role and convince Bob that I was right for it. Bob's initial reaction was lukewarm, but I kept after him. I set up meetings. I sent letters. I told him that I was sure I knew Dorothy as a character and that I could do the part justice on-screen.

At one meeting, we put it all out on the table, Bob's reservations and my convictions. "Dorothy was a classic victim," he said. "She let Paul control her, right up until the end. I don't see you that way."

"Maybe not," I said, "but I know everything about avoiding conflict by trying to please people." I didn't have a specific Svengali-type influence in my life, I explained, but my whole childhood had worked that way: avoid conflict by doing what you were asked or told, don't rock the boat, try to be liked, allow others to mold you in exchange for whatever seemed like love.

Bob listened carefully. He nodded. "One other thing," he said. "You're not a voluptuous person."

I had an answer for that too. In years since, everyone just assumed that I got breast implants so that I would get the role, and while it's true that I might not have gotten the role without them, I was planning on getting them anyway. My whole adolescence, I had always felt masculine. I was too tall, too skinny, not curvy enough. Idaho was all about being a boy: being outside, being active. Even without the pressures of Hollywood's beauty standards, I had made up my mind, though I can't say that I was completely invulnerable to them. I had started to ask around about doctors. But when I mentioned it to Bob, he had his assistant refer me to a plastic surgeon.

The doctor who did the procedure was wonderful. He tried to convince me not to do it at first, because I was so young, but I wasn't going to be dissuaded. Back then, there were three different sizes—small, medium, and large—and I insisted on a set that was even smaller than the small size. It was exciting, not frightening at all. There's something kind of nice about medical attention when you're not sick. The only strange thing is that you're completely normal, and then you wake up in pain. For months, I went around showing them to everyone: Sarah, Bryan Bantry, random photographers who would drop by the set. It was almost as if they didn't belong to me.

*　*　*

WHEN I GOT THE ROLE, I didn't know who else was going to be in the movie with me. Bob Fosse read tons of actors for the role of Paul Snider. Richard Gere read for it. Mandy Patinkin read for it. Fosse really wanted Robert De Niro, which I thought was a great idea. I was in love with him from *The Deer Hunter*. I thought he was a god: so handsome, such a good actor, such a genius at picking roles. I also thought that I would be the one to convince him to do *Star 80*: I would make the case about how important a film it was, about how it showed all the dark seams of the business we were in, what a great opportunity it was for him, how perfect he would be.

I found out that De Niro was staying at a hotel in New York on the west side, and I called someone who called someone else, and all of a sudden it was Robert De Niro on the phone. He had a very thick New York accent, and he was a little brusque, but I didn't care. I asked him if he wanted to meet, and he agreed.

He came over to where I was staying, a posh Upper West Side apartment of a wealthy woman I knew from Idaho. "Robert De Niro," he said. "I'm here to see Mariel Hemingway."

But he didn't look anything like the Robert DeNiro that I was in love with. He was fat and unpleasant and talking in that thick accent. I started telling him about *Star 80*, and he just blank-faced me. And then, even worse, he started to hit on me. I started to see what I was dealing with, which was a guy who had no interest in the movie I was describing, who had come across town only because some young actress had invited him, who was probably thinking about getting laid.

After De Niro left, I still loved his acting, though the bloom was off the rose a little. Years later, we had another audition together, and he wasn't very nice; and then a few years after that, we auditioned together again, and he couldn't have been lovelier. It wasn't until that

third meeting that it hit me: Each and every time, he had been playing a role. The first time, he had been playing Jake LaMotta. The second time, his character had been an asshole, which meant that he
had been an asshole too. The third time, his character had been nicer
and more normal. That's my advice if you ever want to meet Robert
De Niro. Check to see what movie he's about to make.

* * *

I WASN'T PLAYING JAKE LAMOTTA, but I was playing a real person too, and so I set about immersing myself in Dorothy's life. I
watched lots of tape to observe her mannerisms, but I wasn't interested in mimicking her. If you're playing a person who's internation-
ally famous, such as Jackie O, then the physical trappings of your
performance have to be right on. It's too distracting if your posture
if wrong, or if you are constantly tilting your head up when the person in question constantly tilted her head down. But if you're playing
somebody like Dorothy, who wasn't as well known, it's more important to interpret her. And interpreting her was a terrifying proposi-
tion. I had talked to Bob Fosse about the dark seams of Hollywood.

Just as we were starting rehearsals, I was staying at the Beverly
Hills Hotel, and Bob came to have a drink with me in the bar downstairs. He was doing the world's best Bob Fosse impression: talking
excitedly about his vision for the movie, chain-smoking like a mad-
man, gesticulating in ways that seemed manic but were also effortless
and graceful. Every once in a while, he would dissolve into a coughing fit, and everyone would look over at us with concern. "Let's go
upstairs and have one more drink," he said, and I went gladly. It
was a relief not to have to worry if he was going to die right there
in the bar.

The elevator let us off at my floor. I let us into my room. And then, for the next fifteen minutes, I ran rings around the couch while Bob Fosse chased me for purposes of sex. "I have a boyfriend," I said. That didn't dissuade him one bit. He started talking shit about Robert: He's washed up. His reputation is inflated. He can't even write that well. "Well, I'm not interested," I said.

This stopped him for a moment. He steadied himself on the couch and looked at me. "I have never not fucked my leading lady," he said. He paused theatrically. "No," he said. "Wait. Once. And it was a disaster. That was Shirley MacLaine, on *Sweet Charity*. But there has never been a leading lady in a good film who didn't sleep with me."

When I spoke, my voice was at least two octaves higher than normal. "Meet the first," I said.

"It's going to happen," he said.

"No, it's not," I said. "I don't think I could be naked every day on this movie and then come home and be naked with you." Fosse stood down and stopped chasing me. It was like a miracle. He went out of the room coughing, still making Fosse-like gestures.

*   *   *

IN LIEU OF DE NIRO (or Gere or Patinkin), the role of Paul Snider went to Eric Roberts, a young actor who had done great work in films including *King of the Gypsies* and *Raggedy Man*. Carroll Baker played Dorothy's mother, and Cliff Robertson played Hugh Hefner.

The movie had lots of energy, most of it originating with Bob. For all of Bob Fosse's personal flaws, his movie sets were something to behold. I loved it. I got along wonderfully with him. We understood the character in the same way. And he had a specific genius when it came to the mechanics of moviemaking. Bob had started in the theater, of course, and was completely conscious of body move-ments through time, which meant that he choreographed every scene as if it were a dance. In the rehersal hall, which was a huge space that had previously been a church, he got a stopwatch out and timed action down to the second: this is where Dorothy stands during the conversation, this is where Paul turns and makes his ap-peal, beat, beat, pivot. We were drilled on places and cues, which meant that when it came time to actually act the scene, we could concentrate on issues of emotional nuance.

Bob wasn't just a taskmaster when it came to the physical aspects of the film. He was an emotional tyrant too. There were days when he was kind and supportive, and other days when he would look at me icily and say, "You're such a manipulative little cunt." He was pro-voking me, not entirely seriously, but he was also feeding into what he felt the film needed.

Whether he was being superficially nice or superficially mean, I always knew that he was deeply committed to making the movie work, and that made me work harder. I had a desire to make him happy so that he would shoot me well and direct me well, so that my best work would end up on film. We shot much of it in Vancouver, which was safe and calm. When we got back to Los Angeles, life was more claustrophobic and more demanding. I had Bob during the day, yelling at me, tweaking me, and Robert's drug-fueled neuroses at night.

As the film went on, I drew as much from my sisters' lives as from my own. Margaux, of course, had a life that was in some ways very similar to Dorothy's: she had been singled out for her beauty, had been controlled by men who at first seemed to have her best in-terests at heart but who turned out to be more self-interested (though none, thankfully, in as wicked a manner as Paul Snider); she had struggled as she tried to understand if she had any talents beyond

her appearance. There was even a little bit of Muffet in my character-
ization. Of all of us sisters, she was probably the one who had most
acutely felt the pressure of the Hemingway name. She had worked in
the literary world and had traded on her sophistication and elegance.
Her husband had unquestionably tried to mold her, to protect her
by treating her as a kind of trophy—though, again, it had been in a
largely benign way. And because of Muffet's illness, I had watched
the other end of the process, they way that people abandoned her
when they could no longer profit from their association with her.
There was a tremendous loneliness in Dorothy that worked as a kind
of paradox, because the only way she could ever have felt less lonely
was to spend less time with others. She never figured that out, and
she surrounded herself with people who not only eroded her sense
of self but snuffed it out. It frightened me, at times. It felt too close to
losing your mind, too exposed. Dorothy's movement through Hollywood, her desperate need to be seen but her desperate lack of control
over how she was seen, didn't seem like much of a life at all; it was
death in life, and then it was death.

And then there was all the actual exposure. I knew going in that
nudity was a central part of the film. There was no way to avoid it if
you were going to play Dorothy Stratten. I knew her life inside and
out by then, and I knew how much of her identity came from being a body: how it advanced her career and attracted the attention
of men, but also how it shielded her from certain emotional responsibilities and prevented people from dealing with her forthrightly.
I tried hard to separate myself from the role. It wasn't a role that I
wanted to consume me completely. But it was impossible to set all
of it aside: there was too much in what I was doing that bore some
resemblance to what she had done, and the fact that we were creating something analytical, something that attempted to explain her
life, was only a partial correction. Add to that the fact that we filmed

some of the scenes in the same house where Dorothy Stratten and Paul Snider had lived, the same house where Dorothy had died. I was a victim for months, and then the last two weeks of filmimg I had an exploded face from where Paul had shot me, so I had to wear this gross prosthetic on my jaw. I tried to walk around like a normal person, but it was nothing close to normal from inside that thing. I saw how people looked at me, the disgust and pity, and still, underneath that, the glimmer of attraction—the face may have been blasted, but what about that body? It was my body, but it was a new body that I had taken on, in part, to become Dorothy's body. Was it our body? Was it anyone's? Sometime during *Star 80*, that body took a short, strange trip back into the past. We were on a brief break, and I got word that we needed to do some last reshoots for *Personal Best*. I had to bind my chest so that my implants wouldn't be too conspicuous.

Star 80 was grueling in every way. I had never played a movie opposite someone whose character was going to murder mine. The closest experience I had was *Lipstick*, and that had been difficult because of how much I had liked Chris Sarandon, because of how kind and decent he had been to me between takes. Eric Roberts started out that way. He was a dream during rehearsals.

Just before we started to shoot our first scenes, he asked me to go out with him. I said no. I didn't say it brusquely or cruelly. I just told him that I thought we were both about to pass through one of the most grueling experiences of our lives, and I couldn't imagine how claustrophobic it would be to double down on that with a personal relationship—not to mention that I had a boyfriend. I thought it was a perfectly valid explanation, but it turned him into a monster. He wouldn't look at me until cameras started, or he would stomp down on my toes just before a close-up. He even spit in my face once, and I let it happen because I knew that his character was all about freakish possessiveness and moments of petulance. But it was exhausting, and more so because he also clashed with Bob Fosse. Fosse's intricate set-ups and choreography were hard for Eric. At one point, we were try-ing for a scene for what seemed like hours, and Fosse just exploded with exasperation. "God damn it," he said to Eric. "You can't even go down an escalator without tripping."

Eric wore me out every day. He made a difficult movie more diffi-cult. And then, like magic, his personality switched back. We were at some end-of-shoot event, and he put his arm around me, fraternal at most, and beamed. "Didn't we have a wonderful time?" he said. I re-member being on set for one of the final days of shooting and look-ing around at all of them: at Bob, at Eric, at the crew that was sup-porting their vision, at the other actors who may have been at a later stage in their career, or who may have just been starting up the Hol-lywood ladder. Everyone's ego was on display and also at risk. Every-one's appearance was on display and also at risk. There was drinking and there were drugs and there was sex and there were all kinds of psychological games. Once again, I had worked my way into a crazy on-set family that made my own family—and me especially—look sane by comparison.

*   *   *

CHRISTMAS AGAIN meant home again. Home again meant family again. Family again meant habits again.

"How was your movie?" Margaux would ask, and I didn't know how to answer. Her acting career was in limbo at best. She had done a movie called *Killer Fish* with Lee Majors and Karen Black, and Karen Black had a kid on set who was four years old and still nurs-ing. "Tit, Mom," the kid would say. I had gone from *Lipstick* to an Oscar nomination. She had gone from *Lipstick* to *Killer Fish*. I didn't know how to answer, but I knew that any answer would be unkind.

"You're wearing that dress?" my mother would ask, and I didn't know what to do. She was stronger than when the chemo had been at its worst, but that just meant that she had more energy to be critical. When she trained her gaze on you, the next thing out her mouth was likely to be negative. I didn't know what to do, so I smiled tightly and made sure the house was clean.

"I'm going fishing," my father would say, and I didn't know when he'd be back. Though he was less tormented during those years, his peace of mind seemed to be directly related to the fact that he was spending less and less time with the rest of us. He withdrew from the family as a survival strategy. When he was out in the river or on the mountain, he found his bearings. I didn't know when he'd be back, so I went for a walk myself.

"I'm going to meet some friends," Muffet would say, and I didn't know where to look. She was home, fulfilling the caretaker role that had fallen to me earlier, and the more it became clear that her own life was disappearing inside my parents' house, the more elaborate her stories became. She would spin an incredible tale about meeting friends at a restaurant, maybe going away for a week. I didn't know where to look, so I looked down.

Around that time, a wrinkle appeared under my right eye. I was standing in front of a small hallway mirror near my childhood bedroom, thinking about how my face had always looked the same to me, and that's when I saw the wrinkle. I had never seen anything on my face that didn't make me look like I was a little girl. Did that mean that I was an adult? I was taking care of my own career, paying my own way in the world. I had built a house for myself. But if time was passing, if things were changing, why did it also feel that everything would always be the same? Big questions for a small mirror.

I touched the wrinkle once, quickly, and went off to sleep.

10

THE FACE IN THE MIRROR

SNIP.

I closed the scissors and a lock of hair fell to the ground. I was in Salmon, in the house I had built, sitting cross-legged in front of the mirror. I squinted at my reflection. The left side of my hair was shorter than the right.

Snip.

Now the right was too short. I went on like that, cutting on the left, then the right, then the left. It was like balancing a wobbly table—or, more to the point, failing to balance it.

Snip.

When my hair got short enough that I could see my ears, I forced myself to stop. The face in the mirror was frowning.

By the early eighties, I had been a professional actress for more than half a decade. Over that time, I had learned the rhythm of a movie, how it consumed you for months while you were shooting it, and then how you left it behind when the shoot drew to a close. But that didn't happen with *Star 80*. It got into my head and stayed there. Dorothy Stratten was a character I played, but she was a real woman also, a woman who had lived sadly and died suddenly. She had been trapped, and playing her made me think about the other women who were trapped too.

I thought about my mother, how her true love was taken from her by the war and how she had to marry again, to a man who she may or may not have loved, to satisfy society's expectations of her. She couldn't quite bear the weight of those expectations. I thought about Muffet and how men—from my father to her husband—had always regulated her life, in theory because it protected her from herself, but with more problematic consequences too, reminding her that she was a person who couldn't exist in a world without extremely rigid rules and patterns. I thought about Margaux and how she lived in a world like Dorothy's world, where a woman's value was determined largely by how she looked and how she pleased the men around her.

Dorothy had been trapped, and playing her made me wonder if I was trapped too. By that point, I had been with Robert Towne for two years or so, and while the first year had its appeal, the second year was dominated by an increasing sense of how wrong everything felt. I realized that I suited him, that he liked having a young girlfriend—for cosmetic reasons, ego reasons, social reasons—but that he didn't suit me at all. When I would go back to Ketchum for summers or Christmas and run into other girls from high school, they would have normal lives, normal boyfriends. They'd be worrying about whether or not they should break up, or make a more serious commitment, or start a family, or take a trip, or have more conversations, or have fewer conversations. Their lives were predictable in some ways, but they seemed organic, legitimate. I just felt so out of step, as if I were spending my time performing a role that might never end. The pressure built. I worried about it when Robert and I were eating dinner, when we were in bed, when we were walking together outside. I couldn't focus on anything other than the overwhelming sense that I was in the wrong place, romantically and psychologically. Did I want to end up like Dorothy? It was a melodramatic question but a relevant one. *Star 80* didn't quite push me toward a breakdown, but it definitely pushed me toward a breakup.

Robert and I went up to Idaho for a vacation: we didn't stay with my parents or in my place in Salmon but rented a condo instead. Robert had a cold, and he wasn't especially happy during our first day there. He went to bed early to try to get his strength back. The next thing he saw was me, hovering over him in the middle of the night, making my stand. "I can't do this anymore," I said. "I need to end this." It was like a replay of the scene with Woody Allen in Ketchum, except that I was getting out of an uncomfortable relationship rather than out of an uncomfortable offer to travel. I don't think that was an accident. Idaho was a safe zone for me, a place where I felt shielded by both anonymity and familiarity. It was my home, as opposed to Los Angeles or New York—places where I was trying, fitfully, to become an adult, with all the trial and error that the process demanded. "I want out," I told Robert. He didn't say anything at first, so I kept going. I listed the reasons we weren't right for each other. I listed the things I needed to do with my life. I had even picked my replacement, a woman who owned a restaurant in Hollywood. "She loves you," I told Robert. "She can be there for you in ways that I can't."

When Robert finally emerged from the haze of sleep and sickness, he was angry. He was being dumped, and he went after me.

"Oh," he said, "so we're not right for each other? Well, let me tell you about you." And then he opened the floodgates. "You're not who you think you are. You aren't talented. You look strange. I didn't even want you for *Personal Best*. You should probably pick a second career now, because you're not going to make it in this business. And that's just professional. Personally, it's even worse—do you know how sick and twisted your relationship with your mother is?" It was a deluge of insult and invective, and as it came at me, I found myself agreeing with it. Maybe I was just trying to avoid conflict, but there was also a sense in which he was preying on the most vulnerable parts of a young woman and succeeding. Maybe my relationship with my mother *was* sick. Maybe I *was* a terrible actress. The angrier Robert got, the less he seemed like a spurned boyfriend and the more he seemed like that experienced writer and director who had dressed me down on the set of *Personal Best*. I blinked and composed myself long enough to tell him that I would drive him to the airport.

With Robert gone, I drove up to my house in Salmon. Excited, lonely, unsure of what was next, I sat down in front of the mirror, and that was when I hacked off my hair. When I was done, I looked like Mia Farrow in *Rosemary's Baby*, except that I was half a foot taller and the look didn't suit me at all. But I was happy the hair was gone. It represented all the things that had accumulated that didn't fit with my innermost self, that kept chafing against my sense of comfort and my sense of what was right and good. I was exorcising Robert and exorcising Dorothy Stratten, doing it theatrically but also sincerely, trying to locate the real Mariel underneath the movie roles and the real-life roles. Even then, there was an undercurrent of anxiety. When Muffet was at her most extreme, she would cut her own hair. The scissors were potentially a tool of liberation, but they were also a warning of where things might go if they all went wrong.

* * *

"BUY THE GOLD ONE," the man said.

I was back in New York, feeling rudderless. When I had lived there before, my social life had revolved around my best friend, Sara. We would walk around together, shopping or stopping for food, and once a week we had watched our favorite movie, *Breakfast at Tiffany's*. But Sara had gotten married quickly, after a whirlwind courtship. And so, back in the city, with my short hair and my lengthening sense of dread, I paid a kind of tribute to Sara, even in her absence—I went by myself to Tiffany to do some window shopping.

At the time, Rolexes were the hot watch, and I bent down over the case where they were kept and imagined what life would be like if I had one. My favorite was the two-tone, silver and gold. I must have said something under my breath about how beautiful it was.

A voice sounded at my back. "What? You should get the all-gold."

I turned around to see an older man. He looked like a Greek shipping magnate, all mustache and shine. "I like the two-tone," I said. "If you like the all-gold so much, buy it for me."

"Okay," he said. He didn't even seem fazed by it. I felt certain that he recognized me, but he didn't say anything about it.

"No," I said. "No, I'm kidding. Don't buy it for me." He insisted. He was probably there buying watches for a dozen mistresses. I put up a fight. "You know you're not going to get anything in return," I said.

"I'm shocked," he said. He wasn't.

"Anyway, I don't like the all-gold one." I left the store.

Down the block—I don't even think I had made it to Fifty-sixth Street yet—I heard someone calling me: "Miss! Miss!" The man who had been waiting on the Greek tycoon was walking briskly toward me, a box in his hand. "This is for you," he said. It was the gold and silver watch.

"No," I said.

"It's all paid for," he said. "The gentleman insisted."

I went on down the street feeling paranoid. Was this some kind of test? Was the clerk following me, seeing if I was actually dishonest enough to walk away with the watch? Had *Candid Camera* come back on the air? By the time I was home, my paranoia had faded, and all that was left was a strange glow. Life felt charmed. A stranger had done something generous for me with no expectation of anything in return.

That lasted about an hour, and then the sense of confusion and emptiness crept back in. I sat with the cat by the window and got older.

*   *   *

IN THE SUMMER, there was a reunion party for my high school class. When I say "high school class," I need to put the phrase in quotes. I had left school early, moved to New York with two years still to go, and I often wondered what would have happened had I stayed like a normal girl. Would I have become more confident? More popular? Who would have been my friends?

At the same time I wondered about Idaho, Idaho wondered about me. Around the time of *Personal Best*, they made me an honorary graduate. Certain flyers got sent my way. Certain calls were placed. The same people who hadn't given me a second thought in ninth or tenth grade suddenly felt as though their high school experience wouldn't be complete without me there. And so, in that spirit, I went back to Ketchum, me and my short hair and a slightly revised attitude. I figured that if I was being invited solely because I had become famous—and that was pretty clearly the reason—that I was going to act the part. Maybe acting famous would work to my advantage.

Even before I got to town, I was thinking of Sean. He was on my mind because he was always on my mind, ever since he came to the Sun Valley Opera House late and held my hand. I didn't see him for the first few minutes of the party, and I panicked. I almost lost the famous-actress cool I had been practicing. But then he was there, over on the side of the room.

I walked over. "Hi," I said.

"Hi," he said. "How's life?"

"Well," I said. "You know. It was hard to get up here with work. I just finished a movie." I was still in character, copping a slight attitude.

Sean just smiled. "Yeah," he said. "Me too." It took me a second before I realized that he was tweaking me, and that's when I actually relaxed. I may have been putting on a show, but Sean was acting the way Sean always acted: he was completely genuine, unimpressed by the fake me and fully capable of reaching the real me.

"I suck," I said. "What kind of person pulls rank by talking about the movie they were just in?"

"Let's dance," he said, extending his hand. I took it and followed. As soon as we got to the middle of the dance floor, I was having more fun being the normal Mariel again than I ever imagined I could have being the self-important Mariel. All my dreams about what Sean would be like as a man had come true.

The night passed with more dancing, a long conversation outside, and then one thrilling moment where he learned over and took me by the shoulders. "You want to?" he said.

I wanted to. I did. The sex was amazing. I had never had good sex before, not really. I was unprepared and poorly matched for the brief affair I had on the set of *Personal Best*, and sex with Robert always felt a little out of step and claustrophobic. Sean was awesome, comfortable and exciting and athletic, both soulful and playful in the right proportions. He was completely normal—and, as it turned out, I liked normal.

So we were dating, or something like it. Our fling continued. The amazing feelings continued, whether they were during conversation or during sex or during the joking and laughing that bridged the two. I had a boyfriend: a bona fide, in-the-flesh, my-age-exactly boyfriend.

When Sean and I got together, I was about to start a new film. For the first time, it hadn't been easy to find the next part. I had read scripts that I thought were right for me but faced resistance in lining up an audition, or I had been targeted with scripts that I thought weren't right for me at all. Again, it seemed at least partly due to the way that people were responding to *Star 80*. Most of the people who saw it felt that it was a powerful film, but it wasn't an easy film to digest. It had unsettled me deeply, and it seemed to be having a similar effect on others. The movie wasn't just a psychological portrait of one woman and her difficulties with men. It was a slap in the face of the industry, a mirror held up to the worst aspects of the movie business. *Star 80* had a clear argument at its heart: if you're a woman, the movie argued, don't come to Hollywood and expect to make it without also expecting to give yourself away. It was, if you'll pardon the expression, a fuck-or-die movie, and no one in Hollywood wanted to look at themselves or their profession that way. Wherever I went after *Star 80*, whatever I did, the movie's tone clung to me a little bit.

For a little while, I worried I would never work again, but then I read a script for a movie called *Creator*, which was based on a novel by Jeremy Leven. *Creator* explored some of the same themes as *Star 80* but through a completely different lens. It was a comedy of ideas about a brilliant scientist who tries to clone his late wife. Along the way, he enlists the help of a quirky young female assistant—and then, just as he's about to successfully clone his wife, he realizes that he has feelings for the young woman. Peter O'Toole was going to play the scientist, and I wanted to play the young woman. I was excited about the role because I would get to show a completely different side of myself—my character was a kind of nymphomaniac, silly without being too broad, smart in unexpected ways.

I told Sean about *Creator*. "Come down and see me," I told him. "You can visit me on set. It'll be so exciting. Pick me up and then we can spend evenings together."

"It's a date," he said. The corners of his mouth turned up just enough to let me know that he was excited too.

I went back to Los Angeles. After a sane interval, he followed. And then, of course, when he got there, I completely ignored him. He was staying with friends, and he called me when he arrived. "Oh, hi," I said. "I have to go do a reading for this script tonight. Can I call you tomorrow?" The next day, I waited until dinnertime. "Crazy day," I said. "I'm worn out from this work. Can we do something tomorrow instead? Or maybe Friday is better." I made excuse after excuse, most of which he accepted with equanimity. Eventually, he went back up to Ketchum, and our perfect little fling was perfectly over.

Why I rejected Sean—or, at the very least, hid from him until he rejected me—required some explanation, even to myself. For weeks after Sean left, I went back through the circumstances of his trip and tried to think about what put me off, what made me duck and cover.

I decided that it had something to do with the division between my personal life and my professional life, and specifically the way that I couldn't reconcile the two sides of that divide. I couldn't be both the shy and gawky girl who laughed at all his jokes in a high school gym in Ketchum and an up-and-coming actress who was preparing for her fourth consecutive starring role in a major motion picture.

Or, rather, I could have, but I didn't feel like I could. I had been diverted into this other existence, into the movie world, and that came with its own set of demands. You could see them through the pessimistic prism of *Star 80* or through the optimistic prism of *Creator*, but they were inescapable. My career in Hollywood depended upon people noticing me in certain ways—not just men, but largely men, and not in exclusively or even overtly sexual contexts, but in ways that were related to sex. With Robert Towne, it had become actualized. With Woody, it hadn't. With Bob Fosse, we had run in circles around the couch in the Beverly Hills Hotel until I told him in no uncertain terms that I couldn't be both his leading lady and his girlfriend. How would Sean's presence change that? I was embarrassed by all the attention I got but protective of it at the same time. Somewhere in the back of my mind, I felt that I had to keep myself open or at least create the impression that I was available. Weren't young actresses hired in part so that directors could project fantasies onto them? I'm not sure how much of this I fully understood at the time. I didn't have friends who were wise enough to help me investigate it at any depth. But it was all sensed and acted upon skittishly.

Right after Sean left, something happened that proved my point, in both good and bad ways. During *Star 80*, we had to re-create a nude photo shoot that Dorothy Stratten did for *Playboy* magazine. It was a big part of her fame and central to her character, and so Bob hired *Playboy*-style photographers to come out and take pictures of me in the predictable *Playboy* poses. You know, naked in a white wicker rocking chair out on the lawn—the way a girl always sits around the house. Just before the movie came out, Bob leaked those photos to the actual *Playboy* for publication. In my mind, this was a tremendous betrayal, not to mention a confusing one. Those weren't my nudes, not exactly—they were Dorothy's. I had appeared in them in character, dressed (or undressed) as her, in the service of the story. To take them out of the world of *Star 80* and return them to the real world, and the real *Playboy*, was unacceptable. But it was also par for the course for *Star 80* and for the themes of the film. I may have complained to my agent or cried to friends. I may have felt private rage and public shame. But in the end, after I ground my teeth, after I cursed out Bob Fosse's name in my head, after I worried and wondered how it would all affect my career, I realized there was nothing I could do, and I just let it happen.

* * *

CREATOR, BLISSFULLY, THANKFULLY, was a bit of sunlight after the cloud of *Star 80*. It was a light movie, a cheery and original comedy, and I was thrilled to step away from the darkness. And the brief affair with Sean, even though I wasn't able to sustain it as a relationship, had liberated me. I was freer as an actress and as a person. Things didn't seem so desperately important.

My sense of freedom extended beyond work. There was an assistant director on the movie whom I liked. He was a big guy, masculine, and the two of us flirted throughout the shoot. One of the last nights of the movie, we found ourselves alone on set. "Want to get a drink?" he asked.

"At least," I said.

We had a beer—I sipped at mine, mainly just to show that I was up for socializing—and then I went back to his place. It was my first one-night stand, and it was everything I needed it to be: uncomplicated, breezy, exciting. The next morning, still in bed, I found myself laughing, not as a result of the pleasure of it but for a more abstract reason. I had, almost by accident, stumbled into a decision that I hadn't turned over obsessively in my mind. I had discovered, in myself, a previously unknown spontaneity. The night hadn't been consequential, and that was the most consequential thing about it.

II

THE MAN IN THE RESTAURANT

MY FRIEND RICHARD wanted to go to a movie. "Let's meet early," he said, "and get some food at the Hard Rock Cafe."

"Forget it," I said. "I'll go to the movie, but that's all." The Hard Rock wasn't my scene. It seemed gross, too much fame on display, and for all the wrong reasons.

"Just meet me there," Richard said. "Some other friends are coming too." So there we were, before the movie, a group of us talking about our lives and what was missing in them.

After *Star 80*, I had resettled in New York and resumed my normal existence, such as it was. I hung out with friends. I read scripts. I did a little theater. There were moments of celebrity here and there—people recognized me on the street, and one spring I was invited to the Met Ball, the lavish event to benefit the Metropolitan Museum of Art's Costume Institute. But I was lonely. I had never really been in love. My plan, I said, was to solve it all unconventionally, artistically, the way my grandfather would have: I would move to Paris, smoke tons of Gitanes, and have a baby on my own, in the most bohemian manner imaginable.

The other people at the table either nodded or shook their heads. Some of them encouraged me, asked me which *arrondissement* I'd live in. Others objected, on various grounds. Richard got especially upset. He said something rude about Paris and then sank into a kind of churlish silence. I assumed that he had some problem with Paris or single motherhood. I learned years later that he had feelings for me and was hurt by the prospect that I might run off like this. At the time, that never occurred to me. I thought he was gay.

As we were talking, a guy came up the stairs at the other end of the room. He drew my attention immediately, because he looked like he was from Idaho, or at least some movie director's idea of Idaho— he was wearing a periwinkle blue button-down shirt, cowboy boots, and sunglasses, and he had long reddish-brown hair that reached to his shoulders. "I would stay around if I met someone like that," I said, pointing.

This didn't do anything good for my one friend's mood. He got even quieter. "That's just stupid," he said.

I went on. "Yeah," I said. "That guy seems cool. That's the kind of person I'd like to fall in love with and marry." He passed close by our table and went into the back. We left and went to the movie, after which we compared notes on the Hard Rock and both decided that it wasn't our scene: too much wanting to be noticed, too much flash, not enough soul.

The next week, another friend of mine, Liz, invited me back to the Hard Rock. "I know some people who worked there, and I can get us into a special VIP area."

"Forget it," I said, again. The only thing that sounded worse than going to the Hard Rock was going to the VIP area at the Hard Rock.

"Do it for me," Liz said. "Please." Liz had a high-class American accent—classic Upper East Side—and always reminded me of Holly Golightly, which gave her elevated status in my mind. Liz was only a couple of years older than me but seemed to be far more pulled together. She wanted to be a writer and had a very grown-up apartment on lower Park Avenue with beautiful furniture that was expensive but not gaudy—a Biedermeier desk and a side table that was made from a stack of old Louis Vuitton trunks and suitcases in cream and brown leather. How could anyone be so elegant without trying? I wanted to have her style, though it was probably far too precious for me. Even her hair dried perfectly straight. Liz seemed to live effortlessly.

When I got to the Hard Rock, they whisked me upstairs to the roped-off room. Liz was running late—elegantly late—and there were no cell phones in those days, so I did what you always did back then when you waited for someone: I sat alone at the bar, drank Perrier, and tried not to look too bored.

After a few minutes, I noticed the guy from the previous week, the one with the cowboy boots, cutting through the far corner of the VIP room. He noticed me noticing him, and he came up and introduced himself.

We ended up talking most of the night. No one got to the movie. I even forgot how much I dreaded being in a bar. The man's name was Stephen Crisman, and he was one of the managers of the Hard Rock. He had been with the restaurant from early on, in London, and had come to the States to open up the New York branch. Come back to the States, to be more precise—he was from Virginia. Mostly, that first day, he talked about spending time on the Potomac with his dog. That led to him telling me his dog's name, Black Thorn, and then showing me a picture of Black Thorn, which he carried in

Top: Elsa and me hunting in Idaho. I'm eight.
Bottom, left: Mom, Dad, Margot, and me in the Grand Tetons, Wyoming.
Bottom, right: At Dan and Mary Kay's house in Oregon.

SEP • 73

At a lake in the Tetons with two of my mother's friends. I'm on the far right.

Top: My mom, in a happy moment during a period of remission.
Bottom: My dad fishing in the seventies.

Arrived in Idaho: Margot, my parents, and me outside of our new house in the late sixties.

Top: The kid doesn't completely stay in the picture; with the whole family.
Bottom: Muffet holds me up while Margot holds a teddy bear I got for my second birthday.

Top: My eventful second birthday.
Top, right: Me at age three.
Bottom: My daughters Langley at age four (left) and Dree at age six (right) with Muffet.

Top: Me, Margot, and my mom in the Tetons.
Middle: Muffet with me after my christening. What hair!
Bottom: Another christening picture, this time with the whole family.

Top: My sisters at the airport in Hailey, Idaho.
Bottom, left: Margot playing bride in Mill Valley, California.
Bottom, right: Muffet's high school photo in Mill Valley.

Top: Margaux's wedding to Bernard Faucher.
Middle: Fixing up Margaux's hair for the wedding
Bottom: The 3 M's—Margaux, Mariel, and Muffet.

Top: Me and my mother.
Bottom: Me and my dad at Margaux's wedding.

Top: Dad and me at the Cannes film festival in 1979.
Bottom: Posing at Cannes.

Top: Dad walking me down the aisle at my wedding in 1984.
Bottom: A family photo with Stephen's mom, Dorothy Crisman.

Top: Me and Dree snuggling. She's five.
Bottom: Dree and Langley in Idaho.

Top, left: Shot from a yoga photo session.
Top, right: In the garden for a *Mariel's Kitchen* cooking shoot.
Bottom: With my daughters at a New York City premiere, 2010.
(Photograph © Jason Kempin/Getty Images)

his wallet like a picture of a child. Black Thorn was a Belgian Ter-vuren—that's the Belgian sheepdog, midsize, highly intelligent, and highly active—and Stephen said that he loved to watch him run through Central Park. We talked about dogs for a while, and then other animals, and then places you might go with those animals: hikes in the mountains, walks in the forest.

It was ten, and then it was eleven, and Stephen raised his hand to get the attention of a waiter and asked me if I wanted a real drink. Though I never really drank, I asked him what he thought we should have, and he said champagne: a blink later, a bottle arrived at the table. I drank because I didn't want to seem like the kind of person who couldn't be casually social, though I limited myself to a half glass and flushed it down with probably a gallon of Evian. When Liz showed up, she said hello to Stephen, like he was an old friend, and I did quick reconnaissance to make sure that she wasn't interested in him. "No," she said. "Not me and Steve. He's just a friend. Have fun."

Stephen and I stayed there talking until long past midnight. Other friends came and went, but I never saw another soul. Finally, Stephen asked if I wanted him to walk me home. Sure, I said, and he told me that he'd take me through the park. I had always stayed away from the park at night. A girl couldn't walk through there alone. But with her own urban cowboy to escort her and protect her? I felt fear-less and excited. We walked slowly, and he showed me the statues he loved most: a dog near Strawberry Fields and an *Alice in Wonderland* statue that we sat on. He held my hand like Sean had in the Sun Val-ley Opera House.

At one point, while we were walking up a hill toward the res-ervoir, he grabbed me and kissed me. I literally felt my legs buckle and the blood rush out of my head. He put his hand on my back to steady me, and I felt more than safe: I felt located. We didn't get to my apartment until almost four in the morning, and at the stairs he kissed me again. I kissed him back and thanked him, and he asked if he could come up and I said no. "You have to leave," I said. It wasn't only prudishness that made me send him away. It was love, and I wanted to be alone and let myself feel it. I bolted my apartment door and went to the window to see if he was still there. He was, down on the street, looking up at the window. The expression on his face was the same one I thought was on mine—satisfaction and a little bit of wonder.

I hoped he would call me. I may have even prayed. He did, apparently, but I missed him, and finally Liz got in touch with me and said that Stephen was looking for me. We met that night for dinner, and the next night and the night after that. A week later, he was going to see his parents in Virginia, and he asked me to come along. We walked and walked, and ended up on a bridge over the Potomac where he had played as a kid. He turned to me with a look in his eyes that I had never seen before. It seemed momentous and a little terrifying. "Mariel," he said, "I want to take care of you forever." I almost fell into the water. I didn't know if I had been proposed to, technically, but the offer seemed perfectly tailored for me: I had spent years taking care of other people, and here was someone promising to reverse that pattern. This was love. I was sure of it. Suddenly everything was clear. Stephen's offer was basic emotional math, as simple as one plus one.

People say that when you get seriously involved with someone, you get involved with his whole family. In that regard, Stephen was a good match. His family was normal, or at least normal enough. His mother was a little bit controlling and neurotic, but she was kind, and she loved Stephen tremendously. His father was a nice man who had PTSD from combat action, and he was a little stern, especially when Stephen started to participate in the great social experiment of the sixties. But those were minor wrinkles in a generally smooth fabric. Stephen had a brother who worked with him in the restaurant business, and they got along well. When I was young and would spend time in other people's houses, I would often wonder if they were really happy, deep down. The Crismans seemed to be.

But if Stephen's family elevated him, what did that mean about me and my family? I was in a phase during which I kept my distance from them. Right around the time I got together with Stephen, Margaux went to rehab. She had been through a bad period in her career—modeling offered diminishing returns and was destructive to her sense of self, and any hope she had of starting a second career as an actress had been scuttled by poor performances and poor choices—so she turned to the bottle. Well, she turned back to it. She drank because she always drank, because she was a Hemingway and came from a family with Wine Time. Alcohol was so much a part of her everyday life that no one in my family understood why she'd need to go to rehab. My parents, I think, figured that it had to be some other substance—drugs, maybe—because alcohol alone wasn't a problem. What was the problem? If you thought you were drinking too much, just water down your wine with ice. That's what they had done. The shame of it was that their own relationship with alcohol prevented them from seeing what Margaux really needed, which was support—support in the abstract sense, support in the concrete sense, a sympathetic ear, time spent in conversation, whatever version of it seemed like it might work. There's lots of literature about middle children, about the ways in which they get lost between difficult older children and favored younger children, and Margaux was a nearly perfect example of this. My parents had poured so much energy into Muffet, both in terms of worrying about her and in terms of the resources needed to keep her afloat. And during that period when Muffet demanded all their attention and all their worry, Margaux seemed like she had figured everything out. She left Ketchum and turned up as a supermodel. My parents must have watched as she signed her million-dollar contract and thought that she was set for life. But they didn't have any real concept of money at that level—how much actually found its way into Margaux's hands, how much was taken by managers and agents, how much of it was promised but never actually delivered. By the early eighties, she had almost certainly burned through all of her money, but the things that she did to keep herself in the orbit of the fashion world—appearing on talk shows, being in *People* magazine—made it look like she still had it. Margaux got the same message I did: Your mother's sick. Your sister's crazy. Your life is fine on the surface, which is as far as we're willing to look.

For my part, mostly, I saw Margaux's life as sad. I didn't see how it was going to get better. And Margaux was difficult for me in different ways than Muffet was. She wasn't an easy person to get along with, and she represented certain kinds of behavior that terrified me. She was the adventurer, and the libertine, and the one who was unashamed to be self-absorbed in certain respects. And though all those things were part of her charisma, they were also warning signs for me. At one point, she was out in Idaho visiting my parents, and she did a television interview in which she looked awful. I must have said something out loud, because Stephen always treaded a little lightly around the idea of Margaux. He knew that I had issues with her. Again, most of the issues were danger zone issues. When she gained weight, I felt panic, as if that virus of disorderly living might infect me too. But I wasn't mature enough to go directly to the source and try to make her better—or, more likely, lead her to someone else who would make her feel better. I just took aggressive steps, and sometimes even obsessive ones, to prevent that part of my life from resembling hers. Was it selfish? I suppose in a sense it was, but I worried that if I was sucked into the vortex of her life, I would never get my own in order. I paid special attention to my diet. I started new exercise regimens. I doubled down on clean living. "No, thanks," I'd say at lunch, to dessert, and feel like I was getting my hands around the largest problems in my life. It was self-deception, certainly, but it kept the day moving forward: tick-tock, one small controlled decision at a time to ensure that the world didn't spin out of control.

I also became obsessed with monogamy. Up to that point in her life, Margaux had been through a number of relationships, always with maximum drama. Sex was part of her life in obvious and not always pleasant ways. I hadn't liked it when other kids had teased me about her, or when people made offhanded comments about her life as a model, and so I went to great lengths to make sure that I wasn't that kind of person. The second that I had a serious boyfriend, especially one I loved and who had pledged to take care of me, I locked into the relationship. We became inseparable. I came to meet him at the Hard Rock, despite my problems with the place; I hung out with a book or a journal while Stephen wrapped up work. We went away for the weekend to the Hamptons and stayed with friends who would become central to our lives for years—writers, publishers, artists, journalists. It felt vibrant and meaningful, the opposite of the sometimes hollow loneliness that New York had represented before I met Stephen.

What was it like to have a new girlfriend who was a working actress? I think about that often, how Stephen balanced his sense of pride in me, not to mention the reflected glory of fame, with his insecurity and possessiveness. It couldn't have been easy. It didn't feel easy from my end. In 1984, I was hired to work on a film called *The Mean Season*, a thriller directed by Phillip Borsos. Phillip was a recognized talent in Canada, where he won a series of awards for short films in the seventies and then broke out with his first feature, *The Grey Fox*, in 1983. That movie starred Richard Farnsworth as Bill

Miner, a famous Canadian train robber, and *The Mean Season* was a serial-killer story set in Miami at a time when the city was threatened by an oncoming hurricane. The film was based on a novel by John Katzenbach, a *Miami Herald* columnist, and none of it was groundbreaking, but it was compact and competent, and Phillip seemed like the kind of talent who could make something of it all on the screen. Plus, there was the matter of the casting. I would be playing Christine, the girlfriend of Malcolm Anderson, the protagonist and reporter played by Kurt Russell.

Working with Kurt was a dream, and a different kind of dream than I had ever really experienced. Whereas Eric Roberts had been intense in all the wrong ways, and Woody had been quick to establish a weird kind of intimacy, Kurt was as solid and sane a person as I had ever met, in Hollywood or out. When I met him, it was like meeting a brother: we didn't have any sexual chemistry, despite the fact that we were supposedly playing lovers, but he was comfortable beyond anything I could have imagined from an actor. He was all about the work. He loved his job. He showed up on time, had fun, kept the crew loose, asked smart questions, did a great job, and left for the day. It was crazy, by which I mean it wasn't crazy at all. For me, it was a rare glimpse of what normal actually meant and how it could coexist with artistry. And I really liked that. Part of me longed to be that: to do the work as a professional and be seen in that light by everyone around me. Kurt's strategy for life appealed to me much more than De Niro's, for example. I didn't want to become another person. I wanted to use acting to get better and better at being myself.

There's a famous story—people say that it's apocryphal but I will continue to believe it—about the making of *Marathon Man* and a scene for which Dustin Hoffman was supposed to play sleepless and strung out. Being a devoted Method actor, he stayed awake all night and showed up on set looking awful. Laurence Olivier, his costar, asked him if something was wrong, and Hoffman explained that it was his way of getting in touch with the character. Olivier started to speak, stopped for a beat, cleared his throat. "Why not try acting?" he asked. "It's much easier." It reminds me of *The Mean Season* and Kurt Russell, and the way he represented an alternative to the tortured-artist model that seemed so prevalent on sets.

Kurt's sanity illuminated something deeper too. At home, for most of my childhood, I saw a family of Eric Robertses rather than a family of Kurt Russells. My parents had to alter their states significantly to have any chance at self-expression. They were so repressed—by circumstance, by genetics, by a misguided marriage—that they couldn't be themselves in any healthy way. To express themselves, they took extreme measures, with the help of alcohol. They thought they were getting the poison out when in fact they were putting more of it in. When they blew up at one another, when they said horrible things, when they retreated to their corners hurt and alienated, they never did it with any real ability to control the effects, and so the damage spread. Why not try acting? It's much easier.

Because of Kurt—and Phillip, who had a similar philosophy—shooting *The Mean Season* went quickly. The film came together beautifully in the editing room, and it ended up the way I thought it would, as an elegant bit of pocket Hitchcock. Sadly, we were working with the wrong studio. Because of various corporate shifts and sleights, they didn't put very much money behind the P&A—that's the Prints and Advertising budget, basically the entire public promotion of the film. And when it finally came out, it had to compete with a surprising surge in quality dramas—*Witness, The Killing Fields, A Passage to India, Amadeus*—not to mention now-classic teen movies like

The Breakfast Club and huge comedies like *Beverly Hills Cop*. It didn't
do much business, but it remains a fond memory and a fine film.

*　*　*

ABOUT A MONTH AFTER WE MET, Stephen and I took a trip to the
Bob Marshall Wilderness Area in western Montana. He wasn't much
for the trip at first; he played the city boy trapped out in the middle
of nowhere, complaining about where he could get a hamburger or
a beer, about how it was miles to civilization. We went out hiking,
and his complaining took on a different tone. All of a sudden, he felt
sweaty and a little sick. He had chest pains. The guides got out their
first aid kits and started to work Stephen over, and they decided that
there was a very real chance that he was having a heart attack. His
heart was beating hard for a prolonged period of time. The guides
were worried—beyond that, they were stunned. They had no idea
what to do. I called a nearby ranger station, and within about twenty
minutes a helicopter came and landed in the middle of the forest: the
pilot was a Vietnam vet who knew how to get into and out of precar-
ious places. One of the nurses on the chopper recognized me. "Are
you?" she said. I stared back at her, maybe a little more coldly than
was necessary, but it just seemed so out of place.

There was only room for one patient on the helicopter, which
meant that I couldn't go with Stephen, and when the blades started
whirring and the helicopter lifted off, I thought that maybe that
was it. I had found my true love and then lost him in the wilderness. I might never see him again. That night, I couldn't sleep. I woke
up around dawn and got the horse saddled to take me back to the
ranch. But the horses were't allowed to run, and they knew it. I gave
the reins back to the guide and took off running myself. It was fifteen miles, which was a considerable distance but not impossible—

after all, it was a life-and-death situation, and people run marathons every day.

When I arrived at the ranch, I was wiped out, both physically and mentally. The first person I saw, coming up the road, was Stephen. He looked fine. I was rooted to the spot with disbelief. Was it a mirage? I was glad to see him and thrilled that everything seemed fine and out of my mind with confusion and fury. I ran up to him and punched him in the stomach. Stephen took the punch with equanimity. He explained that he had experienced something that they called a benevolent phenomenon. To this day, I haven't looked it up to see if it's real. When they took him to the hospital, he was all hooked up to an EKG machine, even though he was starting to feel better. There was a man next to him, another emergency patient, and that man died: he went into cardiac arrest right there and couldn't be revived. That was enough for Stephen. He pulled out all the tubes and simply walked away. He did what he wanted to do from the moment we got out into the Bob Marshall Wilderness Area: he bought himself a McDonald's hamburger and went to a bar to drink a beer. Then he went back to the ranch.

This answered none of my questions. Was he okay? Did he think he would have health problems later in our marriage? Was I going to be widowed prematurely? Or did he make up the whole thing so that he could have a hamburger?

To recover from our Bob Marshall trip, I took Stephen to my house in Salmon. I knew that it would fix everything. The place was magical—I had created it with a mix of love and excitement, and then I had found a person who could be there with me, completing the space. But that went about as well as Bob Marshall. Stephen didn't understand Salmon at all. My phone there was a party line, which I loved—you might pick up the phone and hear Shirley from across the street, three hundred pounds and in curlers, just chatting distractedly with her daughter in town, and you'd have to clear your throat to get her to vacate the line. Stephen didn't find that as charming as I did. He didn't find it charming at all. Plus, he was worried about his heart. He never went for walks. He didn't want to explore in town. And there were sex issues too. He wouldn't initiate, and he kept his distance when I did. I loved him, and I wanted nothing more than closeness, but his health scare was a barrier between us.

After a week or so in Salmon, we drove down to Ketchum to meet my parents. I hoped that it would be the magical mirror image of when I had met his parents in Virginia—not that everyone would get along, but that it would lead to another moment of pure intimacy between me and Stephen. That didn't happen. My mother took an instant dislike to him. "His hair is too long," she said, but she seemed to have a bigger problem with his air of confidence, which she dismissed as swagger. My father was polite, like he was to everyone, and the two of them stayed up late and sparred intellectually. I was up in my bedroom, and I could hear my father's voice, like it was one of the dinner parties from when I was a kid: "People say that modernism started in the twentieth century, but all the people who started it had roots in the nineteenth century. Nothing's new, really. 'New' is just a word people use when they don't want to understand what came before."

I wasn't waiting for Stephen to come upstairs. He wasn't allowed. Mom made Stephen sleep in the guest room. I pretended that Dad and Stephen were making too much noise with their conversation, got Stephen in a clinch, and whispered to him that he should come up and visit me after everyone was asleep. He did, and I snuck him out before anyone woke up.

Morning started with coffee. The smell was sharp and bracing. I was so happy that I was almost whistling: I was in the house where

I grew up with the man I loved. My mother appeared, but before I could say hello she scowled and shouldered me out of the way. "You smell like sex," she said.

I was shocked. "How would you know what sex smells like?" I returned. She raised her hand and almost slapped me, but she just huffed off to her room instead. I was furious and embarrassed, but most of all I was sad. My mother probably hadn't been held in years, sexually or otherwise, and I had an impulse to run upstairs after her and hug her.

Stephen and I did our best in Ketchum during the summer. Muffet was at the house, and he watched her with a kind of professional curiosity, observing her Wine Time and her long walks. She was doing well during that period, staying bright-eyed, though she was still an eccentric. A simple question could trigger a lavish, spiraling story. I took long walks of my own, hiking Bald Mountain almost every day by myself. The summit is at almost ten thousand feet, and when I got to the top, my face beet red and my heart thumping, I felt a surge of something that I can only describe as immortality. Stephen came once, but he didn't want to push himself, and I got too far ahead of him. But his irritation ebbed, and I kept at the mountain, and by the time we left we were relaxed and focused, if not exactly blissful.

And then, it was back to New York, back to life as an actress and some kind of celebrity, learning how to renegotiate all of that from within a serious relationship.

That fall, Annie Leibovitz was assigned to shoot me for *Vanity Fair*. She had recently joined the magazine as a staff photographer after years at *Rolling Stone*. Around the time of *Personal Best*, we had done a great photo shoot where she took pictures of me in an all-white racquetball court. She had seen the *Playboy* pictures of me (by which I mean the *Playboy* photos of Dorothy Stratten) that Bob Fosse had leaked, and she wanted to photograph me topless too.

I agreed—always the people pleaser—but as the issue got closer to publication, I got more and more nervous. I was a woman in a serious relationship now, not the carefree young person I had pretended to be just a few months earlier. What would Stephen think of the photos? I got on the telephone and started to pester *Vanity Fair* to pull the photos from the issue. I raised every kind of stink: I appealed to their sense of decency, wheedled, maybe even bullied a bit (though I was a completely ineffective bully). *Vanity Fair* didn't listen. Or rather, they listened, but then went ahead and published the photos anyway. Stephen didn't say anything directly, but I could tell that the whole situation made him unhappy.

There was plenty to make him happy too, including the fact that we were continuing to move toward marriage. Plans solidified to the point where we told my parents. My mother delivered a classic Puck response: "If you have kids," she said, "they're going to be retarded." I think she was a little shocked that Stephen and I were so serious, that it wasn't just a passing fancy. I would have liked her to have a real conversation with me about it—about Stephen, about commitment, about the good and bad things about marriage. I was still in my early twenties, and though I was sure that I was in love, I was unsure about most everything else. But it wasn't my mother's way to communicate straightforwardly. She did what was familiar to her: fired off a cruel remark and then withdrew into disapproval.

My dad didn't talk to me about the decision either. He might have been receptive to a conversation, but I was too scared to open the door. To me, initiating a discussion would have been a form of inviting failure. If I explored my feelings and the relationship somehow fell apart, then I would be ruining my one chance at happiness—and that's exactly what I believed, that I had one chance, and that if I didn't grab at the brass ring, I was out of luck.

12

THE WEDDING IN THE CHURCH

"YOU DON'T UNDERSTAND," Stephen said. We were at a restaurant in New York, a few minutes after our rehearsal dinner. Our guests had mostly said their good-byes and wished us good luck. We were in the back hallway having a massive fight.

"You don't," I said. "And you never will."

"That's ridiculous," he said. "You're ridiculous. I can't believe I'm thinking of spending my life with you."

"Maybe you shouldn't," I said. "Why would you want to be with someone who doesn't want to be with you?"

"Oh, is that you?" he said. "I thought you didn't know what you wanted."

"Shut up," I said. "I'm going to the car."

I moved to leave. He reached out for me, and his hand closed around the strap of my dress. I turned away from him, and the strap ripped. "You're just lucky that wasn't my wedding dress," I said.

He laughed a little at that. "So the wedding's on?"

"We'll see," I said, and I laughed a little at that. We were both jittery, on the brink of a big commitment, a little raw from fear and intimidated by how much was about to change. Stephen left angry, and I stayed in a hotel in Manhattan by myself. And then, the next morning, without any real resolution from the fight, we met at Saint Thomas Episcopal Church on Fifth Avenue and became man and wife. It was December 9, 1984, just two weeks after my twenty-third birthday.

If you had asked me five years before if I cared about having a wedding filled with pomp and circumstance, I would have said no, that what was important was true love, and that I could have been married by a justice of the peace while wearing a barrel for all I cared. That would have been a lie. The second that it was clear that Stephen and I were really going through with the wedding, my mind filled with pictures of fairy-tale princesses and castles. I had a costume designer, Julie Weiss, make a dress for me that was based on Grace Kelly's wedding gown.

During the service, I realized that Stephen was still a little woozy from the night before: maybe a little dazed, maybe a little hungover. The second we exited the church, he put on a pair of big sunglasses. "Who the hell do you think you are?" I asked. "Michael Jackson?" He frowned, but not like he had frowned the night before. This was a loving married frown.

We drove back to New Jersey, where we lived at the time, for the reception, which was the second part of my fairy-tale plan: I had decorated the whole house like Christmas, white with pink bows, and picked out the perfect wedding cake. It was a great celebration, a big blowout—Stephen was able to get cheap alcohol from the restaurant, and there was plenty of drinking all around.

Getting married, at that point, in my family, was an equivocal thing. Both of my sisters had already been married, and both of them had seen their marriages end. And while they were happy for me, they were also sad in a road-not-taken kind of way. I think that Margaux was especially bothered by the possibility that she might never have children. But I loved having my whole family there at the wedding. Margaux was sober—she had been to rehab recently—though she had gained some weight and didn't look much like a supermodel anymore. Muffet was good, in Muffet terms: she was medicated and living at home, deep enough in the caretaker mode that she could rationalize the absence of a normal life. My mother actually made it too. I suppose I had never seriously considered the possibility that she would miss her youngest daughter's wedding, but she hadn't been to the Salmon house, and she wasn't in the best of health. But she came out to New York and then to Alpine, where she was genuinely impressed by the way that we had decorated, by the house, and by the sense of ceremony. She responded to order and to effort, because it reminded her of what a life looked like when it was purposeful. She could see that I had devoted myself to the project of preparing the place, and that, for her, was as important as the emotional aspects of the wedding.

I'm not sure what my family thought about Stephen, except that they approached him cautiously. My father was nice and polite, as always—he didn't want any kind of tension or friction with anybody ever. My mother was more openly suspicious, but it was hard to tell if she was specifically concerned about Stephen or just generally worried about any movement in my life that took me away from her.

As soon as the party ended, Stephen and I went straight to the airport and took a night flight to London, where we stayed at Claridge's. We could only afford two nights there, and we were in a daze:

Stephen slept most of the way on the plane, and he couldn't snap out of it once we arrive in England. I pouted and felt neglected, a new wife with a husband who couldn't find energy. After two nights, we shifted over to a friend's house in St. John's Wood. Stephen got better the afternoon we checked out of the hotel, but by the time we were at the house, he was in a dark mood, not angry exactly, but brooding. He was having cold feet, it seemed—he tried to explain it to me, but he wasn't very good at articulating his feelings, and I became terrified that he was talking around some larger set of concerns, or some definite reason that things couldn't work. As best as I could tell, he was afraid of what was coming in our life—he wasn't sure what challenges we'd face, or how we would cope with them as a couple.

The second half of the honeymoon, in Paris, didn't clarify matters at all. One afternoon, I went shopping. It made sense to me: I was in Paris on my honeymoon, and there was a dress I wanted. Stephen became so angry that I was shopping that he just shut down. That was how he fought: rather than screaming, he just got quieter and quieter, as if he wasn't sure he would ever speak to me again. I don't know whether he was concerned about money, or whether it was an issue of control, but it seemed senseless to me—I was bringing in most of the money, and it wasn't an extravagant purchase. In Paris, on the street, I had a shock of uncertainty. Maybe I had made a terrible mistake. What if I had married the wrong person? He had been elusive in his own way in the Bob Marshall Wilderness Area. I hadn't understood the way he had disappeared from the scene and then resurfaced as if nothing had happened. But I hadn't seen this level of intense, quiet fuming.

The doubt passed. We returned to New York and resumed our life together. I was finally part of a different family, which was exciting and liberating. It gave me the chance to avoid some of the same mistakes that had plagued my own family—though I couldn't have known at the time that it would also give me the chance to repeat them. Soon enough, the problems of the honeymoon were repaired and replaced by the excitement of newlywed life in New York City. From the start, Stephen and I were great as a pair, in the sense that we worked great together in social situations. When people came over for dinner, we both knew how to switch on a certain energy. He adopted a kind of brash persona and he liked to talk about sex and shock people; I was the more conservative counterweight. But we told jokes to (and about) each other, and we showed affection when others were around.

Even when we weren't at parties, we were together all the time—I wasn't working on a movie, so he could spend his days with me before heading over to the restaurant at night, at which point I could go with him if I wanted to—and it felt like we were getting closer and closer. We talked about everything, except that we didn't talk about anything. The minute the conversation turned to more serious matters—whether it was because we were bumping up against an uncomfortable part of the relationship or business his wasn't going well—he shut down, and when he did, I just backed off. I stopped being open. It was how I was brought up.

In retrospect, I should have lived with him for a few years before we got married. But what can you do about retrospect? He was older, and I assumed he knew better, and I was shy and felt that maybe living together was a mistake. There was a large part of me that believed in the fairy tale that I had created for our wedding day: you could have all the intimacy and all the sex and all the emotion you wanted, but you had to be married first.

Stephen's first marriage also cast a long shadow. His first wife had had been small and dark-haired, very curvy, very English. Whenever he described her, she seemed like some kind of fairy or sprite, a delicate being who moved through the world with a perfectly feminine grace and ease. What was worse, whenever Stephen described other past girlfriends, they were the same type. There was one girl, Gabriela, whom he rhapsodized about. She was his ideal. She was everything he wanted in a woman, except for the part where they hadn't been right for each other. Not long after we were married, we were walking through Central Park, and he gasped. "What?" I said. He shook his head: nothing, he said. But I followed his gaze. "Is that Gabriela?" I said. He nodded reluctantly. The woman he was looking at was—again—a tiny, voluptuous brunette. I was this big blond oaf, an all-American girl without an especially womanly figure (there but for the grace of implants) and a weird voice to go along with my round moon face. Where did I fit in?

Stephen said that I was being silly and that he loved me. "I love you too," my weird voice answered.

* * *

AFTER *THE MEAN SEASON*, I didn't get another job for what seemed like years. In retrospect, it was only a matter of months, and maybe that wasn't the issue so much as the fact that it felt like a beat too long. I had expected to come back to New York after the honeymoon, spend a little while growing accustomed to married life, and then start working again. I guess you could say that I expected marriage to be like a movie set: four intense months figuring out the rules and forging relationships, and then something new. But the something new didn't come. I heard about other actresses my age getting roles that sounded interesting, and about directors I had worked with starting projects without giving me a call or an audition.

My agent at the time was Sam Cohn. He liked to have lunch with me at the Russian Tea Room, possibly because I was a pretty girl, but he didn't give me any substantive career advice. Nobody explained to me how the business actually operated—what kind of roles I should take, which directors I should work with, whether it made sense to do a small part in a certain prestigious project or whether I could survive a high-profile bomb. It was taken for granted that I was in the industry, that I was a working actress with a fairly visible profile, and that was the extent of the discussion.

In the spring of 1985, I appeared in a play at the Manhattan Theatre Club called *California Dog Fight*. It wasn't a success, but it started me thinking more about the craft of acting, and that summer, for the first time, I started to take acting lessons. It wasn't something I had ever thought about. My entire career had been an accident, really. My first job had surfaced because I was Margaux's little sister, and I had sustained and extended that accident. There were probably untapped reserves of talent, I figured, whether comic or dramatic, and an acting coach could help me discover them.

It had the opposite effect. The second I started to get formal instructions, I became self-conscious and stiff. One early piece of advice I remember was "Don't move your eyebrows so much"—that produced a tornado of self-doubt and analysis. What if I moved them? Would I seem untrustworthy? Was that something that they said to all actresses or was it an issue only for me? Were there certain moments when I should just throw it all out the window and move my eyebrows like crazy? I thought about Margaux's difficulties with acting, most of which seemed to come from a surplus of thinking. Wasn't the job simpler than that, at some level? Wasn't it about putting yourself in situations, finding the place in your head (or heart) that could make sense of that artificial circumstance, and reacting accordingly?

Years later, after even more trial and error, I finally found an act-ing coach whose advice made sense to me. "You know how to act," he said. "That's not your problem. But learn more about the roles you're picking, and more about yourself, and then trust that the in-tersection of those two things is okay. Acting's not your issue. It's a more general problem of self-confidence, or feeling like you're where you should be." But that was faraway at that point. Instead, I was taking classes, putting myself out there, going on auditions, and not finding any more success—or, it seemed, any roles at all. I started to think that maybe I didn't know how to get from one place to another, careerwise. It wasn't a good feeling, and the occasional moments of uneasiness I was feeling in my relatively new marriage didn't make me feel any better.

That's when *Superman IV* surfaced. I had seen the first two Chris-topher Reeve movies, like everyone else in America, and I hadn't seen the third, which people didn't like. There was something off in the tone, they seemed to feel, an uneasy relationship between the he-roic aspects of the story and the comic casting of Richard Pryor. But the third one did well enough at the box office that a fourth was or-dered, and the script found its way to me.

I read it at home over a weekend. It was terrible. The story was about a villain named Nuclear Man who was cloned from a hair of Superman's that was being exhibited in a museum. It didn't make any sense on its face, not even in comic-book terms. Still, I agreed to meet the director, Sidney J. Furie, a polite older man who had directed the spy movie *The Ipcress File* and the Billie Holiday bi-opic *Lady Sings the Blues*. He seemed fine, but I was worried about the production company, Golan-Globus, which had a reputation for cheap-looking movies that were rushed out in order to make quick cash. My thought process became a constant balancing act. Con: It's

Superman. Pro: Christopher Reeve is in it, and Gene Hackman—
who had skipped *Superman III*—was back. Con: Have you read the
script? Pro: It's filmed in London. Con: Again, have you read the
script? In the end, the pros won out, not to mention the price tag. It
was paying work in a studio film, and I didn't feel that I was in any
position to say no.

I went to London, where I had this little apartment in Knights-
bridge. I was by myself, mostly—Stephen was back in New York,
and I didn't have any close friends on the cast or crew—so I would
mostly just exercise, jumping rope for an hour or an hour and a
half every morning. The exercise was connected to a growing sense
of food compulsion. It wasn't an eating disorder, exactly, so much
as an intense interest in controlling my intake. I read a book called
Fit for Life, by Harvey and Marilyn Diamond, which was popular at
the time. They believed in the principles of natural hygiene and proposed eating mostly what they called "live" foods, not to mention
those with a high water content.

The diet made perfect sense, but because of how I was, I took it
to an extreme. If the Diamonds advised that eating fruit until noon
was good, then I would eat fruit all day. If they said that you should
never have protein and carbohydrates at the same time, I would store
them in different cabinets. At night I permitted myself to have real
food, which was real only by the standards of a highly regulated
eater: big bowls of salad, mostly. Eating mostly fruit, drinking gal-
lons of black tea, I was probably high on low calories and caffeine,
but I rationalized it all by telling myself that I was making healthy
choices. But every healthy choice was a specific rejection of someone
else's lifestyle. I wasn't going to get sick like my mom. I wasn't going
to have a heart attack like my father. I wasn't going to put on weight
like Margaux or lose my mind like Muffet. I was going to stay on the

straight and narrow, nutritionally and psychologically and sexually and physically and in every other respect.

The movie was preposterous, but it wasn't painful. I found what I could in the part. I could always find something. Maybe it was a little intimate scene with Chris in which I could connect on a human level. The whole set felt a little arch and false, but I had a way of making sense of that: I had just organized a kind of fantasy wedding, and I translated that feeling to the set, told myself repeatedly that it was just a game of pretend—a consequential and expensive one, maybe, but a game nonetheless. There was something about the life of a superhero that appealed to me. I had spent my life hiding personal pain, thinking my way through how I appeared to the outside world. Equating that with Superman's life was grandiose and a little bit silly, but it also made a certain kind of sense.

There was an ethical issue too. I always believed that once you have agreed to do something, you are obligated to let go of your doubts. If you're doing a job for money, you can't complain all the time. You can't be both in it and out of it. Just find the reasons that keep you located in the work.

For me, finally, what made the project worthwhile was the city, the paycheck, and above all the opportunity to work with Gene Hackman. Gene and I had some great conversations about acting, but he was just as interested in talking about my grandfather's writing. Specifically, he was interested in making a film of *Across the River and Into the Trees*. He would have been perfect for it. The character he projected on-screen was authentically a part of his personality. He was a man of action who was also highly sensitive, a thoughtful person who could occasionally be impulsive in the name of action (which was good) but also in the name of greed or lust (which was bad). I experienced this firsthand. At some point during the shoot,

Gene hit on me somewhat—nothing too drastic, but he made it known that he was interested—and that soured me on him. It probably shouldn't have. He had the right to be interested, certainly, and he never treated me with disrespect. I didn't know his arrangement with his wife or whether he was even entirely serious. I just got flustered because I flustered easily.

But *Superman IV* helped my marriage, in a sense. Whenever Stephen visited, I was excited to see him. And when he was away, I felt better about him. In my mind, I created a happy life that went along perfectly so long as we stayed within the boundaries of what made us happy. Challenges were threats, so I decided that the best way to avoid threat was to avoid challenges.

* * *

"COME IN," I SAID. "Welcome to Sam's Café." And they came in: Robert De Niro, Kevin Bacon, Walter Cronkite, and more.

Right after we got back to New York, Stephen and I opened a restaurant. In the press, people talked about him as one of the creators of the Hard Rock Cafe, which was a little bit of a stretch. Isaac Tigrett had founded the business, though Stephen had been instrumental in things from early on—he had created the guitar bar. But he had been in the Hard Rock business for almost a decade, and he was frustrated. Isaac was almost a stereotypical eccentric multimillionaire, always flying off either to pursue enlightenment or to party—sometimes both—and Stephen felt, at times, that he had been reduced to a babysitter. And then there was the way the marriage affected his ego. I could tell, at times, that he didn't feel like he was keeping pace, that he worried he was too small-time to be with a Hollywood actress. After weeks of deliberation, we came up with the

idea that he should open his own restaurant. It was an exciting prospect for both of us. We got his brother to be our general manager
and found a location on the Upper East Side.

For me, the most enjoyable part was imagining the look of the
place. That was always where I went, whether it was as a teenager
sketching out the Salmon house or a bride-to-be designing my own
wedding. The idea I had was to make it rustic, a rural refuge in the
middle of the city. We decorated with pictures of cows and hung
quilts on the walls (including an early American quilt that Woody
Allen had given me when we made *Manhattan*). People thought the
name came from *Casablanca*. It didn't. In fact, the name came from
Stephen. If we were out walking in the street, or shopping in the grocery store, and he wanted to get my attention, he had learned not to
call out to me. My name was rare enough that people would turn
around to look. So he had picked up the habit of calling me Sam,
which I liked—it was nondescript and androgynous, a little sexy.

We opened the restaurant in 1986, and it quickly became a hot
eighties hangout, with young Wall Street guys stopping in for dinner
on their way home, or celebrities dropping by. Ahmad Rashad gave
People magazine a quote about how much he loved our pasta. I liked
that first wave of attention, but once we were set up and established,
my interest waned. I wasn't the kind of girl to stay there until closing
time. Stephen had to be there whenever possible—restaurants are a
cash business, and his oversight was needed to make sure that everything was working, even down to checking that bartenders weren't
underpouring or overpouring. Our days began to diverge. There
were plenty of times when I was waking up as he got home. That was
an additional complication: late hours in the restaurant world meant
that Stephen would drink, and my childhood had made me defen-
sive and withdrawn around people who drank.

* * *

IN THE SAME *PEOPLE* magazine article that includes Ahmad Rashad's praise of our pasta, I talked about the restaurant as a break from movie work. I think I called Sam's a "diversion." But I was starting to worry that I wasn't in high demand as an actress. I had expectations about the kind of roles I deserved; after all, I had worked with Woody Allen and Robert Towne and Bob Fosse. I didn't want to start grabbing wildly at movies that weren't right for me. But I also didn't want to pass on movies out of a misguided snobbery; plenty of young actresses were making names for themselves by picking projects that seemed like riskier choices.

My first acting job after *Superman IV* was a miniseries called *Amerika*. Even though I was still on the fence about TV, I jumped at the opportunity because my character got to do some song-and-dance work, which was always a dream of mine—as a kid, I was obsessed with variety shows like *The Sonny & Cher Show*, and I loved the idea of being able to do that kind of thing on a set. The plot was fairly complicated, a post-apocalyptic story about a band of rebels trying to re-create a democratic republic.

Amerika was a difficult experience, and not just because we filmed in Nebraska in the grip of a vicious winter. The cold had a deeper dimension too: I was acutely aware of how alienated I was becoming from the day-to-day business of things. When the camera was on and the director called "Action!" I loved being there. I became animated and energized. But when the director said "cut," I immediately felt exhausted. If you had been on set, you would have seen me over by the side, head down, motionless. I just didn't have the energy to participate in the process when I wasn't actually on camera.

Back at home, the feeling of disconnection didn't go away. I re-created the New York I had known as a teenager: lots of time by myself, long walks, exercise. I read *You Can Heal Your Life* by Louise Hay, one of the pioneers of the self-help movement, and started to write daily affirmations in a journal: *I, Mariel, love and accept myself. I, Mariel, am healthy, h-appy, and successful. I, Mariel, am healthy, happy, and skinny.* It was obsessive-compulsive, though I wouldn't have put it that way at the time—or for a long time after that. All I knew was that when I wasn't doing those things, I went slack.

And so, over the months, I began to find myself more and more at the empty center of my days. When I was helping out at the restaurant, I did a perfectly competent job, but I kept a certain emotional distance from the work. When I was at home with Stephen, I played the part of a good young wife, even as I saw that we weren't interacting enough with each other. I was occupied but not fully engaged, there but not fully present. I was, not for the first time and not for the last, performing my own life.

13

THE SPIRIT IN THE ROOM

"HOLD THE POSE," the yoga teacher said.

"Can you sense the increase?" the healer asked, pressing the crystal into my hand.

"Know yourself relaxing," the hypnotist said. "Know yourself dissolving and reconstituting."

"The last time, you said that you had an injury," the energy worker said, flattening a palm against each of my shoulders. "This time, I'm just going to place my hands here. Try to let your body communicate."

Some people feel under the weather, and they go to a doctor. Other people feel like they're out of shape, and they go to a personal trainer. In the late eighties and early nineties, I felt uncertain in nearly every part of my life. I wasn't happy in my marriage: fault lines had already opened up between us and exposed a basic lack of communication. I wasn't happy in my career: the sense of unlimited promise and expansion I had felt in my early movies was gone, and I was feeling stranded. I wasn't happy with my body: I was thin but always wanted to be thinner. I wasn't happy with my mind: I had left high school, bypassed college, and hadn't really found an intellectual challenge that kept me focused. And behind it all, my family still hovered as an original problem that I hadn't quite solved.

Was I rudderless? Was I depressed? I don't know that I thought about it in specific terms. But I was starting to get a little lost, and I went looking for answers. In Hollywood, in the late 1980s, that meant participating in various spiritual endeavors. Some were straightforward. Others were less so. But all were potentially ways out of my malaise.

There was some precedent. Throughout *Personal Best*, I was in physical pain. The training was grueling and the hours long. One of the guys on the set told me about a masseuse who was also a healer, a guy who did bodywork but also released personal trauma. I went to see him, and it was a kind of epiphany. During the massage, I would be focused on the stretching and the soreness, but then all of a sudden there was a welling up of some underground sorrow, and I would find myself crying deeply. I didn't know where it was coming from.

I knew, though, that I loved the feeling. It was a purification, a setting aside of all the imperfections of my life. Up to that point, whenever I had felt that way, it had been as a result of discipline. Cleaning my room obsessively was one kind of discipline. Taking long hikes in the mountains was another kind. Exercising for hours was another.

The most common form of discipline in my young life was food control. Fat, for me, was a visible sign that something else was wrong: it was connected to Margaux's unhappiness (because unhappiness made her drink too much, which made her gain weight) and Muffet's craziness (because her episodes made her take tons of pills, which made her listless and puffy). My mother was thin, but she had always been thin, even before the cancer, and deep down that was probably the role model who made the most sense to me. So I turned to food strategies, which meant turning away from food. I never had bulimia, because of my mortal fear of throwing up, but I did every other obsessive thing with food that was humanly possible. One month, I might take a popular diet to the extreme, eating raw vegetables for all three meals. The next month, I might eat one meal a day of snack food and otherwise subsist on towering cups of iced coffee. It was obsessive. There's no question about that. But the alternative, which was feeling unregulated and out of control, was unacceptable.

But in the late eighties, as a new wife who ran a restaurant with her husband, turning away from food seemed less and less possible. Instead, I started to turn back to yoga. Yoga was something that had been around since the early seventies—I remember going to a session with Margaux when I was staying with her in New York during the promotion of *Lipstick*. In the eighties, I started to get more into it, and like everything else, I didn't exactly do it in moderation. Whatever other people did, I would do fivefold. If something was healthy, then more of it was healthier, right? Of course, when I threw myself headlong into yoga, I didn't exactly pull back on my other obsessions. I kept eating mostly fruit and drinking tons of coffee: in other words, sugar and caffeine, not a great combination for settling your mind. And so, when that didn't make me feel calmer, I tried to find other programs, other gurus. I started going to healers and other spiritual counselors. I wasn't especially selective about which kinds of programs at first, in part because I was searching, and looking at different programs was part of the search. I was eager for deeper connection, and that meant trying however I could to find the spirit in the room.

Most of the visits were secret visits. It wasn't that Stephen was a total skeptic. He was receptive when it was his idea or connected to someone he knew. Isaac Tigrett was into various Eastern mystics, including Sathya Sai Baba—Baba, a beatific-looking Indian man in his fifties, was a guru who was said to be the reincarnation of an earlier spiritual master, also named Sai Baba. Stephen had this big portrait of Sai Baba in the apartment he shared with his Hard Rock friends, but when we were married and I started talking about similar things, yogis and spiritual paths, he dismissed them. In retrospect, his policy was pretty clear: he was fine with whatever choices I made, so long as they didn't take up too much of my time and take me away from him. If he had only been able to say that, we could have fought it out and maybe solved it. But he wasn't straightforward, and I wasn't perceptive.

I started going to different kinds of healers, and I developed a complicated relationship with their ideas. If someone brought me a healing crystal, I didn't exactly believe in its powers as described. But I was also a good audience member and a willing participant, and I wanted to keep enough hope alive so that the possibility felt good to me. There was also a performance component, of course, because I was an actress, and there was a sense in which the sessions with healers were directly replacing movie sets as a means of measuring my own personality development. Ten years earlier, working steadily, I might have processed my own insecurity and fear through a role. Without as many roles, I started to overinvest in the spiritual side of things. I might take the crystal in my hand and say that I thought I felt the crystal's power, or that I thought I was getting a faint glimmer of a past life. And then, in the wake of that admission, the economics of the process kicked in. Healers and energy workers affect a certain altruism, but most of them are businesspeople, and they have a vested interest in setting up a circuit where you're paying them to preserve this illusion.

At one point, Stephen and I sought a higher spiritual source. We went to India, to Bangalore, and because of our relationship with Isaac Tigrett, we had a private audience with Sai Baba. As wide-eyed as I could be back in the States with a palmist or a crystal healer, I was a little skeptical with Sai Baba, the founder of the Sathya Sai Organization. There was a long history of people falling under the spell of charismatic Indian gurus, only to become disillusioned later. I was well aware of how John Lennon had come to feel about the Maharishi Mahesh Yogi, that he was a skirt-chasing charlatan preying on all these gullible Western celebrities. We had our audience with Sai Baba. My back was up. But he was just a calmly intense man in his late fifties with an orange robe and a big Afro. He looked a little bit like Jimi Hendrix. He spoke to me. He had insights about my life and how it might be brought under control with more mindfulness. They weren't especially specific insights, but they were broadly helpful, in that they reminded me that I was in charge of my own life. I was calmed by him more than I was changed by him. But even with Sai Baba, there were parlor tricks that belonged in a magic show more than in a spiritual session: he materialized ash in his hands and then produced these giant diamond earrings for me. They weren't real diamonds, of course—you can't run a business giving away real diamonds.

* * *

WHEN YOU SEARCH FOR MEANING, there's always a tension between looking to the outside world and looking within yourself. For a woman, of course, there's a third option, one that combines elements of the first two: having a baby.

When Stephen and I had visited the Bob Marshall Wilderness Area, I had thought that I was pregnant, though it turned out to be a false alarm. But we always knew that we wanted kids, and we never took any precautions. At some point, we got more serious about making it happen: I started taking my temperature, keeping track of ovulation, that kind of thing. And then, in the spring of 1987, I found out I was pregnant.

Stephen and I were ecstatic. For that whole summer, we were like newlyweds again. If the honeymoon had exposed some of the cracks in our partnership, the prospect of a baby sealed them all right back up.

I had always told myself that my obsession with food was really an obsession with health, and I used my pregnancy to prove it. I ate normally, and along with that I made sure to stay in the best shape possible. Whatever exercises were recommended for pregnant women, I tried them. When there were medical tests, I went into them with a conquering attitude, like I had stayed up all night cramming for an exam.

Right after I found out that I was pregnant, I read for a role in a movie called *Sunset*, a kind of old-Hollywood Western mystery that costars Bruce Willis and James Garner. The movie sounded a little chaotic, but it had a secret weapon: it was directed by Blake Edwards, who had made *Breakfast at Tiffany's*, a movie that was almost like a religion for me. I couldn't pass up the chance to work with him. When I got the job, I was beside myself. "Do you know who this is?" I said to Stephen. "I mean, really. Do you know who this is?"

Blake's first act as idol and oracle was to order me to cut my hair. I wasn't thrilled about that, mainly because it reminded me how superficial life could be: I felt completely disoriented with short dark hair, like a different person entirely. But even that different Mariel was thrilled to be working with Blake, and the rest of the cast was great. The movie was a strange beast, not exactly a comedy and not exactly a postmodern Western and not exactly a masterpiece. Bruce played Tom Mix, the famous actor, and James played Wyatt Earp, the famous Western lawman. In 1929, in the heart of Hollywood, the two of them were forced to become a kind of crime-solving team when they got mixed up in a web of murder, prostitution, and corruption. I was Cheryl, Wyatt Earp's love interest, though the real Wyatt Earp had been much older and very married. Hollywood.

Sunset forced me to confront one of my greatest fears, one that had haunted me since I was a girl: vomiting. The pregnancy wasn't problematic for the most part, but I had terrible morning sickness. Some days I would spend an hour bent over a toilet, panicked because I was thinking the unthinkable. I couldn't be the kind of person who vomited. I had designed my whole life to avoid it. When I think about it now, it makes me laugh. I was focusing on the wrong part of the process. It was the baby who would change things, who would help to remake my life and my sense of myself—not the remnants of my childhood phobia of throwing up. But at the time, getting perspective on my morning sickness was as difficult as learning how to speak up in fights or to deal with my own anger, which is to say that it was impossible.

*   *   *

IN EARLY SUMMER, I had to take an AFP test, which let the doctors measure alpha-fetoprotein and look for abnormalities. It came back low. I have since learned I just test low for nearly everything, but this was my first baby, and the doctors were slightly concerned— low AFP can be a sign of Down syndrome. An amniocentesis was ordered as a follow-up test. Results would take three weeks.

Before I heard the results, I had to leave the country. It was July 1987, and the studio flew Stephen and me to London for the premiere of *Superman IV*. We had pride of place at the premiere and ended up sitting right next to Prince Charles and Lady Di. Diana was very reserved, the princess I had expected. But Prince Charles was friendly, even jovial. "Oh," he said every time Superman appeared. "This is wonderful."

"Well," I said. "I'm not sure about that."

"It's perfectly charming," he said.

"If you say so," I said.

The third time he said something was wonderful or amazing or lovely, I turned to face him. "Maybe I'm going to get in trouble for saying this," I said, "but I think this is probably the worst movie I have ever seen, and certainly the worst one I have been in."

He blanched. "Oh, no," he said. "It's quite something."

That night in the hotel, Stephen and I were laughing about the prince. Suddenly, Stephen's face went rigid. "I just realized that we're about to be parents," he said. The thought really seemed to hit him hard. He set down his glass of wine.

"I know," I said.

"And that test," he said. "I hope everything is okay."

"What if it's not?" I asked him. "There's no turning back now."

"Not even if it comes back with bad news?"

"I don't think so," I said. "I can't imagine getting rid of this baby. It feels like a person."

He nodded, but I thought I saw doubt flash in his eyes. It didn't matter: within a few days the hospital contacted us say that everything was fine and that we would soon be the parents of a healthy baby girl. I was beside myself with joy. I wanted a girl. I understood girls. I was a girl.

*　　*　　*

AUTUMN IN NEW YORK WAS PERFECT—it had been my favorite season ever since shooting *Manhattan*—and in early December, we welcomed Dree Louise Hemingway Crisman. She was a long baby who looked like she would become a tall woman, and when she put her tiny hand around my fingers, or Stephen's, she overpowered us completely. When we brought her back from the hospital, she filled the entire apartment. It was a new kind of spirit in the room.

The first few months of motherhood were bliss: difficult bliss, but completely transporting. My whole life was about this small person—feed her, clean her, change her, watch her—and that was a relief, not to mention instant focus. It cured the sleepwalking feeling that had come over me on movie sets, at home, in the street. When there's a baby, you snap to it.

I had trained for films, and now I was training for parenting. I read books. I asked for advice. I did everything I could to do the best job possible. And it was my job—that much I understood. Stephen was preoccupied with the restaurants. By that point, we had a second Mahattan location, a larger space at the Equitable Building on 51st Street, and locations out of town too. That left me at home with Dree, which was just how I wanted it.

When I would talk to friends with babies, they would talk about how tired they were, and I nodded and agreed, but the truth was that I wasn't tired at all. Motherhood rejuvenated me. In large part, that was because it let me rethink the process of taking care of another person. When I was eleven, when my mother had shattered her leg on the ski slopes, I had become a caretaker almost overnight, and my responsibilities had only intensified when she was diagnosed with cancer. Being put in that position was never easy, but I was so scared that if I didn't do everything I could, my mother would die. I was enslaved by my own terror. Dree helped reset that circuit. Caring for her reawakened some of the feelings of taking care of my mother but also scrubbed them clean of resentment or confusion. When I spoke to my mother on the phone, I loved to talk about how occupied I was with motherhood, partly because I wanted to prove to her that I had matured into the healthy version of the eleven-year-old caretaker I had been.

In other ways, the specter of my mother's cancer remained, a dark cloud over everything. One afternoon, Dree was in her crib, swatting at a mobile and laughing hysterically. Stephen was at the table, looking through some paperwork, his brows furrowed. "I'm never going to get sick," I said.

"What?" Stephen said.

I shook my head. I hadn't planned to say it. When I said it, I knew that I had made a mistake. I didn't want to say it a second time. I mumbled something about a cold and how I had to make sure I had enough vitamin C. But it wasn't about that. It was the other *C*, the one that had taken over my mother's life.

When I was a small girl, my mother was engaged and focused. I wouldn't ever have described her as warm, not exactly, but behind closed doors she could be wonderful and loving. After her cancer diagnosis, though, she became a patient more than a mother, and expecting her to be a source of comfort and support suddenly seemed unfair. At twenty-six, with a new baby, I was hanging in the middle between being the child who could remember the burden of a sick mother and the mother who vowed never to become that burden herself.

The focus shifted away from me, from questions of my own happiness. The focus shifted toward Dree, toward her happiness. This was a virtuous cycle. During the pregnancy and the first year with Dree, I worried less about my own depression. I slept better. I was normal with food. I ate meat and carbs. I didn't load up on fruit and caffeine. My body took care of itself. Mentally, I felt such relief. It was like being on a movie set, but even more intense: I had cues and lines and a call sheet a mile long.

* * *

FRIENDS WERE OVER at the apartment. We had finished dinner. I had cooked and now I was cleaning, doing dishes in the kitchen while people said final good-byes and collected their coats. "That was delicious," a man's voice said.

"Thanks," Stephen said. "I agree."

"Amazing," a woman said. "Kiss the baby good night for us."

The front door opened. The front door closed. I finished with the dishes and turned around. Stephen was sitting on the couch, a glass of wine in his hand. He was still going from the party, smiling broadly. "Did you have fun?" he asked. "I think we did great. I felt bad that we talked so much to Mary. Susan and David really wanted to talk to us."

"It was fun," I said. I went to the couch and sat next to him. A silence opened up in the room and widened. He wasn't saying anything now. His smile was still there, but it seemed more inward somehow. He was smiling into the glow of the memory of the evening. "What do you want to do now?"

He didn't answer. I got a magazine and started to page through it. He sipped his wine silently as I replayed the evening in my head. Stephen had been a good host, warm and welcoming. But when the party started, he got boisterous. He made lots of sexual jokes. It bothered me, because I thought people could see right through them. I thought the jokes were like a sign that said "They Don't Really Get

Along. This Is For Show. They Don't Even Have Sex That Often."
My mental picture of the evening thinned until it was transparent,
and then it was superimposed over the picture of another evening:
my parents, twenty years earlier, after a dinner party of their own.
I knew that Stephen and I were different from my parents. Voices
weren't raised. Bottles weren't thrown. Dree, in her crib, had no reason to be afraid. There would never be a loud fight that would make
her pull the covers tight around her shoulders. My parents hadn't
gotten along. They couldn't communicate. Stephen and I were doing better than that, weren't we? Maybe he was right. Maybe we were
great. Maybe friends couldn't wait to come over and spend time with
us. When I surfaced from thinking, Stephen had already left the couch.

14

THE SISTERS IN THE KITCHEN

MY MOTHER HAD BEEN DYING for years. She was always spending the day in bed because she was too weak to go downstairs to eat, or going downstairs because she felt better, but laboring under the grim knowledge that another day in bed was only a few weeks off. It was like extending a thick gray line: no month was worse than the month before it, but no month was better either.

Stephen, Dree, and I were living in Idaho, in a house about two miles from my parents', and I went to see my mom every day. The baby cheered her up.

Most days, my mother was as she had always been: sharp and judgmental. "This tea is too cold," she said. "The television isn't getting good reception. Where are my slippers?" She had aged out of stylishness and mostly wore Madras-print skirts with elastic waistbands. "I don't need anything," she said, "which is good because your father doesn't spend money on me like he used to. But that's fine with me. He can have the fancy car." My father's fancy car was an old Peugeot: my mother drove an anonymous Taurus and never passed up an opportunity to mention it. "It gets me from place to place," she said. "What else is a car for?"

One morning, Dree was playing on a blanket in my mother's bedroom. My mother was sipping from a glass of water. She raised the glass, lowered it, and looked at me directly. "You're good," she said.

I looked up, surprised. I wasn't even sure she was talking to me. "What?"

She rotated the glass slowly in her hands. "You're a good mother, I mean," she said. "And Dree is a very lucky girl."

It wasn't a long speech. It wasn't especially emotional. But receiving that kind of compliment from my mother was remarkable. "Thank you," I said. I drove home on a cloud.

When the phone woke me the next morning, and I heard my father's voice, and I saw that it was still dark outside, I knew instantly that my mother was dead.

I drove over to the house. My father met me at the door. We walked upstairs in the quietest house I can ever remember. My mother's body had fallen off the bed, and that was all that there was anymore: a skinny little body straight and hard on the floor. I don't think she had even screamed or called out a name. My father had heard a single thump and that was all. I stood over her and felt no fear or repulsion. She wasn't in an awful position, physically or spiritually. There was a peace to it. The coroners came and did whatever they do—made sure she was gone, checked out the scene. And then men in uniforms took her out in that empty bed.

I went home, fed Dree, cleaned up the kitchen, and went on a three-hour walk by Eagle Creek. I walked down to the very end, by the avalanche area, and then just sat on a rock for an hour trying to cry. I couldn't. Tears wouldn't come. I had cried about my mother so many times over the years, mourned her in my mind so many times, that the reality of it was numbing. I played through her entire life in my mind, or at least the life I knew about: her childhood, her first marriage, her years with my father, the difficulties with Muffet, her illness. Beneath all of that, there was a loving woman, a woman I loved. And then one specific memory surfaced: the time I had brought Stephen home, after we had been to the Bob Marshall Wilderness Area, and how she had narrowed her eyes at him and pushed by me in the kitchen with a cutting remark about how I had let him come and sleep with me the night before. My whole life had been a process of warding off that woman while I tried to find my way through to the woman underneath, the calm and quiet and loving one. I thought back to when I was a teenager, and how I had wished that other people could see my mother's good side—the side that looked at you lovingly, that hugged you when you needed comfort, that laughed when you made silly faces in front of the television. She kept that side close, didn't let it out often, which hurt others but also hurt her. I wondered if that secret self, the one she hid from others, was hidden from herself too. A tear or two finally fell.

They say that grief happens in the strangest places. Years later, when I would watch movies, some older woman would remind me of my mother, and I would burst into tears. It was rarely a woman who looked like my mother, or acted like her—Diane Keaton in *The Family Stone* was an especially powerful trigger. I think I missed twenty minutes of that movie from sobbing.

*   *   *

IN SOME FAMILIES, grief is a rallying point for the survivors. In my family, it was more of an opportunity for people to retreat to their corners. Muffet's meds were so intense that they had dulled everything about her. Her response to my mother's death was medicated, almost as if she were operating with a mute or a baffle. "It's sad," she said. "But she had a nice life, and she lasted for a long time after she was sick." She was sweet but not visibly sad. She sounded like she was narrating a documentary about my mother.

Margaux was the opposite. "I'll be right there," she said when my father called her in New York. She flew in the next morning, and I met her at the airport. The drive back was like every drive back with Margaux: a long and not entirely successful process of assessing how much she would try to refashion the situation so it became about her. The whole time she was home, she tried to tell stories about her relationship with my mother, things only she remembered. Some of them were true. All of them went on at length. "I can't hear that now," I said. We weren't very nice to her. But we didn't want her to take the focus away from where it needed to be.

After the funeral, we had a small event at the house. Friends came to the backyard, and my father spoke. "She had years of struggle," he said. "I think she's good where she is." He was quiet otherwise, very contained. He was sober, and in sober times he knew his limits and his losses. And while he wouldn't have said it, he was really relieved. He had cared for her for two decades, even though there may not have been a true love at the root of their relationship. We had all cared for her. And even though we had cared for her, she had suffered mightily, and the end of her suffering meant that a weight had been lifted—from her, from us all.

* * *

THE SISTERS were in the kitchen, gathered around a table of things.

My mother had spoken, over the years, of what would end up where. "I want you to have the china," she would say. "I want Margaux to have your grandmother's necklace." Now chains and rings that somehow represented my mother—that were all the evidence that remained of her—were arranged on the dining room table in Ketchum, and Margaux and Muffet and I were dividing them up.

Muffet went first. "I'll take these," she said, pointing at the costume jewelry. After she came back to Idaho, much of her life seemed to be about playing dress-up. She liked gaudy things, bright scarves and funny shoes. They lit up a life that was in danger of becoming flat and gray. "These are just lovely," she said, gathering them up. "Wonderful."

Margaux was next. But Margaux didn't want to be next. "You go ahead," she said to me. She stepped back into the corner of the room and watched.

There was one ring I liked, a tiny platinum wedding band stamped with the date of my parents' wedding. That was the thing I wanted, so that was the thing I took.

"Wait," Margaux said. "Why do you get that ring?" That was her way. She lived with the idea that she was being overlooked. Being less important meant that she needed to engineer her survival. She would never have noticed the ring except for the fact that I had picked it, and suddenly it became the most valuable thing in the room. I had miscalculated.

"Oh," I said. "Whatever." I set it back down. Margaux swooped in, collected the pieces of jewelry that looked like they might be something. The ring stayed there for me.

*   *   *

WHEN MY MOTHER PASSED AWAY, my father hit the road. He had a huge gray-green transport van that he outfitted with a bed, a satellite dish, and a top-of-the-line sound system. He was going to drive around the country, listening to classical music and fishing. I thought it was a great idea, and I told him so. He nodded. "Muffet will be fine here at the house," he said. "And I'll be fine out, not here at the house."

We had one long conversation before he went. "I wish things had been easier," he said.

"No one could have done anything about it," I said. "It's cancer."

"Not that," he said. "I wish I could have been a more hands-on father. I tried. But I wasn't raised that way, and I didn't always know how to do it right."

"You did fine," I said. "You helped me kill a rattlesnake."

"What?" He tilted his head quizzically. I reminded him of the walk we had taken in Salmon, and how he had told me that I needed to take a rock and crush the snake. He protested. "I wasn't saying animals should be killed."

"I understand," I said. "I understood. But I liked that you liked the idea of the house in Salmon."

"And I like that you like the idea of the van," he said. And he climbed up into it and drove away.

15

THE WEIGHT IN THE EYES

ONE OF THE HEALERS I consulted recommended going back to work. "When there is a trauma," she said, "the body wants to go home."

And so I went to Santa Fe (where I hadn't been very often) to a movie set (where I had) to make a TV movie called *Into the Badlands*. I stood on desert ground and looked up at mesas and tried to either lose myself or find myself. Either one would have been okay.

But it was different. Something had changed. I couldn't use the set to distract myself the same way I had a decade before, and I couldn't easily locate myself there either. In the past, I had adopted the cast and crew as a family. I had gone out to eat with them, become fast friends, had intimate conversations, imagined we would always be in one another's lives. In New Mexico, I kept my distance, ate meals alone, thought mostly about going home.

The movie wrapped. I went back to Idaho. And then, slowly but surely, I panicked. Every morning I made breakfast. Every afternoon I took Dree for a walk. All the while, I was gripped by the fear that I was disappearing inside domestic life.

When I shared my concerns with Stephen, he nodded. "Why are you nodding?" I asked him.

"Because I agree with you."

"You agree that I'm finished as an actress?"

He shook his head. "No, no. I just think that you mishandle things somehow." Now I was the one shaking my head. This wasn't the conversation I wanted to have. But he was already moving forward into his main point. "You're not mysterious enough," he said. "That's why people don't see you as a movie star. You need to create a real sense of mystique, so that people wonder about you even when you're not around." I told friends what Stephen had said, expecting them to condemn him, but they laughed indulgently. He's just doing what men do, they said. He's just trying to solve things, they said. He doesn't know any better, they said.

One evening, with Dree in my lap and Stephen next to me on the couch, and with a movie starring someone else on the TV, I pledged to myself that I was going to do whatever it took to work things out. I was going to flush out the tensions in the marriage, even if it meant that there would be no more marriage. I was going to find my way back to work, even if it meant adjusting my idea of motherhood. None of it was easy, but who said life would be easy? Sometimes you had to hoist a rock and stare down the rattlesnake.

And then I got pregnant again.

It was an accident. I wasn't happy. It's a strange thing to say about a child who would bring me so much joy, who continues to do so today, but the first glimmerings of our second daughter did not come at a happy time. I said it was great news, but the smile was frozen on my face. Stephen and I were fighting all the time, I wasn't working as much as I needed to, and I was sure that a second baby would extend the marriage, hold me there against my will while the professional coastline receded. The boat I was on bobbed in the water, and I couldn't see land in any direction, no matter how hard I looked.

*　*　*

THE FIRST TIME my father climbed into his van and drove away, he was gone for a few months. The second time, he stayed out on the road only a month, and the third time only a week. His plan had changed—or rather, someone had changed his plan. A woman named Angela had befriended Muffet during one of his trips, and then she befriended my father when he returned. Soon enough, she was spending more time with him than with Muffet, and then he was spending more time with her than with Muffet. And then Angela wasn't my father's girlfriend anymore. She was his fiancée.

It was a summer wedding in 1989, just over a year after my mother's death. All the sisters were there. Muffet and I wore pink. Margaux wore green. The two of them carried flowers, and I wore flowers in my hair. Dree wobbled around, clutching her bottle. I was highly pregnant with the second baby, and in some of the photos I'm wearing a worried smile, as if I'm not quite sure what's ahead of me. When I look closely at my face, I remember how I felt. There's a weight in the eyes. In those same photos, my dad looks wonderful: happy, dapper, glowing with the promise of something new.

He and Angela moved into a new condo together, and Muffet got her own apartment. "It's great for her," my dad said. It wasn't. Pretty quickly, it was apparent that Muffet couldn't be on her own. She started to drink more heavily—thirty years of Wine Time had created habits that were hard to break—and she seemed to take her medication only when the mood seized her.

I remember coming back after some time away, visiting Muffet's apartment, and stopping at the door from shock. It was like a crack house, with jugs of Gallo wine everywhere and cigarette burns in the furniture. For years, she had been the one who kept order in the house, but it was order kept for others. On her own, she went completely slack. I helped her clean and tried to talk to her about it, but her stories were becoming more outlandish again. She was waiting for money from someone in Russia, she said. "A prince, I think," she said. "It's all coming in pretty soon, and then I can take care of all of this."

And then she was walking down the street in Ketchum, knee-high socks bunched around her ankles.

And then she was standing on the corner of the street, telling stories to people she didn't know.

And then it was a man from Atkinson's, the local butcher, calling my father to tell him that Muffet was stealing meat. "We don't want to make a big deal out of it," he said. "But it does have to stop."

Within a year, Muffet went to live in a home in Twin Falls. As angry as I was when I heard about it, it was the best thing for her. She had a caretaker who watched over her, who gave her money for coffee and books, who made sure that she remembered to call everyone else in the family and let them know how she was doing. "I'm coming home soon," she would tell me on the telephone. "Daddy says I can live there again."

*   *   *

OUR SECOND DAUGHTER was born in August 1989. We named her Langley, which was a name Stephen and I had picked years before—on the Bob Marshall Wilderness Area trip, in fact. We had played a kind of first-love game: what will we name our babies? We both liked Langron, which was a boy's name from Stephen's side of the family. Late in the pregnancy, I sensed it was a girl, and I changed the name a little bit. Neither of us, I don't think, ever thought of the CIA connection, even though Stephen had grown up in Virginia. Langley Fox Hemingway Crisman joined the family.

But the family was changing. When Langley was two months old, I moved with the girls from Idaho back to Los Angeles, to a small house on Betty Lane in Coldwater Canyon. The thought was that Stephen would spend most of his time in New York, managing the restaurants, and I would spend most of my time in Los Angeles. We would see each other whenever we could. We weren't separating, but I had reached a point where I couldn't justify being distant from the movie business. If I passed into the limbo that claimed many actresses, it wasn't going to be for lack of trying.

What I was trying for, at first, was comedy. Of all the movies I had done in recent years, the one that had given me the most satisfaction was *Creator*. I liked comedy. It let me escape from my own mind. It let me exaggerate aspects of my own personality. It let me have fun. There was a script circulating about a soap-opera writer who was losing control of the show that he created. Network executives were meddling. Actors' egos were rearing their ugly heads. He tries to escape to the country, gets into an accident, and wakes up inside the fictional world of the soap opera. John Candy was starring, and I wanted one of the female leads.

The movie, *Delirious*, was directed by Tom Mankiewicz. Tom was Hollywood royalty. His father was Joseph L. Mankiewicz, who had been responsible for some of the most important movies in the history of American film—he had produced *The Philadelphia Story*, written *All About Eve*, and directed *The Quiet American*. Tom had been a successful writer and was then debuting as a director. When I expressed interest in the part, he resisted. He didn't really want me. He didn't see me as a comedienne: in *Manhattan*, the most famous comedy I had done, I was mainly a foil for Woody, the young girl who laughs at his jokes and cries when he says he can't see her anymore. But I kept at Tom until he let me audition, and when I went in to read, I was really good.

Tom was about twenty years older than me, and everything about him was old-fashioned. He ate classic Hollywood lunches at classic Hollywood restaurants and had classic Hollywood whiskey along with them. He was a throwback to the Golden Age of Hollywood, but he was also a throwback to my grandfather's generation. He was intelligent, erudite, and effortlessly interesting: during lunch, he might start a story about Bette Davis, or James Mason, or Humphrey Bogart, and you knew you were getting an insider's perspective.

On set, Tom was a gentleman director, which meant that he thought and cared deeply about what he was making but didn't rule with an iron fist. That left it up to the actors, which was fine with me. In the opening scene of the film, my character is in a phone booth, calling her mother, and she accidentally knocks all her change off a ledge. While she's down on the floor getting it, John Candy's character—who is late for a meeting to protect his show—barrels through the lobby. She's reaching for change. He steps on her hand. He helps her up and tears the sleeve off her dress. It was madcap comedy, which was almost an athletic endeavor. You had to be in the right part of the frame at the right time, which meant moving fast and with precision.

Delirious was also an opportunity to work with John Candy. It was easy, as an audience member, to take him for granted: I had seen him, like everyone else, in *Stripes* and *Splash* and *Planes, Trains and Automobiles.* But I hadn't seen the personal side of him, and that was the revelation. John was one of the best people I have ever worked with: loving, normal, generous to everyone on set. At the end of the night, he bought pizza for the crew. He loaned money to people if they needed it. At the same time, you could see that he was tortured, in a sense, because he never went home. He stayed with the crew, slept on set. *Delirious* was one of five movies he did that year.

We shot mostly in Los Angeles, but the beginning and end of the film took place in New York, so I went back home on a work trip. It was almost the polar opposite of the careful, quiet alienation that I had experienced when Stephen and I had last lived there together. We saw each other. We had a great time. I worked all day, and after we wrapped for the day I brought the whole cast to our restaurant, at which point I got out of the way and let Stephen charm everyone in sight. I watched him from a distance, in love with him again in some ways, and more hurt than ever in others. Why couldn't we be warm and easy with each other when we were alone?

The movie wasn't a hit. But I have a soft spot for the film, not just because of my fondness for Tom and John, but because the story has a strange emotional resonance. John's character revises his own life, which seems like a wish-fulfillment story, but there are darker aspects to it. What does it mean to obsessively revise your own existence? Does that prevent you from living it? And since the rewrite conceit of the film is so clearly fictional, what did that mean for real-life change? I also thought about my grandfather and the way he had built his own myth as an obsessive rewriter, as a man whose genius lay in revisiting his writing continually until he found the perfect word or phrase. How much thought and rethought were really necessary? How important was instinct? How irreversible were decisions?

A few years after *Delirious*, in the middle of making a Western called *Wagons East*, John Candy died in his sleep on set. Tom called me to break the news. I wasn't shocked. John had never been in good health. But I was tremendously saddened, because John had been such a warm, loving, generous person, and the story could have ended differently. Or could it?

*   *   *

"I'M DONE," STEPHEN SAID. I was sitting in a chair, a book in my lap, and the letters went all out of focus. Did he want to end the marriage?

"What?" I said.

"This restaurant business is ridiculous," he said.

"Right," I said. "Restaurants." I knew that business was bad, or at the very least immensely stressful. Stephen was always under the gun. He was always on the telephone, putting out a fire or lighting a fire under someone. No matter how many locations he opened, no matter how packed they were, we never seemed to make enough money from it. At some point, he had discovered why. To oversee the restaurants' business operations, he had hired a veteran controller, but the man had a gambling problem, and he ended up skimming money out of the restaurants to pay off his own debts. Stephen didn't press charges because the man had a family, and it seemed unfair to add insult to injury. But the skimming just deepened the sense of financial despair and further fractured the relationships on the business side of the restaurant. And Stephen never complained to me about it until he announced, one day, that he couldn't go on.

"I'm just exhausted," he said. "I feel like I have poured my life into these restaurants, and I have nothing to show for it."

"What are you going to do?" I said.

"I was thinking about being a film producer," he said.

"Great," I said. He had dabbled in it already: the two of us had coproduced a small movie called *Suicide Club*, a modern-day adaptation of a Robert Louis Stevenson short story. I had worried about Stephen encroaching on my world, but *Suicide Club* had been a good experience—I was creating, and he was seeing me create, and it lessened the tension between us.

"Yes," he said, and that was the extent of the conversation. Between the late eighties and the early nineties, communication between us had worsened. We had become so distant from each other emotionally that it didn't seem possible that we could work together. There was hardly any intimacy left, conversational or otherwise. And sex had become the one thing I thought it would never be: a Cold War battleground. When I would mention that to girlfriends, they assured me that marriage always took its toll on sex. "It becomes a routine," one would say. Another one would nod excitedly: "That's why you have to tell him what to do. Specifically, I mean. Tell him what you like and what you don't."

I tried being explicit once. We were in bed, and he was down under the covers. "You know," I said, "I don't really like that. I mean, I like it, but not right away. Let's do something else first." I started to explain what I wanted. Stephen wasn't saying anything. I looked down at him. His expression was frozen. He wasn't looking at me or even through me. It was like he was looking at nothing, like he would always be looking at nothing. That was the last time I tried to clarify what I wanted.

More and more, I receded inside parenting. I had loved being with one daughter, and two was even better. Get Dree fed, get Langley fed. Get Dree dressed, get Langley dressed. Motherhood was a list of tasks I could check off in my mind. The one part of the day that thwarted me was playtime. "Let's play house," Dree would say, leading me by the hand into the yard. You'd think that child's play would be easy. But I couldn't just stand there by the plastic play set and pretend that I was a doctor or a waitress or a mommy. It was too strange to me, both familiar and foreign, not real but also in a sense too real. I said a few lines halfheartedly and then took Dree by the hand and led her back into the house.

16

THE MAN IN THE MIDWEST

"YOU KNOW ROCK STARS?" my agent asked.

"I know of them," I said. "Which one?" I was at home, in the kitchen. The phone cord was stretched out across the room. Dree was eating. Langley was in the other room, starting to wake up.

"The one with the long name. Mellencamp."

"John Cougar Mellencamp?"

"He doesn't use the Cougar anymore, I don't think."

"I know him. Why?"

"He wants to meet with you. For a project."

"A music video?" I moved closer to the base of the phone. It seemed like the call might be ending quickly.

"No. A movie. He's directing."

I was intrigued. I stopped moving toward the phone. "A real movie?"

"Completely real. Larry McMurtry wrote it. And he had you in mind while he was writing."

I turned and stepped back into the kitchen. This was something else entirely. Larry McMurtry had written *The Last Picture Show*, one of the best movies of the early seventies, and his books had been the basis for movies like *Hud*, *Terms of Endearment*, and *Lonesome Dove*. "Tell me more," I said.

The movie, *Falling from Grace*, was a semiautobiographical vehicle for Mellencamp: he was playing a rock star named Bud Parks who brings his wife and child back to his hometown for his father's eightieth birthday. While he's there, he ends up having an affair with his high school sweetheart. When I heard the plot, I assumed I'd be playing the girl from high school, but in fact they wanted me for the wife, Alice. When I read the script, I was in: it was Larry McMurtry through and through, which meant that it was smart and sharp and emotionally complicated. Alice seemed like a great role: she and Bud were genuinely in love, but he was also being pulled back into his past in ways he couldn't control. Characters were flawed without being unsympathetic.

John and I met at someone's huge house. He hadn't directed a movie before, so he wasn't on stable footing, and his attitude was pitched halfway between insecurity and arrogance. "Are you right for this part?" he asked me.

"I think so," I said. I felt like I was perfect for it, but I didn't want to seem overeager. "Hold on," I said. "Let me call home and make sure my babies are okay. The nanny has been having trouble feeding them."

"Your babies?" he said. He frowned. "Are you interested in this?"

"Of course," I said. "But I want to make sure that I understand exactly how it's going to work."

"I'm not sure how checking in on your nanny helps with that," he said.

We talked more, and he opened up a bit. He planned on filming the movie in Indiana—in fact, in Seymour, the town where he had grown up. "We want it to feel almost like a documentary," he said. "Or at least to feel like it isn't some Hollywood idea of Indiana."

"That's what appeals to me," I said. "I love small towns. I grew up in one too. And I especially like the idea of taking something so artificial, like a movie, and putting it in a place that's so genuine."

"Okay," he said, standing suddenly. I was struck by how short he was: taller than Woody Allen, but only by a bit. "We'll talk soon." I expected him to give me a phone number, either his or an assistant's, but before I knew it, I was out the door.

I spent several days worried. Had I seemed too distant? Maybe I had talked too much about other movies and not concentrated enough on his. Or was he bothered by the height difference? Finally, John got in touch with me and told me that he'd like me to be in the movie.

I had told John that I loved small towns, but even that didn't prepare me for how I felt arriving in Seymour. The streets were wide and unlined, and you could look down them and see for miles. The land was flat and the sky was huge. I rented a cookie-cutter house in a cookie-cutter neighborhood with cookie-cutter furniture, including a bulky couch that smelled like a new car. Something about the facelessness of the place comforted me immensely. I had a bicycle with a baby carrier behind me, and on days when I wasn't working, I took the girls into town and we shopped for antique quilts and swing sets. Stephen was still in New York, still extricating himself from the restaurant business.

Even when the girls weren't with me, I biked everywhere I could. I loved to feel the burn in my legs after a long day. If I had been a healthy eater after Dree was born, after Langley I went back to my preoccupation with weight and body image. After *Delirious*, I pledged to myself that I was going to get as thin as possible. I lived on pots of black coffee, Folgers mostly, because that was all they had in Seymour. It wasn't gourmet, but I came to love the dirty-water taste. As for food, it was a breakfast of oatmeal that I made the night before and cooled in the refrigerator, or steamed vegetables. I ate according to rules and obsessions, and the result was that I ended up skinner than ever, and proud of it. When I looked in the mirror, I felt like I was achieving again: down to fighting weight, away from the madness of Hollywood, and starring in a movie with a rock star.

And John was quite a rock star. He was royalty in Seymour, of course, but also a local boy. Since we were playing husband and wife, he thought we needed to spend days together away from the set. He picked me up from my house on his motorcycle, and we rode around for hours, zipping along the edges of farms, stopping in small diners where he sopped up gravy with biscuits and I drank more black coffee. On set, we had great chemistry. And even on days when I wasn't in scenes, he would ask me for my opinion on framing a shot or adding a piece of dialogue.

After about a week, I found myself thinking about him when he wasn't around. I may have even dreamed about his motorcycle. One day, as I was hitching the baby carrier to my bicycle, it hit me: I was falling in love. The movie was so free of problems that it took me back to a time when my opinion was valued and I could get as close as I wanted to the heart of the creative process. And I felt that kind of thing distinctly lacking in my dealings with Stephen. When I talked to him on the phone, in fact, I would test him, interject my opinion about the restaurant to see how he would take it. He didn't take it well.

During the third week of shooting, John and I had to do a scene in which we were walking somewhere. It was simple, just fake husband and wife, hand in hand. It was nothing that I would have thought twice about. But the whole time we shot, I was vibrating with excitement. During a break, he took me to a corner of the set and kissed me, and I kissed him back. The next morning, when he picked me up on his motorcycle at the house, he was a little cold. Uh-oh, I thought. Is this going to be the end of my fantasy romance?

But it was only the beginning. He would stop the motorcycle out in farmland and pull me to him and kiss me more. During scenes, he would botch a line, and then, when everyone was setting up the next take, wink at me. It didn't get especially physical—there was nothing that would have been out of place in a high school—but the secrecy made it as exciting as if it were a full-blown affair.

Stephen was scheduled to make his first visit to Indiana. As that weekend approached, I decided that I needed to come clean. I was going to tell him everything. I was going to tell him that I was in love with John. I was going to tell him that I wasn't sure our marriage could survive. I was going to tell him that I didn't know what to do, but that I had to be honest about what I was feeling.

And so, that first afternoon of his trip, I brewed a big pot of Folgers and sat on the new-car couch and prayed that the girls would wake up from their naps so that I could avoid the conversation we were about to have. But they slept soundly. "Stephen," I said.

"What?" He looked at me. My expression must have been panicked. "What's the matt—"

I didn't even let him finish. "I'm in love with John," I said. "We've gotten very close during the shoot, and we even kissed a few times. I need to tell you before I cross a more serious line."

I was looking at Stephen the whole time, but I couldn't see his face: it was like a blind spot in my field of vision. I couldn't bear to think that I was hurting him. When I was done, I waited. The next thing I heard was the sound of him laughing. Was that good news?

Maybe he understood something I didn't. He was older, after all. Then his face came into focus. It was ashen and angry. He wasn't saying a word. It didn't seem like good news anymore. Finally, he spoke. "You made a mistake," he said.

"I know," I said. "But…"

This time he interrupted me. "You should have fucked him and not said a word to me. That way you would have just gotten over it."

"You don't understand," I said. "I think it's real."

"No," he said. "You don't understand. This is what happens in a marriage. Sometimes you get your head turned, and you let it play out because you know deep down it's not real." He paused.

I couldn't sleep at all that night. I didn't like the idea that getting close to someone else might just be a passing thing, or that the marriage I was committed to was a sham. It all seemed dirty and depressing and useless.

In the morning, Stephen flew back to New York. "We'll deal with this after the movie," he said. "You do what you need to do."

I cried on the way back from the airport. But then I started to think about the possibility of my own freedom. I had confessed my feelings for John. Stephen had basically given me permission to act on them. Maybe that's what I was supposed to be doing. I made sure I looked good, and I went to set.

That day, though, something was off. I was rushing things.

I started to see that I had created a work fantasy. John was hugely talented. He was nice to me. I think he genuincly connected with me. But he was a rock star, which meant that he wasn't going to change his life for me. When the movie ended, I wasn't going to end up special to him. If I wanted to be with him, it would be as a supporting player.

I tried. I winked at him and smiled when he winked back. But I couldn't find the exhilaration of those earlier weeks. When I caught a

glimpse of myself in the mirror, I didn't see someone who was energized or in love. All I saw was a scared, lonely woman who had jeop-
ardized the safety of her marriage for a pointless fling that it turned
out she didn't even want.

I called Stephen and asked him to fly back. I told him that I re-
gretted saying anything, and that the situation with John was probably more about my own issues.

I had the day off, so we went to a movie. We didn't really watch
it: we stared across the armrests at each other. When it was over, we sat
in the empty theater for an hour, and I apologized for my behavior.

"I'll still take care of you," he said.

I squeezed his arm.

"But listen," he said. "It's like I said. You should have just fucked
him and not said anything."

I was confused.

Stephen slid his arm away from my hand. "That's what I did."

"What do you mean?" I said.

"I've been seeing someone else for a few months," he said. "I have
feelings for her, but I have stronger feelings for you. That's the way it
goes. Other things fall away, and the marriage lasts."

I gripped the armrests. Was that why he had been so cold with
me? When he was making business calls at night, was he calling her?

The next day, when I went to work, I couldn't look at things
the same way. I felt like I was living the story of the film. Alice, my
character, had a husband who cheated because he needed to feel
a jolt of life apart from the marriage that nurtured but no longer
excited him. Every scene with John was suddenly leaden and sad.
In New York, Stephen and I were careful to be kind. We acknowl-
edged that we had been bruised by circumstance, and that made us
tender—and tender toward each other. But it hurts to step carefully
in your own home.

*   *   *

"I JUST WANT SOMEONE I can have a decent conversation with," Sam Baldwin said. "A conversation that doesn't end in weepy tears over some movie."

He was talking about me. I knew it. I sobbed and dabbed under my eyes with a Kleenex.

Sam Baldwin, of course, was Tom Hanks—or rather, the role that Tom Hanks was playing in *Sleepless in Seattle*. He was with me constantly in the period after *Falling From Grace*. At home in New York, in a marriage whose fault lines had been violently exposed, I did what any woman would do in my situation—I watched romantic comedies. That was a glory period for the genre: *Ghost*, *Pretty Woman*, *The Bodyguard*, *Four Weddings and a Funeral*. I didn't go to the theater. It was a private, intimate experience. If there was a romantic comedy on TV, I would watch it from start to finish. I would go to the video store and rent a stack of them. And then I would sit down on the couch and cry the entire time. Sometimes, Stephen would be in the kitchen, pouring himself a drink. Sometimes, he'd be in the bedroom, sleeping. But sometimes he'd be right beside me, watching the same movie, the two of us a foot apart but also a world apart.

My relationship with romantic comedies was complicated. On the one hand, I got lost in them: the improbable coincidences, the swelling music, the way the hand of fate brought two hearts together. Was that what I had felt with John on the motorcycle? I reached for another Kleenex. But just as the plot drew me in, the casting pushed me out. It seemed like every actress in the world who was within a decade of my age got a starring role in a major romantic comedy. Michelle Pfeiffer did. Julia Roberts did. Meg Ryan did. In my mind, I got the lead in every movie I watched, but nobody ever called. I had been up for the lead in *About Last Night*, but it had gone to Demi Moore instead and launched her career.

I was drifting in Hollywood, and I knew it. In the early nineties, there was a script going around town about a policeman who got involved in a destructive sexual relationship with a murder suspect. It found its way to Paul Verhoeven, who was best known in the United States for big-budget action movies like *Total Recall* and *Robocop* but who had started off his career in the Netherlands as a director of adult thrillers. The movie, which was called *Basic Instinct*, was going to be a return to Verhoeven's roots.

Verhoeven already had his leading man, Michael Douglas, and the two of them were deciding who would play the murder suspect. They auditioned a bunch of actresses, including me. I knew I could play the role—and, furthermore, it was exactly the kind of part that made sense for my career. It would put me firmly into adult territory and show that I could hold my ground in a darker, more dangerous film.

Michael, apparently, was impressed with my audition and tried to convince Paul to cast me. Paul was less certain. He wanted an actress named Sharon Stone, who had done mostly television up until that point.

The two of them went back and forth on casting. For days, I'd hear nothing, and then the Hollywood rumor mill would start up again, and I'd get calls from people in the business congratulating me on landing the part. And then, all of a sudden, Sharon was cast. I heard all kinds of things, none verifiable: that she had seduced Michael, that she had seduced Paul, that she had seduced someone at the studio. On the one hand, that kind of gossip is insulting. Is that the only way that women can get parts? On the other hand, those kinds of things sometimes happen, especially when the prize is a career-defining role.

I was devastated when I lost out on the part. I went down that road in my mind for so many years. People tried to console me, especially after the movie came out. "You wouldn't want to do that scene," they would say. "The one where she uncrosses her legs. You're a nice girl." I would smile and nod quickly and go off on my own where I could fume. Acting wasn't about being a nice girl. It was about taking risks, pushing yourself in the business, finding out more about your depths and limits. Sharon got the opportunity, and she ran with it. More important, it helped her become better at her job. When I saw the movie, I was a little critical of her performance. I didn't think she was a great actress. But *Basic Instinct* gave her the chance to work with the directors of her choice, to pick the best scripts—and over the years, she became not only a movie star but a good actress. The woman who starred in *Casino* was worlds away from the woman who starred in *Basic Instinct*. Luck can create skill.

*   *   *

AND THEN, SOME LUCK OF MY OWN: "I have a TV project you might be interested in." In the early eighties, when I heard those words, I passed on *The Executioner's Song*. In the early nineties, I heard those words and went to work for Steven Bochco.

Bochco was one of the real heavyweights in the industry—he had started as a story editor on many of the seventies' cop shows that my mom and I loved to watch and went on to create *Hill Street Blues*. He was executive producing a courtroom drama about Manhattan divorce lawyers called *Civil Wars*. My character on the show, Sydney Guilford, was one of two hotshot divorce lawyers; the other one,

Charlie Howell, was played by Peter Onorati, a handsome TV actor who had briefly been a professional football player.

"This will be a much better situation," I told Stephen after one of the first weeks on set. "The show shoots at Fox Studios right over here. It's not like a movie set at all. I can go to work and then come right back here to be with you and the girls."

And yet, the television series was the hardest work I had ever done. For starters, there was the simple fact of production demands. We had to get a show done each week, which meant long hours every day and then, when time started to run out, truly horrendous hours. Sometimes we put in twenty-hour days. The set was like visiting a new country: or, more to the point, a new kind of country. Series sets provided a stable family, the one that was always there. Week after week, I saw the same faces, had the same deadlines, sat in the same meetings.

Slowly but surely, I remade myself in the image of television. I became more efficient as an actress, more aware of schedules and process. Again, I was a good student. Dree and Langley were still babies, and they would come to the set a handful of times during the week, but mostly they would have to wait until the weekend. Stephen preferred the television-star version of me. I was around more, for him and for the kids. And I was also suddenly paying the bills, which was something that he loved.

* * *

THE SHOW WAS A SUCCESS, though not a huge one. It was on the air for two years and was peacefully put out to pasture. But I stayed on the small screen long enough to kiss Roseanne.

When I try to reconstruct how I got the guest spot on *Roseanne*,

I can't. Maybe the offer came through John Goodman. I had worked with him on a play in Dallas right after *Star 80*, and we had gotten along great, and then he had rocketed to stardom. Maybe it was Bruce Helford, the show's executive producer and writer. Maybe it was Roseanne Barr herself, flipping channels one night and running across a showing of *Personal Best*. Hey, she might have thought, that lady can really play a lesbian like nobody's business.

Whoever thought of me, I want to thank them. It was one of the easiest jobs in the world. All I had to do was play Sharon, the girl-friend of Sandra Bernhard's character, and kiss Roseanne's character in a gay bar. Done and done. I didn't think much of it, other than it was fun and that Roseanne was lovely to work with. She was with Tom Arnold at the time, and that meant that even if you were just a guest star in the show, you could hear them screaming at the tops of their lungs. But she was a pleasure in every respect: smart and aware of others and determined not to make formulaic garbage in a medium full of it.

And yet, the kiss was more than just a kiss. Lesbian characters weren't prominent on network television at that point, and certainly lesbian affection wasn't. Two stations in small markets refused to carry the episode. Editorials were written about our national resistance to same-sex love, or about the liberal obsession with cramming alternative lifestyles down the throat of the audience.

In the years since, the lesbian kiss has become a staple of television shows, especially during sweeps. But at the time it was unprecedented, and powerful. It followed me around for years. In fact, over the course of my career, it's probably become the second-most-common point of contact for fans, after *Manhattan*.

*   *   *

"*AKAPHANA   BINA,   RAPALA   CARANAMA   TA.*" The woman was speaking rapidly, not making much sense. Her eyes were bright. She looked like she was in the grip of some kind of spiritual ecstasy.

"Kids," I said to Dree and Langley, "this is your Aunt Margaux."

We were in Idaho, at home, and Margaux was visiting. We hadn't seen or heard much of each other for a few years: maybe during Christmas in Idaho or the occasional phone call. She was at a crossroads in her career, in the sense that she didn't have much of a career left. Her modeling had tapered off: she had gotten older (though she was only forty), she had gained some weight (though she had lost it), and she had run into problems with alcohol and drugs (though she had gone to rehab). She had also become heavily invested in healing and spiritualism. She learned to be a hypnotist. She studied herbal medicine. At one point, she took an extended trip to India and came back speaking in tongues. When she passed through Sun Valley, she was still doing it. Angela, my father's second wife, had a violently negative reaction to it: it embarrassed her, and she may have thought Margaux had made some kind of bargain with the devil. Dree and Langley loved it, or at least admired it as a kind of bravery. They laughed delightedly.

Margaux wasn't an easy aunt. She loved my kids, but she was awkward around them. It was almost like she was acting the role, which meant that her speech and her gestures were wooden and stilted the way they were when she did line readings. The fact that it was a family role made it even more uncomfortable for her. And there was also a second issue, which was that Margaux's increasing immersion in New Age and self-help practices irritated me. It hit too close to home. It sometimes seemed almost like it was a parody of my own life. Over the years, I had gotten more deeply involved in spiritual and self-empowerment programs. I got involved in something called Self-Realization Fellowship, which was founded on healthy tenets of meditation and yogic principles, mindfulness and kindness to one another. The Fellowship was wonderful—affirming, free of manipulation—but in the wake of that, other kinds of people started to contact me: palmists, energy manipulators, past-life psychics, crystal manipulators. I went to all of them, did my best to feel whatever I was told to feel, concealed many of my visits from Stephen, wondered if I was in fact getting better or just pouring money down a hole. Spending time with Margaux made me think too much about the latter possibility.

Then, one day, a woman I respected greatly told me about a medium in St. Louis. "She's a conduit to the world beyond," she said. "And through that she makes sense of this world." I had been to ordinary psychics, not always completely seriously, and with mixed results—one told me that I would live a very long life, another told me that I would have three children, two daughters and a son—but the St. Louis medium was billed as something special. She had the power, I was told, to bring your whole life into focus. I made an appointment to go see her.

The trip, on short notice, was immensely expensive, and I made up an excuse for Stephen: I think I told him I was scouting a role or meeting with the producers. Whatever it was, I made it sound like work, both necessary for household finances and boring for him to think about. And then I went off the grid: I flew to St. Louis and drove to the woman's house, following a map the whole way. This was going to be my destiny, I told myself, a soul-clarifying moment: I was going to meet someone who would help me onto the right path and then help keep me there.

I found the address, which was an unassuming ranch-style home in a suburban neighborhood. Perfect, I thought. This is exactly the kind of place where life-changing experiences happen: the places where you would least expect them. I pictured a pleasantly soft woman sitting behind a tidy kitchen table, holding my hand and seeing into the center of my soul. I parked the car on the street, walked up the path, and knocked on the door. There was movement inside.

And then the door opened, and all of my hope collapsed at once. The woman who greeted me was grossly overweight, eating even as she stood in the doorway. Her house was chaotic—I could see that from where I stood—and she didn't seem to understand why I had come. Even when we were set up for our reading, at the kitchen table, which was the furthest thing from tidy, she kept shifting in her chair, to the point where I was worried it might break, and saying things that were radically disconnected from the things she had said a minute before, but just as pedestrian and worthless. "There will be a time of crisis," she said. "You are going to need more assistance." All the while she looked at me with a mix of appetite and contempt; she couldn't conceal either emotion. It was a shakedown, pure and simple, routed through some jerry-rigged notion of the supernatural. I went to sleep there with one eye open, worried that something crazy would happen: robbery, kidnapping, a knife at my throat. And nobody knew where I was. I left the next day and slouched back into my home like I had after the Mellencamp incident: uneasy, guilty, even more insecure than before.

*   *   *

"HERE," WOODY ALLEN SAID. "I have something for you."

I wasn't dreaming. Woody and I were in an office in New York City, and he was offering me a part in a movie.

I had followed Woody's career for years. I was like any other fan.

Except for one thing: in every movie of his I saw, there were roles I coveted. I loved the rhythm of the dialogue, the self-deprecation, the flashes of surreal wit. I asked for—you might even say demanded—a meeting with him.

It had been years since I'd seen him. It's possible that we hadn't had a real conversation since I drove him to the airport in Idaho almost twenty years earlier. When I came into the room, he was sitting down, looking the way he had always looked, maybe a little older, maybe a little more frail. But he was nice to me. He was more than nice. We still had a friendly spark after all those years. He described the movie he was writing, *Deconstructing Harry*: it was about an aging writer who has to confront various figures from his past—old lovers, old rivals. It sounded perfect for me. Wasn't I part of his past? He laughed. "Right," he said. "There's a part for you."

I went home and started fantasizing about the reunion. *Deconstructing Harry*, starring Mariel Hemingway? *Deconstructing Harry*, with a special appearance by Mariel Hemingway? I remembered going to the Oscars in 1980, watching Meryl Streep win. Every time the phone rang, I jumped. Was it Woody with the offer?

When they finally got back to me, I was hugely disappointed. The part that Woody had for me was a few lines in one scene. I wondered whether he had some aversion to me because he felt strange about *Manhattan*, about what it had said about him: it was, after all, a film that centered on his character's relationship with a young girl. When he's talked about the movie, he has always been a little dismissive. He'd tell interviewers that it wasn't his favorite. That upset me. My whole life shifted because of it, and he saw it as just another project? Still, I found a way to play it. I imagined that Beth, the character, was the mother of Tracy from *Manhattan*.

I was in New York a long time, maybe three weeks, even though

I was only filming that one scene. I watched the way he worked with other actors. His reputation now, of course, is that he rarely says anything to his actors, that he just wants them to act what's on the page. But I remembered something different. When we did *Manhattan*, he was completely engaged. We talked extensively about my character and what I was discovering about her. It wasn't just me. He was the same way with the other actors. By *Deconstructing Harry*, he had lost most of his confidantes and defaulted to another version of himself—a wonderful director who was a better writer and knew it.

The movie earned rave reviews for Judy Davis. In my mind, I was a complete failure. I had dreamed that Woody would restart my career, that he would relaunch me in my thirties just as he had launched me in my teens, but instead the experience just seemed to prove that I was destined to be out on the margins of the film world.

17

THE SILENCE IN THE LINE

THE PHONE WENT TO BUSY SIGNAL and dial tone in my hand. "Hello," I said, but there was no one there any longer.

I was back in Ketchum, visiting my father and Angela for both homecoming and recharging. I did all the Idaho things I could: hiked, cooked, sat and listened to nature. The girls and I went out onto the north fork of the Wood River with friends and stepped into the cold water. The cold took my breath away, and afterward I stood on a large boulder and watched the wind vibrate the cottonwoods, mimicking the sound of rain.

At my father's house, we knocked on the door, and we heard him call from inside. I imagined the room before I went in: yellow patterned chintz curtains, leopard-printed settee with gold legs. What I couldn't have imagined was my father. As long as I had known him, he had worn fishing shirts and khakis. Now, he was in a smoking jacket, green golf pants, and monogrammed velvet slippers. "Sit, sit," he said. The gaudily dressed grandfather who had once been my fisherman father beamed. The kids all crowded around him, and soon enough he had them transfixed with a story about the war, and how he had parachuted into Normandy to do OSS work but had gotten sidetracked by fly-fishing instead. It was a good story, but a story I had heard. I went to help Angela in the kitchen.

As I went into the kitchen, the phone was ringing. "I'll get it," I said.

There was a female voice I didn't recognize on the other end, speaking softly and deliberately. She asked if I was Mrs. Jack Hemingway, and I explained that no, I was Jack's daughter, and I would be happy to put my father or his wife on the telephone. The voice spoke to me instead. "Your sister has just been found dead," the woman said.

"Muffet?" I asked. I flashed back to when she was running through downtown Ketchum wearing only a scarf.

"No," she said. "Margaux."

"Are you sure it's not Muffet?" I asked again. "Joan?"

"I'm sure," she said.

They were calling from California, from the L.A.P.D. I listened numbly. Margaux had been found dead at home, in bed. She had a back problem, so her legs were propped up, and there was a cushion under her knees. There were candles going. Their first guess of cause of death was accidental overdose: she was taking Klonopin for her alcohol-induced epilepsy, and she had taken too many, maybe in combination with various herbal remedies whose potency people didn't exactly know. "I'm sorry," the woman said.

I didn't hang up the receiver. There wasn't just silence on the line. There was silence *in* the line. The phone went to dial tone and busy signal in my hand. I had spoken to Margaux a week before. She sounded almost normal. We laughed about old stories and about ourselves. She was trying harder to listen to me, to ask questions rather than performing. I was trying to be compassionate, to think about her challenges rather than judging them. Maybe we'll get through our difficulties, I thought. I knew we would never be best friends, but it had started to seem like our relationship would keep getting better, that we could build on it through our thirties and forties and beyond. That had seemed like a comforting idea, and then suddenly it was gone. I didn't hang up the receiver. There was silence in my hand.

My father was in the kitchen. Angela had brought him in and turned the TV to CNN. Margaux's picture came on the screen, with two dates separated by a dash: the year of her birth and the present year. He stood close to the set and then stood farther back and leaned against the counter. He looked small in his smoking jacket. I looked at him and he looked back at me, though he couldn't meet my eye. I knew how he felt. The whole situation seemed surreal. There were many times when it seemed like Margaux was at the end of her rope, or when she made us feel like we were at the end of ours, but now she had gone beyond the end, and there was no coming back. All the air went out of me and then out of the room, and I saw her distantly, objectively: a woman in a bed, no longer living, candles burning around her.

Stephen and I flew to California and visited the coroner's office. We did everything that my father couldn't handle doing: identified the body, filled out paperwork. At first, the coroner judged the death as an accidental overdose. Margaux was detoxing from alcohol and taking anti-seizure medication, and mixing it with various herbs.

As we were leaving, an assistant coroner tapped a spot on the paper where cause of death was listed. "It's still under investigation," he said.

"Investigation?" I said. "Why?"

"We have to look into the possibility of suicide."

I flinched. The thought had crossed my mind, but not in any conscious way.

"Please call us," I said. "Call when you find anything out at all. We need to know before you release it to the press." A few days later, with no call, they released a finding of suicide. A friend called because she had seen it in the newspaper.

I was back in Idaho by then, and the phone stayed in my hand the way it had when I heard about her death. I was overwhelmed, so I did what I always did. I went for a walk. With Margaux dead, maybe by her own hand, I took the longest hike I could. I felt completely numb. It was a form of shock—you know you've been shot, and you're intellectually aware of the pain, but your mind hasn't connected all of your body's dots. I had been that way with my mother, and I demanded something different of myself with Margaux—because I was older, because I should have known better—but I couldn't deliver. I sat on a rock and looked at the sky, and then I looked at the ground.

When emotions came, they weren't exactly feelings of grief. I had thoughts of panic to start with. Oh shit, I thought. She's gone. Mom's gone. Is it my turn now? In the wake of that, I felt hugely guilty. I felt bad that I hadn't reached out more. Why wasn't I more perceptive? Why wasn't I kinder? We had talked a week before, but we should have talked a day before, and maybe that would have saved her. She had never directly addressed her depression, though I knew that she was often in a frustrated frame of mind. But who could have possibly known where it would lead? She probably didn't even know.

I stood, sat down, stood again. I tried to recover a good memory of Margaux, but everything I remembered was complicated. She was never easy, not when we were older, not when we were kids. When she came through the door, everyone gasped a little. We all braced ourselves for her, and she sensed that, and it just emboldened her. Margaux was locked and loaded all the time.

In the weeks following her death, though, the picture filled in a little bit, and what I learned surprised me. In talking to her friends, to people who had worked with her, I heard about a lighter, sweeter person, someone who was generous and kind and not at all maddening. When she came through the door, they were happy to see her. It was the opposite of my mother. With her, I desperately wanted the outside world to look beyond her bitterness and negativity and see the kind person beneath the surface, the woman who sat with me and laughed at the television, the woman who sacrificed herself for her family. With Margaux, the outside world apparently saw nothing but that kind person. That made me angry—how come nobody else suffered with her the way that we did?—and then guilty all over again. And then it just made me sad.

The tragedy of Margaux's death was that it offered the strongest proof yet that my family prevented people from becoming who they actually were. As a child, Margaux was constantly judged for not living up to the standard of elegance and refinement that Muffet set, covertly by my father and overtly by my mother. I was scared of her. And so she became that monster because it was the only way for her to remain part of the family she loved. Inhabiting that role was a survival strategy. But what happens when people don't survive? I mourned my sister not because she was a fully formed person who was lost to the world, but because she was anything but that. She didn't get the chance to finish.

My father never accepted the idea that her death was a suicide. He didn't talk about it much, but when he did, he talked about it as an accident. And there were still plenty of loose ends, not just for him but for all of us. The absence of a note, for example. Margaux was bigger than life. When she was in a good mood, she was self-absorbed and funny. When she was in a bad mood, she was self-absorbed and brooding. But she was all about effect. Her whole life was about getting attention. A Margaux without a dramatic exit made no sense. And yet, whether or not it made sense didn't matter. It had happened. She was gone.

* * *

"YOU'RE TOO CLOSE TO THE EDGE," I said. I was talking to a drinking glass on the counter. I reached over and tipped it. It felt to the ground and shattered. "Good," I said. "Good riddance." Then I went for the vacuum cleaner.

For the first time in my life, I was openly angry. The fights between me and Stephen would start the same way they always had, with a great dinner party and then a period of silence. Any time before, I would have just gone upstairs and gotten into bed, trapped between the fear that things were falling apart and the fear that they weren't.

But after Margaux died, I wasn't willing to let the silence settle over us. "Why are you being so quiet?" I'd demand. "What the hell is the matter with you?" Or: "I'm so sick of your whining about your business. If you want to do something, then do it." Or: "Maybe our lives would be better if you weren't so goddamned focused on me. I don't need you to call me every fucking hour." Sometimes, Stephen fought back. More often, he absorbed my anger, got colder and quieter, and then left the house to run errands or take a long drive. That was a form of jujitsu, and it meant that I was left alone again. In the house by myself, still fuming, I would do two things: break things and clean fiendishly. I made sure to break only certain things, of course: I was obsessive-compulsive even in rage.

From the outside, I'm sure it would have looked comical: my stilted expressions of fury, calculated to cause the smallest amount of damage. But it was the first time that I had allowed myself to come out of my shell (mostly) without fear of consequence. I opened up a little bit wider emotionally, even if I didn't have the experience to turn it toward productive ends.

The one place it helped, I think, was in parenting. Most of parenting small children had been about task fulfillment: dress, feed, drive. But my daughters were growing up, which meant that they were entering a period when they were feeling their way through new emotions. That meant, in turn, that they needed more from me than a checklist. In my own family, growing up, I had always been the baby sister, a little bit removed from my sisters' adolescent turmoil, but memories of it started to return to me. When I looked at Langley and especially at Dree, I saw other images superimposed over them: Muffet flouncing around in scarves, Margot getting drunk with boys. My daughters had been babies and then little girls. They had been on the mat with me, playing, or on my lap. Then, suddenly, they were shimmying into skirts that were too short and talking back to me with fire in their eyes. One day, I sat Dree down for a talk. She was twelve, but she was rapidly outpacing herself: she had all the early signs of trouble with boys, with substances, with self-regulation in general. "Look," I said. "I have a story to tell you about your Aunt Margaux."

She had known Margaux only faintly, and only at the end. I went back in history, told her about Margot before there ever was a Margaux. I told her about how people in families felt left out sometimes, and how that could result in disappointment or sadness but also become something more volatile, a kind of uncontrolled fury. "She started to get the idea that all of her value came from outside of herself," I said. "From how she looked and who she was willing to spend time with, to what she drank and what else she did. She went to extremes to be seen, and they backfired." I told Dree about her aunt's death. I used the word "suicide" with her for the first time. I laid it on thick, the way that Margaux would have done.

By the time I was done, I had scared her a little but softened her a little too. The teenager, temporarily returned to childhood, went up to her room.

* * *

IN 1999, there were several programs and events celebrating the centennial of my grandfather's birth. My dad did most of the interviews and appearances. He held the reins when it came to that kind of thing. I did my part, in one small way: I narrated an episode of A&E's *Biography* about my grandfather. It was called "Wrestling with Life."

The centennial was bracing. It connected me to my grandfather but also reminded me of the weight of his legacy. I felt more than ever that the rest of us were under scrutiny. We were representing him. I was paranoid about ever seeming foolish in public. I wouldn't do PR for film projects if it seemed silly. I wouldn't have a drink when Stephen and I were out. It even kept me in my marriage, in a sense, because it applied pressure for me to keep up appearances.

The Hemingway centennial brought out all kinds of analysis, from close literary readings of my grandfather's work to more general commentary on the way America treats its celebrities. There was one strain of discussion that frustrated me, and that was speculation on his state of mind, especially toward the end, as he grew more and more depressed and eventually succumbed to suicide. It's one thing to be an academic and specialize in literature. Scholars had every right to dissect and explain his works, to situate them alongside F. Scott Fitzgerald and Gertrude Stein and look at the ways in which they informed later masters like Norman Mailer. But the pop psychology was harder to justify. How could anyone imagine that they truly knew the man? How could they wonder aloud about his inner state without a shred of evidence? And yet, questions kept surfacing in the press. Was his depression inseparable from his genius? Had his death been connected to alcohol? To impotence? To a misguided sense of immortality? To simple fear?

I remembered when I was a child, how I learned about my grandfather's suicide: slowly, and with a growing sense of how difficult the idea was for people to process. Local priests, for reasons of their own, resisted calling the death a suicide. My father didn't speak about it very often, and when he did, he used a kind of shorthand with other adults: quick comments, averted eyes. Ernest's decision couldn't be completely explained. No one could ever truly know if it was premeditated or the result of a moment of despair or even intentional at all. It was an unanswered question, an open file in a closed case, and because of that people didn't know quite what to do with it.

During the centennial celebration, as I revisited those memories, I realized that I was doing the same exact thing to Margaux. I had a working theory about the end of her life, which was that she had become immensely famous for something unsustainable, and that she had never really felt that her fame was earned. The person she had become in the public eye didn't match how she felt inside, and as that public persona began to fade, she had nothing to fall back on. She didn't have the habits necessary to reconstruct a sense of self.

More to the point, she had habits that made that reconstruction difficult: not just alcohol, not just drugs, but a lifetime of pushing back
against the dysfunction of our family, defining herself in large part as
someone who produced tension, possibly to distract herself and others from even more painful emotions. And yet, I still couldn't completely fathom that her confusion and depression had taken her to
the point where she had opted for death over life. That didn't mean
it hadn't happened, only that I couldn't bring it into focus. As blurry
as suicide is for the person driven to the edge of it, or over it, it's just
as blurry for those left behind. Suicide blocks everyone from a clear
view, and proximity doesn't make anything easier.

In those years, I thought often about how many other families
were in the same position that we were—how many other families
struggled with the suicides of loved ones, often not even admitting at
first that that's what they were struggling with. The shame of losing
a family member or spouse to suicide is sometimes so powerful that
it distorts everything around it. And then there is just the broad im-
possibility of it all: to those of us enmeshed in the daily business of
life, struggles and victories both, it's hard to fathom that we might
ever want to remove ourselves permanently from existence. Over
the years, I have come to see things more clearly, or at least to recognize that there is rarely any rhyme or reason in suicides. They can be
a cry for help gone wrong, or a punishment to those you're leaving
behind, or one fateful twenty-minute window when you lose your
bearings and can't find the reasons to go on. Maybe, at the end, in
her bedroom, candles going, Margaux was just a lonely woman who
couldn't do it anymore.

As I write this chapter, history has furnished one more sad coin-
cidence. Robin Williams, the great movie comedian, has been found
dead in his house in Tiburon, California, from a suspected suicide.

The news is only days old, and the wheels of speculation are spinning furiously. News outlets are turning over everything he ever said about his depression and his battles with addiction, not to mention more abstract demons. There is a quote that's circulating, something he said in character in a film: "Suicide is a permanent answer to a temporary problem." Personally, I think that's too pat. The truth is scarier, because it reveals something more profound about the ripple effect of suicides, how they leave behind a lifetime of wondering, doubting, and rationalizing, a lifetime of slowly coming to the understanding that there is no definitive understanding, and there never will be. Suicide is a permanent question.

18

THE SPACE IN THE ROOM

"TOMORROW?" I ASKED. "Are you serious?"

"Yes," my father said. "The doctors looked at my heart and didn't like what they saw. There's enough arterial blockage that they wanted to schedule a triple bypass right away."

"But tomorrow?" I was in Los Angeles. He and Angela were in New York, staying at a hotel on the Upper East Side.

"They didn't want to wait."

"I'll come see you right away," I said.

"No need," my father said. "I'll just relax and recover, watch football on TV and write. I'll be fine."

"But I won't be," I said. "Be there soon."

I flew in the day after his procedure and went over to the hospital in the morning. He was there with Angela. He brightened as I came in the room. "Hi, sack of potatoes," he said. It was my least favorite nickname, but it felt like my favorite. The television was on, a little too loud, showing election coverage. It was Bush versus

Gore, with the results still in dispute in Florida. Gore was calling for hand recounts. My father and Angela had become very conservative, and they didn't like that the outcome of the election was in dispute. I watched with him and tried not to say anything that would set him off.

After a little while, he shut off the television and told me the story of his surgery. One of his doctors was a distant relative, and my dad had great things to say about him. "More than competent," he said. "Really understands the whole process, inside and out." As if summoned, that doctor appeared at the door. He shook hands with my father and told me that they had planned a fishing trip together.

When his fishing buddy left, my father got quiet. He was looking at me, and then he seemed to be looking at a spot above my head. He looked smaller, and for a second he seemed sad. "You know everything is going to be okay," he said.

"I know," I said. "The doctors told me the surgery went well."

"I mean it will all be okay," he said. He took my hand in his. "Everything will be fine. I had to take care of things. I'm not afraid."

"There's nothing to be afraid of," I said. At that moment his heart burst. My hand was in his. My eyes were on his face. He tensed and then slackened. It was as if I could see his soul leave his body. I ran into the hall, yelling for the doctors, but they were already there at the door.

From that moment forward, my father was no more. The doctors put him on life support. Angela had a hard time letting him go. I sat with him every day and talked to him. The television was usually on, still tracking Gore and Bush, almost a mockery now. I turned thirty-nine with my dad in the hospital in late November, and on December 1, they let him go. Where he had been, there was just a space in the room.

The doctors were surprised. "He was in pretty good shape for an old man," one of them told me.

"Thank you," I said. A minute later, when he left the room, I felt dizzy. Why had I thanked him? Where was my father? I needed time to think. When my mother had died, when Margaux had died, I had gone walking in Idaho. Now I went walking in New York City. After a little while, I was tired, uncommonly so, and I sat on a bench and tried to cry, the same way I had tried with my mother and with Margaux. But I was older and less interested in the performance of the thing.

Instead, I stood back up and walked to the corner of Central Park. I looked at the trees and thought about how my father had taught me about nature. He had taught me about its healing power, about its ability to settle the human spirit—we were all so small and so temporary compared to everything that was around us. I thought about how the two of us had walked through the park when I was twelve, when he had come with me on my audition for *Lipstick*. We had gone past the Alice in Wonderland statue, and he had stood back a bit and watched me be amazed by it. If my mother's death had seemed almost like an afterthought, an ellipsis trailing away from the sentence of her life, the cancer and the frailty, my father's death was a hard stop that I could not quite get beyond. It sent me back to other losses. It made me think about Margaux, about my grandfather, about all the people who had been important to all of us and who were no longer on the earth. It hurt in ways that I couldn't quite explain to myself, and I had to stand at the corner of the park just to remind myself that it was real. It was a little while before I told Muffet.

My father was buried in the cemetery with the rest of the family. Angela wanted him placed next to Ernest, which meant that he was buried far away from my mother and my sister. There wasn't much speech-making at his funeral. He would have been the one to do it. Later, I took *A Moveable Feast* down from the shelf and turned to a passage about when my father was a baby in Paris:

> *My wife could go to work at the piano in a cold place and with enough sweaters keep warm playing and come home nurse to Bumby. It was wrong to take a baby to a café in the winter though; even a baby that never cried and watched everything that happened and was never bored. There were no baby-sitters then and Bumby would stay happy in his tall cage bed with his big, wonderful cat named F. Puss. There were people who said that it was dangerous to leave a cat with a baby. The most ignorant and prejudiced said that a cat would suck a baby's breath and kill him. Others said that a cat would lie on a baby and the cat's weight would smother him. F. Puss lay beside Bumby in the tall cage bed and watched the door with his big yellow eyes, and would let no one come near him when we were out; and Marie, the femme de ménage, had to be away. There was no need for baby-sitters. F. Puss was the baby-sitter.*

The cat was long gone. The *femme de ménage* too. And my grand-mother who had played the piano in a cold place and my grandfa-ther who had written about it and now my father too, under the earth in Idaho, where he would be forever.

*　　*　　*

MY FATHER'S DEATH wasn't a tragedy, not exactly. It was crushingly sad to be there with him in the hospital, both at the moment the doctors rushed into the room and for those weeks when he lay still in bed. But he was an elderly man who had lived a full life. He had survived his wife and one of his daughters. He had remarried and enjoyed his old age. I left Idaho after his funeral with some peace in my heart.

And yet, there was significant discomfort too, not because I was saying good-bye to my father, but because I was saying hello to a version of myself I wasn't quite prepared to face. As long as my father was alive, I could tell myself that I had something positive to look forward to: a conversation on the telephone, a visit when I could show him pictures of the kids. I could look through family photo albums and share memories with him. With my father gone, all the memories were suddenly my own, and that meant that I had to try to own the truth of those memories as well.

What was that truth? In part, it was being clear with myself about the fact that my family had tremendous difficulty expressing straightforward love, especially during my childhood. My parents had both found themselves in a marriage that didn't suit them, and they had reacted accordingly: my mother by affecting a pose of critical bitterness, my father by retreating into abstracted affection—and, at the same time, by retreating physically into the basement. My parents were so preoccupied by their own problems and the secondary problems that resulted (simmering resentment, compensatory drinking) that they didn't always have energy for parenting, and what limited energy they had was quickly drained by Muffet's struggles with her mental health. The result was that Margaux and I, in a sense, were neglected. The situation was complicated all over again by serious health problems, first my father's heart attack and then my mother's cancer, both of which put my parents at the center of the family and pushed the children to the margins all over again.

As I moved through adolescence and into adulthood, I often

looked to my parents for protection and guidance, and every time I found them all too willing to leave me exposed. When Woody Allen invited me to Paris, they didn't object the way I wanted them to. When I decided to move to New York, they didn't force me to stay and finish high school. The sense of neglect thickened, and the result was that I became preoccupied with forging a new kind of order for myself. I grew obsessed with food issues and body image, conflicted about love and sexuality, compromised in matters of straightforward emotional communication. I was extremely efficient in all things but not necessarily engaged in my own life. Every time I had experienced a major loss—my mother's death, say, or my sister's—I wondered why I couldn't feel simple sadness. And every time I made a major commitment—to a film, to a marriage—I wondered why I couldn't feel simple joy. Was I angry at my parents? Was I too empathetic to their frustrations? Did I both love and hate the way that my family had shaped me? Finding those emotions was like reaching through a gray curtain.

When my father died, though, that curtain parted. For the first time, I let myself take in the full sweep of my life—the good and the bad and everything in between—and recognize that every single one of my experiences helped make me who I was. In mourning my father, I began, in real ways, to mourn my sister and my mother, to come to terms with my own limits and choices. When I was a child, I used to press myself against my bed to try to become invisible. I didn't want to be seen amid all the chaos of my home, and maybe I didn't want to see it. When my father died, I began to think about how I might tell my own story—first to myself, and then to others—and how telling that story would, for the first time, make myself visible within it.

19

THE PAIN IN THE HEAD

"MY HEAD HURTS," Stephen said.

"Did you take aspirin?" I said.

"Not in my head," he said. "On it." He bent down and pointed at his crown. I felt around. There was a tender spot around the size of a nickel. "Weird," I said. "How long has that been there?"

"I'm not sure," he said. "I think I should go to the doctor." My heart skipped when he went out the door. But the doctor waved it off: not a problem, probably just a mole, nothing major.

The pain persisted, and six months later Stephen was at a different doctor who didn't wave it off. A second doctor was called in for consultation. A biopsy was ordered. We went home with grim expressions and couldn't sleep for days. One afternoon, Stephen got a call from the hospital and took it in his office. He came out shaking his head. "It's melanoma," he said. "Stage IV."

Stage IV meant that the cancer had spread. Stage IV meant a five-year survival rate of less than 25 percent, on average. I spent days

reading the literature and learned that melanomas were more severe when they occurred on the sides of the feet, the palms of
hands, or in the nail beds. I learned about the difference between
punch biopsies and shave biopsies. I absorbed all the information
I could. And then I went into savior mode. I was determined to
do everything for the man I loved, for the father of my children. I
called the best surgeons directly or used my fame to figure out how
to get to them. I was consumed by the challenge of getting Stephen
the best care possible.

We were pretty quick to tell the kids that we were in the middle
of a battle. When I used the word "cancer," I made sure not to say it
so quickly that they wouldn't think I was afraid of it. The plan, we
explained, was to operate and hopefully get the whole tumor out of
Stephen's head, after which they would look at the lymph nodes and
assess the spread. The surgery was brutal. They had to dig into the
skull to get all of it. They wrapped his head afterward. He looked
like a half-mummy and had to sleep sitting up.

Initial results looked promising. The spread was minimal. But
cancer isn't just about tumors or blood tests. It's about gauging your
power (or powerlessness) in the face of a largely unseen adversary. It's
your attitude. It's your environment. And it's your intake. It was this
last component that I focused on, mainly. My obsession with food
hadn't started when my mother had gotten sick, but it had intensified then: that's when I had started to develop my ideas about foods.
When Stephen got sick, I was working with a holistic healer who was
also a chiropractor and spiritual teacher. He was big on how sugar
feeds illness, and how internal organs need consistent detox.

The hospital let me down—not with the surgery, but right afterward. I remember the first meal Stephen was served during his re-
cuperation. He hadn't eaten in days, and his first tray was filled was
the most disgusting food: a piece of chicken with every last nutrient

boiled out of it, a tiny carton of milk, a cup of green Jell-O, and a slice of chocolate cake. Wouldn't a hospital know that he needed green vegetables? Was that what the Jell-O was supposed to be? I confronted the doctors, who responded with blank faces. They hadn't studied nutrition since college, and even then it was for two weeks at most. "I'll take care of your food," I told Stephen. "I'll take care of you."

* * *

"QUIET," STEPHEN SAID. The girls weren't being noisy. I wasn't, either. I could hear wind going through the trees outside the window. But Stephen put his head in his hands. "I need total quiet."

When he came home from the hospital, Stephen was difficult: demanding, short-tempered, intolerant. It sent me back to the early seventies, in Ketchum, when my father returned to the house after his heart attack. Like my dad, Stephen wanted to make sure that he was king of his castle, that his authority was never challenged. It was a ridiculous situation—and yet, he had cancer. How was I going to make a case that he didn't deserve what he was asking for? And so I told the girls to be quiet. I told them to help their dad. I bit my tongue whenever his requests became unreasonable. Above all, I swallowed my own doubts about the marriage.

The last of these was the bitterest pill. Our holistic healer, who also fancied himself a kind of therapist, was quick to make sure that I understood my obligation to Stephen. "I know you don't always want to go on with this," he said. "But you can't leave him, of course."

I had two answers. Here was answer one: "That's only true until you're unhappy for two decades."

Here was answer two: "You're right."

The second one was the only answer I let anyone hear. It was also the answer with the deepest roots. Thirty years earlier, cancer had forced my father to set aside any thought of ending his marriage to my mother. Stephen's cancer restarted that entire cycle. Cancer was the ultimate anchor. All of a sudden, it wasn't a question of whether or not your relationship was bad. It was a question of whether you were making good on the marriage contract: for better or worse, in sickness or in health.

It was an extreme time. There were days when I felt completely connected to Stephen. I made appointments for him. I planned his diet. And then there were days when I felt desperate and trapped. I hadn't done a single thing to solve the problems in my head—my trouble finding out what I really wanted from life, my inability to communicate, my tendency to do a good job whether or not the task really mattered.

One day, exhausted, confused, and resentful, I sat on a chair in the kitchen and thought about ending it all. It was mostly melodrama. I don't think I had any real intention of killing myself. I certainly didn't have any specific plans. But I was so out of my depth. I felt like I hadn't chosen any aspect of my life, like everything since childhood had been sent to me and I had neglected to send it back. I had no real ownership of it, no control, no productive solitude. I had nowhere to turn, and so I turned inward, but I didn't like what I found there either. The day in September that planes flew into the World Trade Center, I watched the news as if in a trance. It was my former home—my Manhattan—under attack. I huddled in a corner of my couch and wondered if anything would ever be okay again.

My moment of despair passed. Stephen helped it pass, in part, by coming around to a better way of thinking. That first year, he changed his lifestyle. He calmed down. He began to exercise regularly. He quit drinking. After nine months or so of mindful living, his body responded by returning to health. By the end of that first year, he was cancer-free.

But even with a healthy husband, I needed to work. Money was suddenly a huge priority, both to deal with Stephen's treatment and to pick up the slack for the months when he couldn't work at all. I took any job that I could get my hands on, including projects I never would have considered a few years before. I acted in TV movies, straight-to-video productions, strange Canadian films that no one would ever see—just because there was a paycheck.

* * *

"DON'T DO IT," I SAID. The doctors had just left the hospital room. I didn't expect an answer from Stephen. I gripped his hand. "I'm begging you," I said.

After the year of remission, Stephen reverted to his old ways. He started drinking again. He ordered pizza late at night. I tried to enforce healthy eating, but I could only do it when I was around. If I went out of town to work, he was in charge of the house and the girls, and he ate what he wanted.

In late 2001, his cancer came back. Doctors found little spots in his liver and his colon. They met with us, faces even grimmer than the first time around, and recommended aggressive chemo and radiation therapy. They were lined up on either side of his bed: like pallbearers, I thought briefly, and then banished the thought. When they left, Stephen just looked at me and took my hand. He started to talk and stopped.

"Look," I said. "You know where I stand on this. Chemo and radiation are killers. They might kill the disease, but they might kill you too, especially if you don't pay attention to diet and meditation and exercise."

"If you say so."

"This isn't about me," I said. "You have to want to do this. You have to want to eat the right food."

"I'll do it," he said. "But I want to talk to more doctors too."

"We'll talk to them all," I said. "We'll learn everything about every cutting-edge treatment. We'll find other options."

He nodded. As it turned out, there was an option—a trial in which cancer patients were injected with cells harvested from their own bodies. The thinking was that it would trigger an immune response and teach the body to fight the tumor. It was incredibly painful for Stephen, having needles jabbed into his thighs, and painful for me to watch. But it started to work, and it seemed to me like the effects were accelerated by the diet. After four months, the results were promising. After six months, there were guardedly optimistic smiles from the same doctors who had stood grimly at Stephen's bedside.

Stephen's second bout with cancer had a short-term boost for our marriage. He also believed that the diet had accelerated his recovery, and it changed his opinion of me. I wasn't some diet-obsessed, New Age–susceptible nut job. I was a levelheaded wife with insights about the way the world worked and maybe even a special wisdom. I remember being at home once, coming into the kitchen or going out of it. Stephen was sitting on the couch, and he heard a fork clink against a plate. The noise brought his head up. "Hey," he said. "Thanks." It was short and simple, but it was completely genuine and unconditional, and it filled me with warmth and hope. That's how the pattern went: bleak months stretching into bleak years and then, at unpredictable intervals, fantastically affirming moments that made me think that everything would be okay.

We fought less about the marriage in those days and more about questions of parenting. Dree was spirited, headstrong, stubborn—all wonderful qualities that didn't always seem so wonderful when they were powering a fifteen-year-old through the world. Stephen indulged her. He went easy on her. And she took the temperature of the room, decided how she could best play her parents off of each other, and tried to make her life easier. She reminded me of myself at twelve.

But I had also been a quiet kid who went off on my own to avoid tension. In that way, Langley reminded me of myself at twelve. She stayed in her room, drawing or reading. I tried to go by at regular intervals and knock on the door, or ask her if she wanted to come out for a snack, but she was adamant about protecting her solitude. I'm sure, too, that she felt we were focusing on Dree while neglecting her. When you have one child who demands a disproportionate amount of energy, it's sometimes hard to be there for the others. As parents, you say all the right things. You say that you love them both equally. You say that they're both important. You say that the squeaky wheel doesn't always get the grease. But saying it doesn't make it true.

* * *

"WOW, MARIEL," the therapist said. "You're powerful."

The marriage had continued to decline. As Stephen returned to health, he lost some of his softness and his kindness. He depended on me less and seemed to resent me more. At some point, I told him I thought I wanted to end the marriage. I must have said it with enough seriousness that it got his attention, and we went to see a marriage therapist.

It was a typical therapy office: impersonal palette, Kleenex boxes, comfortable leather chairs to help you deal with the uncomfortable things that everyone was feeling.

"Tell me," the man said. "What's your main concern?"

"It seems like everything is all bound up together," I said.

"You're worried about your career," Stephen said.

"That's not it," I said. It was, at least in part. My most recent role had come in a TV movie about the political ascendancy of Arnold Schwarzenegger—I played his wife, Maria Shriver.

"You think you deserve better," he said.

"Also not true." It was also true, at least in part. Since Stephen's first diagnosis, I had felt more and more trapped.

"And sometimes," Stephen said, "I feel like you wanted me to get sick, because then you'd be able to get free."

I had been on autopilot, but this got my attention. "What?"

He backtracked, but only a bit. "I don't mean that you wanted me to get sick, but the way that you act—the way you want me to notice you but you never really come forward—creates this environment where everything that's poisonous is held inside. Who knows what the results of that are? You talk all the time about healthy diet, but that's the only thing that's healthy."

I was surprised by Stephen's eloquence. I even saw the truth in some of what he was saying. But to blame me, even in an indirect way, for his cancer was beyond the pale. I looked at the therapist. He looked at me. A smile creased his face. "Wow, Mariel," he said. "You're powerful."

Neither Stephen nor I said much on the ride home. I was grateful the therapist had backed me up, but it was also a shock to see how critical and negative Stephen was. That night, in bed, I realized why it bothered me so much. I hadn't become my mother—he had.

＊　＊　＊

"EXCUSE ME." It was a woman's voice. I started to turn toward her. Usually, when people excused themselves in advance, it was the prelude to an autograph request. Dree and I were boarding a plane for

New York, where she was studying with the New York City Ballet. The woman who had excused herself pushed past me at the edge of the jetway, crushing my toe with the wheel of her roller bag. If she recognized me, she didn't show it.

We found our seats. Dree put on headphones and turned toward the window; I closed my eyes and tried to sleep. The flight was smooth, but there was plenty of turbulence. Months, even years, had passed by in a whirl of loss, anxiety, and disorientation. I hadn't had much time to focus on my career. And yet, I was also under financial pressure to keep working. The result had been a string of less-than-memorable projects: a female version of *In the Line of Fire* called *In Her Line of Fire*, a Russian thriller called *Time of Change*. I thought of them as "get me by" movies, but it was a risky gamble: when you take projects just to get by, you're making a move in a chess game where you can't see the other side of the board. Sometimes you can move from that to a more substantial role. Sometimes people start to see you as somehow synonymous with those kinds of roles.

On the plane, in the midst of that turbulence, I did what many people do on planes. I tried to communicate with a higher power, or at least a clearer inner power. Just help me find a direction for myself, I said. I wondered where I was headed in the industry, whether I could reenter it on my own terms, and whether, in the broader scope of things, that even mattered. Thirty thousand feet above the ground, movie sets were even smaller and farther away. Maybe the things I had learned about myself, my family, and healthy living were more important. Maybe there was a career shift that put those things in the foreground: I could teach yoga, or work as a nutritionist, or confront the challenge that scared me the most, which was learning how to tell my family's story to a broader audience. When the plane landed, I had more questions but also the beginning of an answer. The woman who had pushed past me on the way in also pushed past me on the way out.

20

THE TIME IN THE DRIVEWAY

"INDIA?" I ASKED HIM.

"India," Stephen said.

"Are you serious?"

"I'll show you how serious I am." Stephen went to his computer, opened up a website, and India appeared before me: an illustrated itinerary that took us through a half-dozen cities in as many weeks, highest-level accommodations the whole way. The girls were even allowed to bring friends along for part of it. I was flabbergasted. I wondered how much it all had cost and where Stephen had gotten the money, but I didn't ask questions.

We stepped inside the pictures on the computer. We went to India. It was amazing. The family visited ancient temples and went on hikes together, and though Stephen and I were uncomfortable when we were alone together, it was still one of the most meaningful experiences of my life. The country was teeming with people, and it had majestic examples of nature; it was half a world away, and when you were there you felt like you had never been anywhere else.

And then it got better. "We have a private audience," Stephen said.

"What do you mean? With who?"

"With the Dalai Lama," he said.

A private audience wasn't exactly private. What it meant was that Stephen and the girls and I, along with a small group of other pilgrims, got to travel to Dharamsala and sit in a room with the Dalai Lama—monk, Nobel Laureate, and spiritual leader of the Tibetan people.

The day of the audience, we arrived at the Dalai Lama's residence in McLeod Ganj, or Little Lhasa, the uppermost settlement in Dharamsala. Cell phones were confiscated in exchange for check slips. We were shown down a hallway and into a waiting room that could have been a dean's office in a university, except for the large portrait of the Buddha. Outside on the porch, there was a long line of pilgrims. We waited. Others in our party shuffled papers and jotted down notes. Guards instructed us on how to greet the Dalai Lama: how we were to stand, what posture we were to use when we offered him the traditional kata scarf as a gift.

A ripple went through the crowd outside. "He's here," said Dree. Langley craned her neck to see. His Holiness had arrived, and he was working the line. A guard came and moved us from the waiting room to the porch, and suddenly we were face to face with the Dalai Lama. He led us into his office, which was filled with chairs and sofas. I ended up right next to him. I had seen pictures of him a hundred times: the shaved head, the calm but slightly playful expression, the red and yellow robe. But now he was only a few feet away. An interpreter explained the rules, and the audience began.

I was nervous at first, but he was so delightful: attentive, serene.

He smiled and barely spoke, but when he did he seemed to radiate pure wisdom. Others in our party had prepared questions for His Holiness. "How do we bring peace to the planet?" "What is the role of business as the world moves forward?" I didn't have a question. I was too nervous. But I watched him watch the room, now and again looking at me directly, which made me giggle every time.

The time passed quickly—or maybe it's more accurate to say that it didn't seem like time existed at all. We had turned in our gadgets and devices. No one dared check their watch. Questions were asked and answered. Pauses were allowed to settle into the room.

Finally, the translator let us know that the audience was drawing to a close. At that point, the Dalai Lama leaned toward me and put his hand on my hand. He looked me directly in the eyes. "You're okay," he said. That was all he said, but as he spoke I realized it was all I needed to hear. After all those years of searching, after all the attempts to find myself, one of the wisest men in the world was telling me that the search itself was unnecessary.

* * *

"I NEED THIS TO BE DONE," I said. We were in the front hallway of our house, Stephen and I, and I was suddenly disoriented. I couldn't remember if we were coming or going. All I knew was that I wanted out.

Stephen's response was to book us into a Tony Robbins seminar. It was the most advanced program in the entire Tony Robbins arsenal: the six-day Date With Destiny weekend in Palm Springs. "Let's go to this before we make any decision," he said. "It'll help us think our way through things."

I didn't have much experience with Tony Robbins—he was one of the few gurus I hadn't encountered. I knew a little bit about Date

With Destiny from friends: I knew that they divided the five thousand or so participants into teams, maybe twenty-five in all, and that each of those teams participated in a series of exercises designed to maximize achievement and fulfillment. I was terrified that somehow the event would become a referendum on my marriage. I even went so far as to draft a letter to the seminar organizers: "I'm going to attend," I wrote, "but please don't make this about reuniting me with my husband."

From the first moment we were assigned to a team, I had an uneasy feeling. There was a diagnostic stage, and it was determined that I was "significance-driven" while Stephen was all about love. Everyone else on the team nodded.

I returned from the Date With Destiny weekend worse than when I had gone. The jury had returned with their verdict, and I had been convicted. The problems in the marriage were my fault. I was the one who had made things untenable. The whole ride home, I apologized to Stephen. And his reaction only made things worse: he just accepted my apology silently. It was like he was finally hearing the things he had wanted to hear for years.

I gave it another year. It seemed like a lifetime. We went back to therapy. I kept a journal. I tried, in every conversation, not to be too significance-driven. And then, one day, in the front hall of our house again, I turned to Stephen and said what I had said a year before. But this time I meant it. "I'm done," I said. "For real. I just can't do this anymore. Maybe I am the problem, but I can't work it out. It's beyond me. I'm leaving."

Stephen held up his hand. "If you do this, there's no turning back."

I looked at the man I had lived with for twenty-five years, the man who had been by my side for my mother's death, my sister's death, my father's death, the man who I had seen at night and in the morning and in bed and in the hospital for our daughters' births and in the hospital again for his surgery. I tried not to blink, because I was taking it all in before I gave it all back. "That's right," I said.

Dree was twenty, still studying dance in New York. Langley was a few days away from turning eighteen. We were living in Santa Monica, staying at a house that was way too expensive for the money we were bringing in. We only had a month or two left on the lease, so Stephen and I stayed together for a few weeks—him in the guest room, me in the master bedroom. Dree supported the decision, of a fashion: "I thought you guys should have gotten divorced years ago," she said. Langley was devastated. I sat on her bed and tried to comfort her. "I totally understand," I said. "I hope that someday you forgive me. I hope that someday you understand."

After a few weeks, Stephen got an apartment with Langley, and I found a little house in Topanga. There was a phase when Dree got angry at Stephen, and the two of them passed through a period of estrangement. There was a period where Langley and Stephen bonded and I was briefly the villain.

One of my first days in Topanga, I went out to the car and sat in the driver's seat. I felt both hollow and full, as if someone had pulled all of my insides out and filled the space back in with a substance I couldn't yet identify. When I backed the car down the driveway, I checked the rearview mirror and saw only my own face. There was no one else in the car. Nobody was going to tell me where to go or what to do. Nobody was going to check in on me every hour. And it wasn't just that no one was calling for the next hour, or the hour after that: no one would check in on me in that way ever again. It was just time in the driveway, just me and my time, not owned by anyone, not owed to anyone.

I was so excited. Everything I did had a sharp outline. I went to a yoga class and the grocery store. I went to a restaurant by myself. and I loved it. When I was leaving the restaurant, I saw a woman on crutches moving slowly across the parking lot. I fantasized that she would cast them aside and walk. I remembered when my mother broke her leg. Forty years of habit dissolved. I went back to the car and sat in the driver's seat.

*   *   *

IN WASHINGTON, a wineglass sailed past my face.

When Stephen and I split up, I set aside all the unhealthy patterns that had bedeviled me for decades. I vowed that I wouldn't feel the need to accommodate other people and suppress my own desires. I vowed that I wouldn't romanticize silent and moody types. I vowed that I wouldn't get into another relationship too quickly.

In the wake of leaving my marriage, I was good about it. I had a close friend who was also a yoga teacher, and she and I hiked almost every day for months. She had more experience with men—dating, sex, arguing—and she spoke while I listened. I had also spent time in a women's group, and while I was heading toward my breakup it had been a source of solace, but afterward I started to chafe a bit. The group environment frustrated me. It worked against the idea I had that I needed to be on my own.

And then, four months later, I worked against that idea too. I started dating a man I met through mutual friends. He was a famous writer, wealthy and decorated. He knew everyone in the political world. He was very smart, had well-formed opinions on everything, and seemed to want to listen to my opinions too. I'm sure that dating a Hemingway was a factor for him. And most important, he was attracted to me—for the first time in years, I felt desirable again.

One morning, we woke up, had breakfast, and then I went to

the bathroom to wash my face. I caught sight of my face in the mirror. I looked good. I looked happy. Maybe I got it right this time, I thought. Maybe we'll get married. My face frowned before my brain could catch up to it. It was my twenty-two-year-old self, sneaking out, filled with naïve optimism, incapable of wisdom or self-protection.

When I slowed down and took a more honest look at the relationship, I saw that my new boyfriend had some issues. He wasn't a terrible person, but he had a strange set of criticisms: he told me that I laughed too often and that it didn't sound authentic. He had stretches when he was alone and cold, hard to reach and not very rewarding once you reached him. The more I looked, the more I saw that he was Stephen all over again: distant, brooding, never really present in the way I needed, uninterested in really challenging me or engaging with me. Once I saw the problem, it didn't take me very long to walk away from it. We started to fight. I made fewer and fewer concessions. When I said good-bye to him, we were in DC. He was jumping rope, badly, in a hotel room, and I laughed at him. That wounded him so deeply that he threw a glass at me. It just missed. "I think I'm going," I said.

When I got back to California, I wrote him a cordial letter. He wasn't to blame anymore than I was. I thanked him for the time we had spent together but was clear about the fact that we would never see each other again. And so it was back to hiking with my friend, and back to hearing about her sexual experiences and her romantic theories.

One day, she told me that she had a new boyfriend, a guy who had come to see her teach a yoga class and subsequently pursued her. "We actually met years ago on a river trip," she said, "but at the time we were just friends. He's like an extreme macho form of you."

"Meaning what?" I said. I wasn't offended—just curious. What did that mean to her?

"You know," she said. "Attractive, strong, into fitness and mindful living. You should meet him."

I picked her up and we went to meet her new boyfriend at a trail in the Santa Monica mountains. We got to the site, and he was already there, sitting in a truck with a custom MTNMN license plate, for "mountain man." He hopped out of the truck and came to greet us. "Mariel," my friend said, "this is Bobby Bobby, Mariel."

We hiked. Bobby was very protective of my friend: she was the least experienced hiker, and he wanted to make sure that she could handle it. At some point, she started to lag a bit, and the two of us started talking. The conversation began with mountains—it seemed like the obvious choice—and wandered through a variety of topics: food, meditation, medication, modern living, mindful living. When he started to ask about my parents and my marriage, it didn't feel intrusive at all, even though he was still a total stranger. My friend had caught up with us at that point, and the discussion shifted into the relative merits of city and country. "I'm not sure I could live anywhere other than a city," she said. "I need that kind of environment. I need to be surrounded by ideas." I loved cities, but I needed to spend time away from them too, to move more deeply into the natural world and discover my own thoughts. Other people's ideas could seem like a static museum or even a prison if you weren't connecting with your own. I was starting to say something to that effect when I noticed that Bobby was making the same point.

A few weeks later, Bobby called and asked if he could take me climbing. "Sure," I said, remembering the rock by the lake in Ketchum. But real climbing was far more arduous, which I proved by falling and coming out muddy and soaked. When I finally got the hang of it, Bobby beamed at me, and a moment of electricity passed between us. I was definitely interested in him, but he was already spoken for, so we became friends instead. Over the next few months, we talked on the telephone, hung out occasionally, always finding our way into long conversations about things I had never discussed with a man: ethics, philosophy, my family's sometimes difficult history. When those moments of electricity recurred, I used them to power the discussions.

One day my friend called me. "We broke up," she said.

"You and Bobby?" I tried not to sound too interested.

"Yeah," she said. "I liked him fine, but it wasn't working out the way I wanted." I waited two weeks and then invited Bobby to visit me in Idaho. We both knew that he wouldn't be making the trip as a friend. It was June 2009, and we have been together ever since.

The November after we met, Bobby took me up to Ojai for my birthday. The first place we went to after the drive was a big health-food store, and we walked through all the aisles, filling up our shopping cart. The second place we went to was a hiking area; we climbed and ate. The day wasn't elaborate. There was no surprise party and no expensive presents. But when we got back in the car, I turned to him suddenly. "This was the best birthday I've ever had," I said.

"I know what you like," he said.

I blinked back tears—of joy, of relief. It was so simple but so true. In my whole life, I had never felt that clean connection between the events around me and my own inner desires. In many—maybe even most—cases, it was my own fault. Since childhood, when I had tip-toed downstairs to clean up evidence of parental discord, I had spent much of my time and energy doing what I thought would make situations better. Those same habits had carried through into my marriage. I tried to keep the peace, did my best to limit tension, and everyone around me let me. This didn't mean that they were bad people, only that they had decided that it was in their interests to encourage that part of my personality. Suddenly, with Bobby, I could do what I wanted, and—more important—I could understand why it was my obligation to figure out exactly what that was. I started to investigate every aspect of my life. I kept more organized journal notes. I retraced my steps through life, trying to look more honestly at the events of my childhood. I sketched out a broad philosophy of exercise, diet, and nontraditional spirituality. For the first time in my life, I truly began to take control of my food and body image issues. I wasn't finished with them, by any means—I don't know if I'll ever be finished with them—but I understood them as part of a broader set of issues.

The effort paid off when Bobby and I cowrote a book called *Running with Nature: Stepping Into the Life You Were Meant to Live*. It was a self-help book, with some of the limits of the genre, but it gave me a newfound appreciation for my own voice. When I saw my words on the page, I knew how far I had come since those days when a confused and frightened little girl pressed herself into the sheets of her bed and tried to become invisible. It wasn't that Bobby was the solution to my problems so much as that he came along at a time when I was ready to be the solution to my own problems.

21

THE LIFE IN THE MOVIE

WHEN MY MANAGER, Tracy, called to tell me about the Emmy nomination, I was clearer on the concept than I had been when my agent called me about the Oscar nomination thirty-five years before. "Thanks," I said, and went to tell Bobby the news. This time, I was nominated not as an actress but as a producer, for a movie about my family I had made with the documentarian Barbara Kopple.

For years, I had resisted the idea of a film about my family. It seemed too difficult, too intrusive, with too much risk of misrepresenting those who could no longer speak for themselves. My friend Lisa disagreed. And Lisa, a round-faced blonde who could have been a fourth Hemingway sister, wasn't just speaking as a friend—she worked for Oprah Winfrey, first for Oprah's talk show and then for the OWN Network, and her job involved finding compelling personal narratives to share with Oprah's audience. "There are so many issues in your family, from suicide to mental illness to alcoholism," Lisa said. "Think of how many people can relate to at least some part of your story."

I demurred. Lisa persisted. Eventually, she did more than persist. "Barbara Kopple is interested," she said.

That changed everything. Barbara, of course, was one of the country's premier documentarians; her work had covered everything from complex socioeconomics (*Harlan County U.S.A.*, about a Kentucky miners' strike) to celebrity portraiture (*Wild Man Blues*, one of the most intimate and respectful looks at Woody Allen), winning her a pair of Oscars in the process. I agreed to meet with her in person. Barbara was clear about her interest in my story without being aggressive. "These are subjects that are universal," she said. "But the particulars of your story give people a foothold and a way of understanding them." Barbara addressed the concerns I raised and—even more important—the concerns I was afraid to raise. "You'll be safe," she told me. "We'll make this together. This is our film." Whether by luck or by design, she had directly addressed my two most pressing anxieties: first, that I wouldn't be protected during the process; second, that my ideas wouldn't be valued. I went home from the meeting, reread some of my journal entries, and meditated on the process of making a film. I don't even think I spoke to Bobby about it immediately. I wanted to make sure that the overall idea of documenting my family made sense, psychologically and emotionally. Would reliving the difficult events of my childhood be traumatic or liberating? Had I come to terms, in any real way, with Muffet's mental illness, with my father's alcoholism, with my mother's cancer, with Margaux's suicide? I didn't know for certain, but the work I had done on myself in the final years of my marriage and my first years with Bobby were optimistic signs. I could start stories about my past, in

my own mind, without a sudden urge to take flight. I was also thinking of the film as a dress rehearsal for an autobiographical project
over which I would have full control: in the back of my mind, the
notion of a book-length memoir was starting to take shape. I called
Barbara. "I'm in," I said.

Making the documentary, *Running from Crazy*, was the hardest
thing I had ever done. It was exhilarating but also exhausting, in part
because it precisely upended everything I knew about movies. As a
young actress, film sets provided me with the stable family I didn't
have at home. My relationships with other actors and crew members were temporary, of course, but that was part of the appeal—
just as people got more complicated or difficult, the shoot was over.
Easy. *Running from Crazy* was the opposite. Barbara and I agreed
that to tell the story fully, my actual family members, including
my daughters and my ex-husband, should be interviewed. Langley
agreed to participate in the project immediately; she was excited, if a
little guarded. Dree was a harder sell. One of the film's main focuses
would be Margaux's suicide, and Dree felt protective of her aunt.
They were both models, both headstrong and confrontational.
I had to convince her that the movie wouldn't betray Margaux's
memory—which meant, of course, that I had to believe it myself.

The film also presented a nearly impossible acting challenge. For
decades, I had appeared in movies playing characters. I knew how to
do that: I read the script, found some aspect of the character I could
identify with, learned my lines, connected with the camera. Here, I
was supposed to play myself, and I wasn't sure what that involved.
On the surface, it seemed simple—just tell the truth—but what did
that really mean? The Mariel in the movie was preoccupied with her
family's struggles and her struggles with those struggles, and though
those were things I had thought about for years, they were only one

aspect of my life. Pushing them to the foreground was inherently artificial. And how did you present a natural version of yourself to the camera, anyway? Did you exaggerate your mannerisms? Did you eliminate them? Did you enter some Buddhist state where you dissolved your traditional sense of self and trusted the camera to rediscover it?

Sometimes the strangeness of the process wore me out. There were days when I would look at the lights set up around my dining-room table and wonder how I could endure another minute. There were times when I saw Barbara setting up a shot and worried that the whole endeavor was deeply flawed, a funhouse mirror masquerading as a regular mirror. And there were times when I heard my own voice as it left my mouth and worried about how false I sounded. But I got through it. Barbara helped me get through it. And when Barbara and I didn't see eye to eye, or when my energy flagged, Bobby helped me get through it—he was always there to hear my concerns and remind me of my broader goals. In the end, we had a product that both of us were proud of, an account of my family's emotional life that was sensitive and nuanced—if not purely "true," whatever that means.

More than that, it was an account of family life in general—of the bizarre dynamics that inevitably crop up when flawed people are placed in close proximity to one another for extended periods of time. When I watched the finished film, I thought about what Lisa had told me when we started: that audience members would connect with different aspects of the story, depending on their own histories. And I thought forward to the story I was now certain I would tell on my own. I began to understand that my story was useful not only on its own terms, but as a trigger for other stories, that autobiographical honesty was contagious. If I was inspired by *Running from Crazy*, others would be as well.

The documentary also helped me develop a new understanding of the movie business. In 2014, I was invited to the Golden Globe Awards to honor Woody Allen, who was receiving the Cecil B. De-Mille Lifetime Achievement Award. Woody didn't attend, of course, so in his place the organizers assembled a table of performers associated with his films. I was nervous before the event. I went through a hundred different ideas about my hair and my clothes. When I got to the Beverly Hilton, my nerves fell away. I felt a surge of warmth. That lasted about four minutes. Then I started thinking again. Mainly, I thought about the strangeness of the industry. Look, there's Drew Barrymore. Why do I see her here rather than bumping into her at the supermarket or in the park? There's Meryl Streep. We were in *Manhattan* together, up for Oscars the same year; was that a lifetime ago or maybe even more? And there's Tom Hanks and Rita Wilson. We used to socialize. Are we still friends in the real world?

And then, late in the evening, Cate Blanchett won Best Actress for *Blue Jasmine*. Her acceptance speech was gracious and funny, and she devoted a section of it to the actresses who had anchored Woody's movies before her, including me. While Cate was talking, I looked around the room. All my questions about social propriety and professional awkwardness vanished. I saw only people who were proud of a colleague. Their pride was the result of the fact that they recognized the worthiness of the award, which in turn was a result of the emotional truth of Cate's performance. Playing a self-deceiving upper-class woman in the midst of a streak of bad luck—a Woody-flavored version of Blanche DuBois—she somehow touched a wide range of viewers. What Cate did with Woody was, miraculously, a type of universal storytelling. I suddenly understood what I needed to do with my own story.

This kind of storytelling is central to human existence, whether or not people know it. Everyone needs to take control of his or her own life by making sense of it. It doesn't matter how conventional or unconventional that process is. Another example: A few months ago the phone rang and I picked up. "Hiiiii," the voice on the other end said, stretching out the word for maximum effect. It was Muffet, calling from Twin Falls, where she lives and is looked after by a lovely woman. "It's so great to hear your voice. I miss you so much." We traded small talk about the last time I had seen her, when I gave her a Starbucks charge card so she could buy herself all the coffee she wanted. "Right," she said. There was a pause. "By the way," she said. "You know what? I could use a bit more money." I waited. Instructions were sure to follow. "Could you send me a check for twenty thousand dollars? Send it here and don't tell Vonda." I told her I'd send the money. "Great," Muffet said. "The money from Russia is on the way. The aristocrats that I've been dealing with, the princes, they're sending me the cash. It's almost here. When it gets here, I'll pay you back." We hung up, after which I sat and thought about how my relationship with Muffet had evolved. There was a time when I would have reacted to her request by getting upset. I would have set the phone down and mourned my older sister, lost in her own madness. But that time passed long ago. It turned into something else: a realization that Muffet, like everyone else, is telling her own story. Objecting to the details of that story would be pointless and even counterproductive. She passes through the world surrounded by her own understanding of it, just as we all do. In her case, the perspective is somewhat unique—very few people live with the mix of fantasy and reality that she does—but it's still central to her life. As a young woman, she was the purest person in the bunch, and that's what she remained.

In interviews, people always ask me what it feels like to be part of the Hemingway family. I never know exactly how to answer, because the truth is that I spend more time thinking about what it feels like to be part of the much broader family of flawed, hopeful, intermittently improving humans. When people see the Hemingway part of my name in boldface, they miss out on everything else: on the fact that I grew up in suburban America in the seventies just like they did, that I sang along to the same Moody Blues records they did and had the same fears about being tall and flat-chested they did, and that I loved and pitied my father and loved and resented my mother. Seeing the Hemingway in boldface prevents them from seeing the divorced mom who loves and is loved by her daughters, or the amateur chef who spends hours in the kitchen cooking for guests, or the pet owner who runs with her dogs in the California hills, or the klutz who drops things, or the voluble e-mail correspondent who uses too many emoticons. Did my family have more than its share of sadness and self-destructive habits? Perhaps, but as I have learned from speaking to groups across the country, sadness and self-destructive habits are everywhere, including the places where you'd least expect to see them. My story is extraordinary in some ways, because of the ways in which my family lived in the public eye, but that should work as a point of contact rather than a point of separation. As I live in the present, make my peace with the past, and think about the future, I am trying to keep this in mind: that we're all here on the same planet, that we're all lifting weights and setting down burdens, that we're all putting our feet where our feet need to go.

A LETTER FROM CUBA

IN 2014, I GO TO CUBA. I am there to play a cameo in a film about my grandfather. Hair and makeup people transform me into a woman of the 1950s: brown wig, cat-eye glasses, cream suit. The whole scene is shot at a table, which means the audience will never see my feet. I wear my own sandals.

I am playing a *New Yorker* writer who may or may not be based on Lillian Ross. I have come to interview my grandfather, laugh at his jokes, record his wise remarks. So here we sit eating roast pig, black beans and rice, fried plantains, and cabbage. It is vile to look at and repulsive to smell, and after six hours I couldn't bear to think about lifting it to my lips, but that's the magic of acting. Grape juice, playing the part of wine, is poured and repoured for every take, though the first time around, the Cuban prop guy fills the glasses with real wine. He didn't see anything wrong with it.

My character's name is Dorothy Evans, and she has one line: "What do you get for a short story now, Papa? A hundred dollars a word?" The line feels heavy in my mouth, and it never comes out in a way that makes me completely happy. It's not the line I want to say. I want to say something meaningful. I want to be there for him. Instead, I feel like an outsider. It's not the fault of the film. The film seems wonderful, which is why I have agreed to participate. It's filled with talented actors: Joely Richardson is playing Mary, my grandfather's last wife; Adrian Sparks, who has played my grandfather several times onstage, plays him here too; and Giovanni Ribisi is Denne Petitclerc, the author of the screenplay, whose friendship with my grandfather formed the basis for the film. When I was young, Petitclerc was always in Idaho. He and his wife, Wanda, had a house in Ketchum. Ribisi is amazing at bringing him back to life. I am honored to be watching them all and to help them bring their vision of my grandfather to life. My boyfriend, Bobby, is an extra, looking more like Don Draper than even Jon Hamm does, and it's clear to me that they'll have to keep the camera off him—otherwise people will be drawn in. This makes me smile, because I love him and always see the power of his presence.

I watch Adrian Sparks especially closely, because I feel I know my grandfather, and I want to see how he's coming to life in the film. But why do I feel that? I never met the man. I have only read books and scripts and biographies, just like everyone else. But that's maybe a twinge of false modesty or strategic democracy. The fact is that I do have a stronger connection to him. I grew up hearing stories and seeing pictures, and I lived through a lifetime with the son he created, my father. Not a day goes by in my life where there is not a reference to Ernest Hemingway in connection to me, and there is a cumulative effect, both for others and within myself. The fact that I never met Papa is secondary to trying to digest his legend and trying to understand whether that affected how my family was in the world. Did he help to create a genetic puzzle that will never be completely solved? The Finca Vigía, where we're filming, where he lived, is a house stamped with distinction. It is not grand, but it has a grand presence, and it holds the man.

Can you know someone without meeting him? When I was eleven, in Paris, Papa spoke to me in the pages of *A Moveable Feast*. That's the book of his that touched me first and most deeply, and now I am producing a film version of it. And more than that, I am writing. I am writing my own story, writing about how he matters or does not matter within that story. And while that could be (should be?) frightening, it's life-affirming. I am a Hemingway in name, in appearance, and in character. I don't go to bullfights or kill big game. But the Papa I feel here at the Finca Vigía is a more familiar type, someone who loved so deeply that it hurt him to show it, a man who was so aware of his own vulnerability that he built walls around it and shunned those closest to him. He loved the children near his home and helped them create a baseball team. But then he withdrew inside himself and abandoned the people who needed him: my father, for one. He abandoned them when he killed himself, but he abandoned them many times before that too. When he left my grandmother, Hadley, shortly after my dad's birth, he weighed a life of normalcy and love against a life of creative devotion. It is said that he loved Hadley more than any woman he was ever with, and that in leaving her he chose to be Ernest Hemingway, Great Writer, rather than Ernest Hemingway, man, husband, father. No one can say for sure, but I imagine that he felt cornered, that he felt that he couldn't have both lives. I have made the opposite sacrifices, choosing family over career or others over myself. Have those sacrifices made me happier than they made him?

I am not a Hemingway scholar, but I am a Hemingway, and to me, that means that I have a ticket to understanding a world of darkness, of courage, of sadness, of excitement, and—at times—of complete lunacy. And yet, other people with other names feel these things too. It may just be that they don't have an American myth to which they can connect themselves. We all live our stories with a sense of panic and, hopefully, come out of them at some point with a sense of calm.

These are complicated ideas with simple results. I have learned, over time, to tell my story, and I have arrived in a place of calm. That means comfort, finally. It means being a woman, being loved and loving when I want, but not feeling obligated to be either. It means being comfortable with my mind and my body, both for their abilities and their limits. It also means being able, whenever necessary, to reinvent myself, to be new. Above all, it means taking responsibility for who I am. I think of a quote by a writer I'm not related to, the poet Audre Lorde: "If I didn't define myself for myself, I would be crunched into other people's fantasies for me and eaten alive." Some days it's a lovely ride, with shafts of light knifing down through dark clouds, and some days a shelf of my mother's porcelain falls and I cry for hours missing the woman I lost to cancer decades ago. I loved her so much and was sad that others couldn't see why. I cry for my sister Margaux too, who was so loved by her friends but couldn't show that part of herself to her family.

The beauty of humanity is in this balance. We hold some problems in and let others go. We reflect at times and express at other times. We accommodate others and we assert ourselves. We learn to live without some things and we sharpen our desire for other things. We forgive ourselves for our fears and we forge bravely ahead. That's what I feel most here in Cuba, that my grandfather learned to express his desire, that he made a world around him rather than simply being turned to powder by his stresses and disappointments. The world injured him, but he moved past that. We have all done that, as best as possible. Over the course or our lives, trapped in our lives, liberated by our lives, we became strong at the broken places.

APPENDIX

RESOURCES *for* MENTAL HEALTH,
SUBSTANCE ABUSE, *and* BETTER LIVING

ONE THING I'VE LEARNED is that just as solutions are imprecise, so are problems. My parents drank, but was alcohol really the cause of my childhood anxiety and adult disaffection? That's hard to say. My sister Muffet suffered from mental illness from a relatively early age, but her problem touched off a domino effect of related problems. My parents felt guilty that they couldn't rescue their daughter from herself. My sister Margaux felt frustrated with all the attention that went into caring for Muffet. I reacted by demonstrating repeatedly and obviously just how sane I was. Suicide, depression, obsessive-compulsive tendencies: none of these exist in isolation. Problems in families are part of an intricate ecosystem. One causes a second or allows a third to grow in suddenly fertile soil.

As a result, when I'm asked what services, foundations, and groups are helpful for family dysfunction, I tend to think in terms of a wide net. I'm more likely to say that something might work than that it won't, and more likely to say that it might work than that it will.

Most of these are services I haven't used personally, so I can't vouch for them myself, but I've heard good things about them.

There's also a real and proven link between mental health and other kinds of health: physical on the one hand, spiritual on the other. It's something that I have believed since I was a little girl. The more I research the matter, the more I'm sure that my initial instinct was correct. That's why I have also included resources for nutrition, exercise, and spiritual balance. A healthy mind goes in partnership with a healthy body and a healthy soul.

Finally, it's important to remember that while these organizations offer help, they can't always offer solutions. Much of the process by which problems are solved, or at least neutralized, comes from within the people who are grappling with them. These organizations work best when they activate something inside your mind, heart, or body: a sense that a solution is possible, the will to move forward with a different perspective, a renewed tenacity or hope.

ALCOHOL

Though I am not an alcoholic, I have known many people who are over the course of my life, and many of them have been helped and even saved by working with the following organizations. I am always moved when I hear stories from friends who have dedicated themselves to the 12-step program or found a truer sense of self by attending daily meetings. Above all, these programs help launch people on a journey to understanding themselves.

Alcoholics Anonymous
aa.org / 212-870-3400

Adult Children of Alcoholics
adultchildren.org / 562-595-7831

Al-Anon Family Groups
al-anon.alateen.org / 757-563-1600

DRUGS

Drugs have never been a big part of my life, but I have seen their destructive effects on people close to me, particularly my sister Margaux, and I know how prevalent drugs are in our society—both illegal drugs and prescription medications. Like alcohol programs, organizations dealing with drug addiction promote mindful and conscious living.

Narcotics Anonymous
na.org / 818-773-9999

MENTAL HEALTH

General mental health is something of a misnomer: most mental health issues, even if they seem general at first, are made up of many specifics. But if you have a problem, you have to start somewhere. I am very connected with the following organizations: I have spoken to groups under the auspices of NAMI and McLean Hospital (where I am an honorary board member), and I try to embrace any and all organizations that promote help and understanding. Again, these groups aren't panaceas. Your needs (or the needs of family members) may point you toward one rather than the other. But once you have located the right environment, it's more than a relief—it's a lifesaver.

National Alliance on Mental Illness (NAMI)
nami.org / 800-950-6264

National Institute of Mental Health
nimh.nih.gov / 866-615-6464

McLean Hospital
mcleanhospital.org / 800-333 0338

Substance Abuse and Mental Health Services Administration
findtreatment.samhsa.gov / 877-SAMHSA-7

OBSESSIVE-COMPULSIVE DISORDER

When I was a little girl, I had behaviors that helped me keep the world orderly. They were good for me until they got too ritualistic, until my own identity began to be compromised by the habits and compulsions. In my case, I overcame some of the habits on my own, but others have OCD that can't be fully controlled without assistance. OCD can be a mental illness, and in those cases it needs to be treated like all others, with compassion and understanding.

International OCD Foundation
iocdf.org / 617-973-5801

DEPRESSION AND MOOD DISORDERS

Depression is more common than anyone realizes. Many people are afflicted by it, at various levels of severity, and most of them don't address the problem because of the accompanying stigma and the fear that admitting depression will cost them jobs or relationships. That's where these organizations come in: they give people a place to start talking about it and dealing with it, to take a closer look at mental imbalances with compassion and purpose.

Anxiety and Depression Association of America
adaa.org / 240-485-1001

Depression and Bipolar Support Alliance
dbsalliance.org / 800-826-3632

Families for Depression Awareness
familyaware.org / 781-890-0220

BRAIN

When we experience emotional problems, they leave a trace in our brain, and Brain Wave Optimization has been an enormous help to me in my life dealing with depression, obsession, and childhood trauma. The program works to balance the hemispheres of the brain through sound and to create new neural pathways. What I love about Brainwave Optimization is its elegance and simplicity. Your brain hears itself in real time and balances via feedback. There are no pills. There are no long conversations or negotiations. The process, which is called allostasis, is like a kind of massage or chiropractic correction, but for the brain.

Brainwave Optimization
www.brainstatetech.com

SUICIDE

Suicide is widely misunderstood, because there is no rhyme or reason to it, no clear line dividing suicidal ideation from intentionally
failed attempts from successful attempts. A suicide can be planned
carefully in advance or can be the result of one panicked day. I
have worked personally with the American Foundation for Suicide
Prevention, but all of these groups do their best both to help people with suicidal thoughts and to support the families who have lost
their loved ones to suicide.

American Foundation for Suicide Prevention
afsp.org / 800-273-8255

American Association of Suicidology
suicidology.org / 800-273-8255

Suicide Prevention Resource Center
sprc.org / 800-273-8255

National Suicide Prevention Lifeline
suicidepreventionlifeline.org / 1-800-273-TALK (8255)

Suicide Awareness Voices of Education (SAVE)
save.org / 952-946-7998

CANCER

Cancer has hit close to home for me repeatedly—it dominated the
last two decades of my mother's life, and it affected my husband in

early middle age. I believe that people need to concern themselves intimately not only with the medical aspects of cancer prevention and treatment but with the lifestyle component. I highly recommend that people supplement traditional medical treatments with holistic methods, and investigate Eastern as well as Western methodologies for healing. I also urge people to visit sites such as Food Matters (foodmatters.tv) to read up on diets that assist with cancer treatment.

American Cancer Society
cancer.org / 800-227-2345

CancerCare
cancercare.org / 800-813-4673

Cancer Support Community
cancersupportcommunity.org / 888-793-9355

Burzynski Clinic Advanced Alternative Cancer Treatment
burzynskiclinic.com / 713-335-5697

Caregiver Action Network
caregiveraction.org / 202-772-5050

DOMESTIC VIOLENCE

Domestic violence affects so many people, and it can take many forms. These organizations are concerned primarily with the safety of spouses and children in violent families. No one should hesitate to seek help.

The National Domestic Violence Hotline
thehotline.org / 800-799-7233

Children's Safety Network
childrenssafetynetwork.org

FOOD AND EATING DISORDERS

My obsession with food began in childhood and lasted for many decades. If I had known of organizations like this, I would have dealt with things earlier and in a healthier manner.

National Eating Disorders Association
nationaleatingdisorders.org / 800-931-2237

Overeaters Anonymous
oa.org / 505-891-2664

YOGA

Yoga, of course, is a Hindu spiritual and ascetic discipline that involves breath control, simple meditation, and the adoption of specific bodily postures and is widely practiced for health and relaxation. From personal experience, I can attest to the value of the practice—and, more to the point, to the joy of the practice. It's a way to process the rush of the world, to learn to trust yourself, and to find a great sense of balance whether times are good or bad. I encourage you and your family to explore different types and aspects of yoga through classes in your local community, online resources, and instructional videos. Yoga is an important part of my commitment to living mindfully, awake, aware, and connected inside and out.

ALTERNATIVE HEALING MODALITIES

These resources share some of the same priorities as yoga: they seek to reduce stress, increase focus, unite body and mind, and engage with Eastern as well as Western spiritual practices.

David Lynch Foundation
davidlynchfoundation.org / 641-209-6404

National Ayurvedic Medical Association
ayurvedanama.org / 800-669-8914

Center for East-West Medicine UCLA
cewm.med.ucla.edu/international

ACKNOWLEDGMENTS

THANK YOU TO: Tracy Columbus—you have been my lighthouse in this journey of storytelling; you are a beautiful and gracious human that I am proud to call my friend. Ben Greenman, for hearing my voice and being humble and cool about it. Heather Reinhardt, for keeping my life together. Judith Regan, for having the foresight to see this project as important and Lucas Wittmann, for negotiating the waters of many opinions. Lisa Erspamer, had you not said I needed to tell my story, none of this would have happened.

Thank you Mommy and Daddy, I know you did your best and I will always love you. Thank you Margot, you suffered greatly and I see that now. Muffet, who still sees the world from a place of love and acceptance, you are always stunning to me. Thank you to everyone in my life that has had an impact on my journey, I am grateful.

And of course, Mr. Bubba.